Christmas 2006

A book you will enjoy
a lifetime.
Daddy

WEIRD
MINNESOTA

Sterling Publishing Co., Inc.
New York

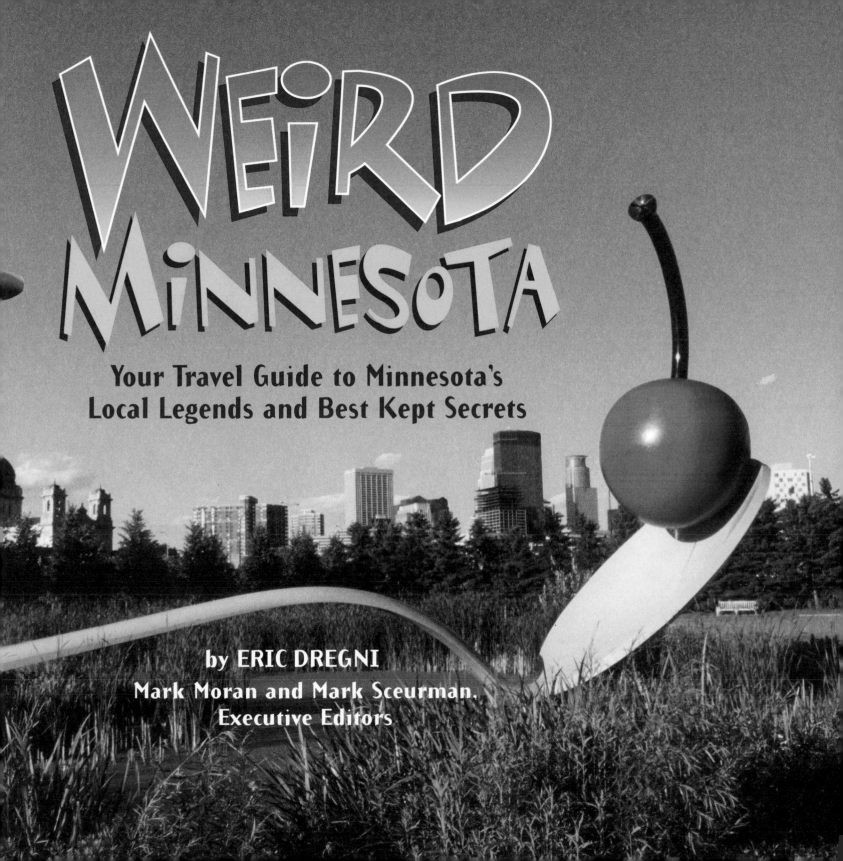

WEiRD MiNNESoTA

Your Travel Guide to Minnesota's Local Legends and Best Kept Secrets

by **ERIC DREGNI**

**Mark Moran and Mark Sceurman,
Executive Editors**

WEIRD MINNESOTA

Published by Sterling Publishing Co., Inc.
387 Park Avenue South, New York, NY 10016
© 2006 Mark Moran and Mark Sceurman
Distributed in Canada by Sterling Publishing
c/o Canadian Manda Group, 165 Dufferin Street,
Toronto, Ontario, Canada M6K 3H6
Distributed in Great Britain by Chrysalis Books Group PLC
The Chrysalis Building, Bramley Road, London W10 6SP, England
Distributed in Australia by Capricorn Link (Australia) Pty. Ltd.
P.O. Box 704, Windsor, NSW 2756, Australia

10 9 8 7 6 5 4 3 2 1

Manufactured in the United States of America

Photography and illustration credits are found on page 255
and constitute an extension of this copyright page.

Sterling ISBN 13: 978-1-4027-3908-8
Sterling ISBN 10: 1-4027-3908-7

For information about custom editions, special sales, premium
and corporate purchases, please contact Sterling Special Sales
Department at 800-805-5489 or specialsales@sterlingpub.com.

Design: Richard J. Berenson
Berenson Design & Books, LLC, New York, NY

Weird Minnesota is intended as entertainment
to present a historical record of local legends,
folklore, and sites throughout Minnesota.
Many of these legends and stories cannot be
independently confirmed or corroborated,
and the authors and publisher make no representation as to their factual accuracy. The
reader should be advised that many of the
sites described in *Weird Minnesota* are located
on private property and should not be visited,
or you may face prosecution for trespassing.

CONTENTS

Our weird journey began a long, long time ago in a far-off land called New Jersey. Once a year or so, we'd compile a homespun newsletter called *Weird N.J.*, then pass it on to our friends. The pamphlet was a collection of odd news clippings, bizarre facts, little-known historical anecdotes, and anomalous encounters from our home state. It also included the kinds of localized legends that were often whispered around a particular town but seldom heard outside the boundaries of the community where they originated.

We'd started *Weird N.J.* on the simple theory that every town in the state had at least one good tale to tell. The publication soon became a full-fledged magazine, and we made the decision to actually do our own investigating to see if we could track down where all of these seemingly unbelievable stories were coming from. Was there, we wondered, any factual basis for the fantastic local legends people were telling us about? Armed with not much more than a camera and a notepad, we set off on a mystical journey of discovery. Much to our surprise and amazement, a lot of what we had initially presumed to be nothing more than urban legends turned out to be real—or at least to contain a grain of truth, which had sparked the lore to begin with.

After a dozen years of documenting the bizarre, we were asked to write a book about our adventures, and so *Weird N.J.: Your Travel Guide to New Jersey's Local Legends and Best Kept Secrets* was published in 2003. Soon, people from all over the country began writing to us, telling us strange tales from their home state. As it

turned out, what we had perceived to be something of very local interest was actually just a small part of a larger and more universal phenomenon.

When our publisher asked us what we wanted to do next, the answer was simple: "We'd like to do a book called *Weird U.S.*, in which we could document the local legends and strangest stories from all over the country." So for the next twelve months, we set out in search of weirdness wherever it might be found in the fifty states. And indeed, we found plenty of it!

After *Weird U.S.* was published, we came to the conclusion that this country has more great tales than can be contained in just one book. Everywhere we looked, we found unwritten folklore, creepy cemeteries, cursed locations, and outlandish roadside oddities. With this in mind, we told our publisher that we wanted to document it ALL and do it in a series of books, each focusing on the peculiarities of a particular state.

One of the states we wanted to compile a Weird book about was Minnesota. Why, you might well ask. Well, because to us, it seemed like such a pure, wholesome, and homogeneous place that we were sure Minnesotans must be hiding a weird side. Anyway, that's the impression people from New Jersey get from the state. When we had the opportunity to travel extensively through Minnesota, we found that it was indeed a pure and wholesome land—more important, though, it was also very weird! Not only that, but much to our delight, we discovered that Minnesotans themselves realize that their home state is somewhat odd. Despite (or perhaps because of) its upright reputation and Midwestern longitude, the state is actually off the charts when it comes to its high density of oddities—and everyone there seems to know it.

So the decision was made to create the book that you now hold in your hand. But whom would we invite to take this fantastic journey along with us? We needed a true Minnesotan to collaborate with—someone who really knew the secret sites and little-known stories that only a local would. As it turned out, we didn't have to find that perfect author, because he found us! Out of the blue, Eric Dregni wrote to us at the *Weird* home office one day last year.

Eric told us that he'd been collecting tales of weird goings-on in Minnesota for years. His enthusiasm for the bizarre people and places he'd discovered was infectious, and so was his gift for storytelling. We soon knew that in Eric we had found a real kindred spirit. There was no doubt in our minds that he possessed what we refer to as the "Weird Eye." The Weird Eye is what is needed to search out the sorts of stories we were looking for. It requires one to see the world a different way, with a renewed sense of wonder. And once you have it, there's no going back— you'll never see things the same way again. All of a sudden, you begin to reexamine your own environs, noticing your everyday surroundings as if for the first time. And you begin to ask yourself questions like, What the heck is *that* thing all about, anyway? and, Doesn't anybody else think that's kinda *weird?*

So come with us now, and let Eric take you on a tour of his state—with all its cultural quirks, strange sites, and bizarre stories. It is a fabled place we like to call *Weird Minnesota.*

—*Mark Sceurman and Mark Moran*

Introduction

We see a pattern in the visits of the many sightseers in our state. The typical guidebook steers folks to a little bronze plaque honoring the town's founder. Then they simply must stop in at the pioneer museum, filled with dusty old artifacts donated by townspeople who couldn't bear to chuck them in Dumpsters. They're urged to visit the quaint covered bridge or the lovely natural rock outcropping nearby. Meanwhile, the kids are snoozing and convinced that Minnesota has got to be the most boring state in the Union.

But wait! What the heck is that? There's a thirty-foot-tall talking lumberjack lifting his enormous arms (thanks to ropes and pulleys) and guessing all the kids' names.

What did you say? One man spent thirty-nine years of his life winding twine into a twelve-foot ball? Why would anyone do that?

Someone stole a million-dollar pair of shoes? Did they catch him? What would you do with such expensive ruby slippers?

A musician in Dinkytown played a concert for twelve hours straight inside a refrigerator box? Cool! How did he pee?

The children have shaken their slumber and are sitting up straight as they learn how the police let gangsters live scot-free in Saint Paul—until some deviant unloaded his machine gun at fellow mobsters at a nightclub in the caves near downtown. The police found no clues, but you can still see the bullet holes. The bodies were probably buried in cement deep in the caves, and ghosts haunt the place late at night.

Not only are the kids awake, but that night, they can't go to sleep. They want to know more about this bizarre state where there are insect plagues, meteors plunging from the heavens, bigamy, arsons, a governor who dreamed of being a woman's bra. . . . What is this place? Is this Sodom?

Hardly. It's Minnesota, where devout citizens walk on water. In fact, we're so holy, we even drive pickups over frozen water, set up shacks over holes in the ice, and sit to fish. Tell this to Californians and they won't believe you.

These sites, people, and events are quintessential Minnesota. Some are oddly interesting. Others point out the breathtaking imagination of our citizens to create the one-and-only "world's largest (fill in the blank)." A few are disturbingly violent and seriously challenge "Minnesota nice."

For years, I've been obsessed with our state's roadside attractions and little-known historical calamities, as well as the generally dubious behavior of many of my fellow Minnesotans. I first reported on weird things in our state when I wrote an article for my high school newspaper, the *Minnetonka Breezes*, about a coven of rich satanists living along Lake Orono in black A-frames with a large statue of Lucifer in the entranceway.

This is not normal.

Weird Minnesota is the result of years of searching for the scandalous, scary, immoral, disconcerting, and, well, funny stories of our state. This book is not complete, fortunately, because Minnesotans keep engaging in questionable conduct. In fact, just this past year, a new candidate for governor appeared: Jonathon "The Impaler" Sharkey, of the Vampyres, Witches and Pagans Party. You can't make this stuff up. And it just keeps on coming. . . .

Turn the page, pick a story, and tune in to the weirdness of our state and all its disturbing beauty.

–Eric Dregni

Local Legends

Legends are part truth, part dreams (or nightmares), and all rumor. Some are scandalous, some are frightening, and others are whimsical.

Why do these stories spring up? Who can say. Certain places, like dark caves and deserted camps, seem ripe to yield bizarre tales of lost souls or sinful mafiosi. Some stories, like the 1862 Dakota Uprising, are so horrible that they're rarely told.

The most famous legend from Minnesota, of course, is that of Paul Bunyan, the mighty lumberjack whose prowess with an ax is still told around many a crackling campfire. And because no one has sole rights to his story, the exaggerations continue.

Untidy woodsman that he was, Bunyan left his personal belongings scattered around the state to become valuable relics and a lure for tourists.

The following legends are only a smattering of the many that have endured, but they give a taste of Minnesota's vast imagination and the power of its word of mouth.

World's Largest Paul Bunyan

Scribes for the Red River Lumber Company near Akeley first put Paul's tale to paper in 1914. Minnesota lumbering was near the end of its peak; much of the forest had been chopped down and the wood carried to mills by oxen and the rivers.

Listening to the fireside stories of bragging woodsmen, authors W. B. Laughead and James Stevens both scribbled notes on this famous French-Canadian lumberjack. Truth was thrown to the wind and hyperbole ballooned with each telling of the tale. Laughead's Bunyan tales were compiled in a promotional brochure for the Red River Lumber Company that claimed "the largest sawmills in the world," employing over seven hundred men. Stevens's stories were published in 1925, at the height of Paul's popularity.

To pay tribute to the hometown lumberjack, the Krotzer family built the World's Largest Paul Bunyan Statue in 1984. Standing thirty-three feet high, Paul juts out his enormous hand for tourists to hop into for a photo. To celebrate their native son, the residents of Akeley pack the little town for Paul Bunyan Days in June every year. Tourists can check out the Red River Museum behind Paul for a tour of the "true history" of Paul Bunyan.

The Original Paul Bunyan

You might think Paul Bunyan was just a big guy with a blue ox who could do some extraordinary tricks, but you'd be wrong. According to historian Karal Ann Marling, Paul was a symbol of "the American worker, grown larger than life in the strength of collective action."

In *The People, Yes,* author Carl Sandburg announced that "the anonymous folk concocted Paul Bunyan out of the genial humor of their collective imagination and their mutual resilience of spirit." Don't tell Sandburg that the first written record of Paul Bunyan was in an advertisement for the Red River Lumber Company.

Everyone wanted a piece of Paul Bunyan, so in the 1930s self-important Bemidji mayor Earl Bucklen posed for a woodcutter's statue three times his size for the Bemidji Winter Carnival. This rigid lumberjack has become the model for all other Paul Bunyans, as it stands over Lake Bemidji at eighteen feet tall and weighs two and a half tons.

Paul was soon accompanied by his best buddy, the giant blue ox named Babe. The eight-foot-high, ten-foot-long cow was built of wire, wood, and canvas at the county highway department and perched on top of an old Model T so that it could be transported to local carnivals. The frightening blue beast blew huge clouds of smoke out of the exhaust pipe hooked up in its nose. Babe's tin horns were too long for Bemidji's streets, however, and got caught in strings of Christmas lights hanging over the town for the annual winter parade in 1937, bringing the procession to an abrupt halt. Thanks to national press coverage, attendance at the Bemidji parade skyrocketed from fifteen thousand that year to a hundred thousand the following year.

Babe soon returned to his permanent position by his master's side, along Lake Bemidji. A local boat company supplied Babe with huge wooden ribs and set the front legs far enough apart so that a truck could drive between them. Paul and Babe still keep watch over Bemidji and remain the most photographed fiberglass in the state.

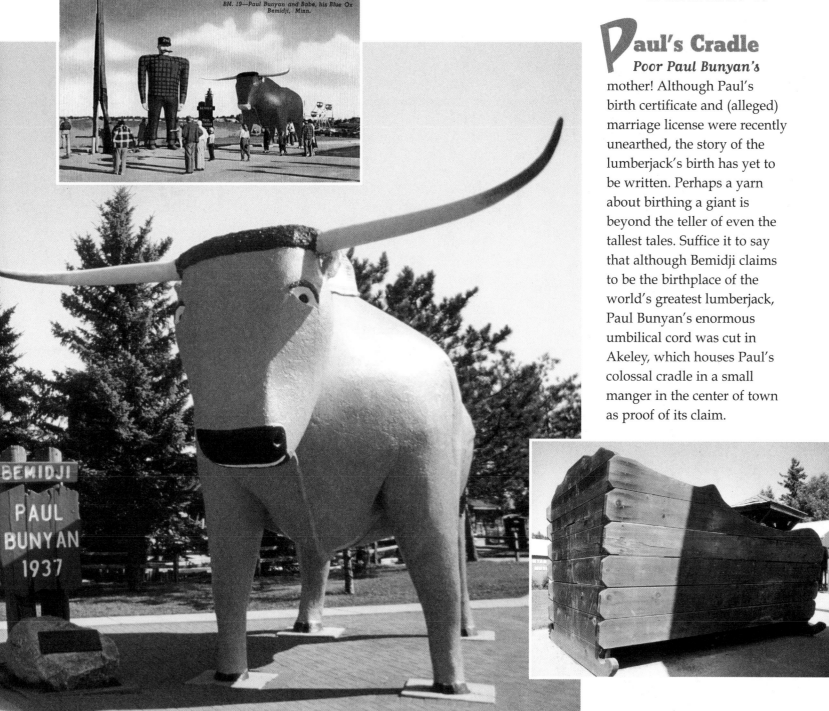

BM. 19—Paul Bunyan and Babe, his Blue Ox
Bemidji, Minn.

BEMIDJI
PAUL
BUNYAN
1937

Paul's Cradle

Poor Paul Bunyan's mother! Although Paul's birth certificate and (alleged) marriage license were recently unearthed, the story of the lumberjack's birth has yet to be written. Perhaps a yarn about birthing a giant is beyond the teller of even the tallest tales. Suffice it to say that although Bemidji claims to be the birthplace of the world's greatest lumberjack, Paul Bunyan's enormous umbilical cord was cut in Akeley, which houses Paul's colossal cradle in a small manger in the center of town as proof of its claim.

The Tall Tales of Paul Bunyan

Paul Bunyan was Mr. Minnesota. While other states, especially Michigan and Maine, also lay claim to the famous logger, Minnesota has cornered the market with enormous fiberglass statues, paying homage to the state's ongoing battle against trees. Paul Bunyan's origins may be lost to the mists of time, but his legend and size continue to grow in leaps and bounds around the campfire. He still tests the embellishing skills of storytellers.

As the tale claims, five storks worked tag team to deliver Paul to his normal-size mother. An entire herd of milk cows were then put to work to pump out enough milk to feed the portly baby Paul. Loggers cleared a lumber wagon of freshly cut timber to make a baby carriage large enough for the toddler. A mere week after he came into the world, he busted his britches and filled his father's shoes and clothes. After that, Paul was left to improvise to cover his huge body, resorting to using wagon wheels as buttons.

Paul was always a member of the clean-plate club, with a voracious appetite that kept his cook, Sourdough Sam, slaving over the stove. Sam would boil up entire lakes just to make a Bunyan-size bowl of soup. To grease the massive skillet for old-fashioned lumberjack flapjacks, he would strap strips of bacon on his feet and "skate" across the sizzling hot metal. If Paul caught the sniffles in the winter, fellow lumberjacks would steer clear since his sneezes regularly blew the roofs off houses. When the mercury fell to record lows in Bemidji, the ingenious Paul bred walleyes and northern pike with lynx so that the fish could grow fur coats and stave off Jack Frost.

Meanwhile, Babe the Blue Ox was downing thirty bales of hay for each little snack. As good a worker as he was, Babe had a minor accident one day when a water tanker he was hauling cracked, forming Lake Itasca; it then inched its way south to form the Mississippi River. Paul and Babe hit it off immediately and could often be seen rassling for fun, which, of course, is how Minnesota's ten thousand lakes were formed.

Paul Bunyan Land

In his day, Paul Bunyan was unbeatable even by roaring chain saws. But competing for space with strip malls almost did him in. When Kohl's department store bought out Paul's property (Paul Bunyan Land, of course) in Baxter at the corner of highways 210 and 371, the world's largest talking lumberjack was suddenly homeless.

South Dakota expressed interest in placing the talking lumberjack in the Black Hills, perhaps as the fifth head at Mount Rushmore. Minnesotans were outraged that this symbol of their state might be transported over the border. Governor Tim Pawlenty quickly went to Brainerd to persuade the lumberjack that there's no place like home.

And so the twenty-six-foot-tall Paul went to This Old Farm, a historic attraction east of Brainerd where visitors can still hear their names called by the five-thousand-pound man with the size eighty footprint.

Kids marvel at the omniscient giant, who somehow knows who each of them is. The giant in the huge split-log crèche wows crowds of tots as he nods, blinks, and tells tall tales of the old logging days. The woodcutting beast bellows out, "Hello, Johnny from Saint Paul!" Ignore the man behind the log cabin and the cashier with the microphone feeding him information.

Before Bemidji raised its Paul Bunyan statue in 1939, Brainerd hosted the first Paul Bunyan Water Carnival with guests of honor Paul and his maybe wife Pauline marching down Main Street in 1935. Following the success of the parade, a Paul Bunyan statue was commissioned from a hobo artist who lived under the bridge over the Mississippi. This little Paul and Babe still stands in front of the tourist information office under Brainerd's castle water tower.

One lumberjack who isn't in Brainerd, however, is the chain-saw sculpture featured in the Coen Brothers' movie *Fargo.* (Brainerd didn't sound quite right for the film's title even though the action takes place there.) The Coens hail from St. Louis Park, but maybe their Minnesota connection wasn't enough to secure rights to use the talking Paul Bunyan in the movie. The Paul Bunyan statue featured in the film was donated to the tiny town of Hensel, North Dakota, for its help with the movie.

Even though Brainerd is short the movie statue, there is no shortage of Paul Bunyan naming rights in town. Just look for the Paul Bunyan

Expressway, Paul Bunyan (bike) Trail, Paul Bunyan Bowl, Paul Bunyan Nature Center, etc. To make up for the dearth of lumberjack art, a series of chain-saw sculptures in memory of Paul Bunyan's early days stands downtown on Laurel Street.

Bowling Paul Bunyan

Under Brainerd's castlelike water tower—which some call Paul Bunyan's flashlight—stands a mini version of Paul Bunyan and Babe the Blue Ox, just a fraction of the height of the old talking lumberjack at Paul Bunyan Land. When the talking Paul Bunyan moved east of Brainerd, tourists still stopped at the intersection of highways 210 and 371 to see him. The owners of Paul Bunyan Bowl (who also owned Paul Bunyan Land) raised a Paul Bunyan armed with an AMF ball ready to topple the timbers and a Babe the Bowling Ox munching on any pins left standing.

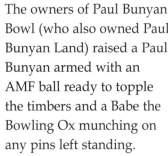

Paul Bunyan's Squirrel

Just as Gulliver became suddenly tiny when he traveled to Brobdingnag, so do visitors to the world of Paul Bunyan. You'll be dwarfed by the wonderland of statues of Paul's immense ax, phone, toothpaste, Zippo lighter, and giant magic mushrooms. Pet the fiberglass Henry the Giant Squirrel, the critter who munched on prune pits at Paul's legendary logging camp on the Big Onion River.

Paul Bunyan's Dog

To keep Henry the Giant Squirrel from getting too frisky, the unstoppable Sport the Reversible Dog keeps him in check. The story goes that the canine was cut in half and hastily sewn back together with his hindquarters upside down. Sport runs along on his front legs, and when he gets tired, he just flips upside down and keeps on trucking, so he can run twice as far as an ordinary dog.

Paul Bunyan's Sweetheart

In 1991, the brisk wind across the frozen waters of Birch Lake whipped up and decapitated Paul Bunyan's wife like a guillotine. Now, no one is exactly sure that Paul Bunyan was married, but never mind. The residents of Hackensack, concerned that Minnesota's lumberjack might be lonely, found a new head for the "bride."

While Brainerd claimed that Paul's girlfriend, or wife, was named the unimaginative Pauline, the residents of Hackensack knew that her real name was Lucette Diana Kensack. To prove their case, the Hackensack Chamber of Commerce displays the official marriage license along with other authenticated documents and Paul Bunyan memorabilia.

The poet Robert Frost even chimed in on the debate and advised that Paul would "thank people not to think of her." In his poem *Paul's Wife*, Frost revealed the gossip behind the giant's love life when he wrote, "Paul sawed his wife out of a white-pine log . . . there were witnesses that Paul was married, And not to anyone to be ashamed of. . . . She wasn't anybody else's business, Either to praise her, or so much as name her."

Frost's advice on Paul's wife didn't stop Doad Schroeder, who owned the local grocery store, from erecting an oversize fiberglass statue of Paul's lady with her hands placed coyly in front of her and a curious Trojan horse–like trapdoor carved into her skirt in case repairs were needed.

Next to his hefty mama stands Paul Bunyan's runt of a son. The human-size boy was named simply Paul Junior. The residents of Hackensack come out in force to celebrate the joyous union of Paul and Lucette every year during Sweetheart Days with a performance of the musical *The Ballad of Lucette* by the Hackensack Metropolitan Light Opera Company. Lucette, still with her back to the lake that once took off her head, watches the scene down Main Street.

Paul Bunyan's Fishing Bobber

Ole the Blacksmith made shoes for Babe the Blue Ox that weighed so much that Ole sank knee-deep into the earth each time he took a step with them. After he finished Babe's shoes, he hammered a huge, sixty-foot bobber for Paul Bunyan to try to catch Sunfish Sally with and haul her out of Lake Whitefish. Just as Sally was about to chomp on the hook, Notorious Nate the Northern took the bait for her and was snagged instead. Paul mustered all of his might to pull the ensnared northern pike out of the water and threw it miles away to the downtown Pequot Lakes. The bobber conveniently landed in the braces built to hold a water tower.

With the ever-expanding number of golf courses in the area, dissidents are advocating painting over Paul Bunyan's bobber to make a giant golf ball. Traditionalists rebut that it's doubtful Paul Bunyan ever had time to play golf, and besides, no one has found his golf clubs—yet.

Paul Bunyan's Walleye

Towns across the Midwest recklessly announce their titles of "capital" and "world's biggest," and there's no authority to crack down on impostors. The huge fish statue in Rush City may not be the world's largest walleye, but this catch certainly would make a fine little snack for Paul Bunyan. The 1,999-pound lunker is nothing to scoff at, though, and has statistics to awe any fisherman:

> Weight: 1,999 lbs. 15.5 oz.
> Bait: thirty-five-pound tiger muskie
> Line: one-inch manila rope
> Rod: sixty-two-foot white pine
> Reel: three-ton logger's winch

As did Notorious Nate the Northern, Paul Bunyan's walleye grew fur to keep warm during the infamous "year of two winters." Come spring, the fish were so hungry that Paul Bunyan easily nabbed this lunker out of nearby Rush Lake.

Cordwood Pete

Paul Bunyan had a brother? Peder le Dang weighed in at a puny hundred pounds and stood barely four feet nine inches. Maybe his growth was stunted. When he was growing up, poor little Peder could never get enough flapjacks at the breakfast table because his big brother, Paul, ate everything in sight. Taller lumberjacks nicknamed le Dang Cordwood Pete because the little lumberjack would rather split cordwood than saw big logs.

When the local opera house in Fosston was bulldozed, a local legend was born again. Under the foundation, a time capsule dating back to the late 1800s was discovered. Inside was the tale of puny Cordwood Pete.

Pete was always raising a ruckus, it seems, especially when he'd hit the hooch. He bragged that he was the mightiest man in Minnesota for his size, which was probably true considering his slight height. Other lumberjacks admired Pete's feisty spirit, but no one would fight the little man.

Pete, like Paul, grew up in Bangor, Maine. When Pete heard that Paul was making a name for himself in Minnesota, he took the next train west. He was tired of the woodcutters in Maine who mocked him for his size and didn't respect his verve. Pete ended up in Fosston in 1883.

One night, Cordwood Pete sneaked into a lumber camp and "borrowed" his big brother's famous double-bladed ax. While escaping the camp, Pete gave the ax a swing, and the blades just kept cutting. Before he knew it, one hundred acres of forest had been felled in a single day. The railroad hired this mini lumberjack with the mighty blade the next day. But Pete had to give Paul Bunyan back his ax after he clear-cut fifty miles of trees.

After that, Pete returned to smaller jobs like woodchopping, which was perfect since he had no Babe the Blue Ox to haul his timber. He had only a trusty little donkey named Tamarack. Peder "Cordwood Pete" le Dang lived to be eighty-four years old and is buried just east of Fosston in the Rose Hill Cemetery.

Uncle Dan Campbell

A homespun Paul Bunyan, Uncle Dan Campbell evoked tales of grandeur and brawn. In Big Falls, a statue of the pioneer stands with his snowshoes, a shotgun, an eagle on his shoulder, and an enormous load of logs that he could surely pull with one arm.

The 1862 Dakota Uprising

"Let them eat grass!" is what an official supposedly told starving Dakota Indians when they asked for food in exchange for the credit owed them by the Treaty of Travers. A drought had ravaged Minnesota in 1862, so food was scarce. The Lower Sioux Agency near Redwood Falls was required to give the Native Americans food and money regularly, but the head of the outfit, Andrew Myrick, kept all the grain for the white settlers and famously blew off the Indians.

Tribal elders were finally persuaded by a fiery young Dakota to attack the group on August 20, 1862. Just as Marie Antoinette lost her head to the guillotine for telling the peasants to eat cake if they had no bread, Myrick's corpse was found with his mouth stuffed full of grass. At least, this is how the legend goes.

The 1862 Dakota Uprising lasted for days. New Ulm was the target of repeated attacks, and Minnesota's most famous doctor, W. W. Mayo, was on hand to treat the wounded. The revolt spread to Fort Ridgley, where the Dakota were held back by a hundred and eighty soldiers. When the battle was finally over, three hundred whites had been killed. No one ever bothered to count the number of dead Native Americans.

Sixteen hundred Native American prisoners were held at Fort Snelling in conditions so squalid that Native Americans still refer to the fort as a sort of concentration camp. The surviving settlers of the uprising along the Minnesota River demanded the blood of the rebels. A list of 392 Dakota were deemed guilty and condemned to death on November 5, 1862. While

SHA-KPE, (Little Six.)
A PRISONER AT FORT SNELLING CONDEMNED TO DEATH.
Engaged in Massacre of 1862, boasts of having killed thirteen Women and Children.

People escaping from the Indian Massacre of 1862, in Minnesota, at Dinner on a Prairie. Photographed by one of the party.

WHITNEY'S GALLERY.   SAINT PAUL.

the Civil War was raging, President Lincoln recognized the blood lust of the survivors but insisted that the list be pared down. The year before Lincoln famously signed the Emancipation Proclamation to free black slaves, the president approved the execution of thirty-eight Dakota—the largest mass hanging in U.S. history.

A special gallows was built to hang all the Dakota at the same time. Fourteen hundred infantry were called up to guard the prisoners; to prevent a riot, alcohol was banned for fifteen miles around Mankato for two days. When the executioner swung his ax, the rope from which the prisoners were hanging wouldn't break. Some in the audience viewed this as a sign from God that the Dakota should be set free. William Duley, who had had family members killed in the revolt, wouldn't hear of it and slashed the rope with his pocketknife in order to execute the thirty-eight.

"The dead were buried in a single shallow grave near the riverfront," according to *The Sioux Uprising of 1862*, by Kenneth Carley. "That night several doctors, quick to seize the rare opportunity to obtain cadavers for anatomical study, dug up the bodies. Dr. William Mayo drew that of Cut Nose and later his sons learned osteology from the Indian's skeleton."

The Underground Wedding Chapel

Things just weren't right around Harmony in southeastern Minnesota. Animals were disappearing, but no rustlers had ever come into the area. When three pigs belonging to farmer Kennedy went missing, he searched all over his land because he knew that the pigs would never miss a meal.

Living in an era before alien abductions, farmer Kennedy kept his head about him and retraced the path his pigs had taken. Deep within the bowels of the earth, he heard a faint "Oink," as though his three pigs had been plunged into one of the nine circles of hell. Farmer Kennedy scoured the ground until he found the small hole from which the oinks were emanating.

The farmer's son was lowered into the pit with a lantern and found the three pigs in perfect shape rummaging around in the dark. When the son shone his torch around, he discovered a beautiful underground waterfall and a series of breathtaking caverns.

Much of the ground around Harmony is karst, a limestone landscape that makes for numerous underground caves, streams, and sinkholes as water breaks through the rock surface. Kennedy's newfound cave was dubbed Niagara Cave because of the giant, sixty-

ENTRANCE TO CATHEDRAL DOME, 150 FEET HIGH, NIAGARA CAVE.

IOWA-MINNESOTA LINE

PHOTO BY NIAGARA CAVE

foot waterfall a hundred and fifty feet beneath the earth's surface.

Soon, the myriad tunnels were mapped out and tours were led through the beautiful caves. A Crystal Wedding Chapel was set up so that lovebirds could tie the knot in the constantly forty-eight-degree church, even if only a few relatives could fit in to witness the event.

As part of the Niagara Cave tour, the guides spin yarns about the history of the cave and farmer Kennedy, who lost his three little pigs. Suddenly, at the end of the tour, the lights go dim and screams echo against the walls of this cave, deep within the earth. Just a little Minnesota weirdness.

Death Star

When the Golden Gophers' home turf at the University of Minnesota, Memorial Stadium, was bulldozed, football fans lamented the loss of their outdoor brick stadium. Architectural ornaments from the old arena were placed inside the new McNamara Alumni Center, but this was too little too late. Besides, the new building on the old stadium site had a disturbing trapezoidal shape composed of forty thousand feet of granite. The university tried to put a positive spin on the building by nicknaming it the Geode. Annoyed U of M students have deemed the building bad luck and nicknamed it the Death Star, as though Darth Vader lurks inside, ready to give them an F if they enter.

Mermaid in Maidenform

"It's the kids from the high school— they do this every year," we're told as we snap photos of Albert Lea's *Little Mermaid* statue on Fountain Lake. The statue promotes the town's Danish heritage with a loose replica of Copenhagen's famous symbol. To tease the reverent Danes, high school students dressed up the naked statue on a rock island a dozen feet from shore. The offending garment was quickly removed—at least until next year.

Punk Rock and the Quadruple Murders

Here's a modern legend that got started by a rock band looking for some free publicity and media anxious to jump on any grisly story it can find—or dream up.

Sixteen-year-old David Brom was a straitlaced student from Rochester who dressed in almost preppy clothes and was considered a nice, normal kid. Somehow, a friend persuaded Brom to let him cut his hair in a Mohawk. A week later, Brom killed his parents, brother, and sister with an ax.

The New York Times reported that Brom had had an argument with his parents and that punk rock records were found at the crime scene. The Broms were described as a devout Roman Catholic family who might have argued over an audiotape that David had been listening to. A week prior to the murder, a feature article in the local Rochester newspaper had reported a connection between violence and music.

Seeing an opportunity, the Oakland rock band Negativland put out a press release saying that "Federal Official Dick Jordan" and "certain federal authorities" who were involved in the Brom case told the band "don't leave town" until the investigation is completed. The implication in the press release was that David and his parents argued about Negativland's song "Christianity Is Stupid," from the band's fourth album, *Escape From Noise.* The feds later denied having had any contact with the band.

Alternative weeklies and music magazines picked up the story that the Brom ax murder was caused by Negativland's song featuring the "found sound" of a 1968 sermon by the Reverend Estus Pirkle, preaching

(probably sarcastically), "Christianity is stupid; Communism is good." David Brom was sent for forensic psychiatric tests, and the media offered the explanation that punk rock music had mentally damaged him.

After that, Negativland, perhaps now worried about the media storm surrounding them, tried to keep mum about the incident. Finally, however, they agreed to an interview on CBS affiliate KPIX in San Francisco, which reached millions of viewers. CBS focused its report on the connection between murder and music and ran only a small section of the interview (cutting out all of Negativland's views on the dangers of sensationalism) over footage of body bags being carried out of the Brom home. After that, the story of how Negativland's music had caused the quadruple ax murder in Rochester gained even more momentum.

Eventually, Negativland released a CD called *Helter Stupid* about how they orchestrated this media virus that then took on a life of its own. The band had issued its original press release, in which they claimed to have been interviewed by federal authorities, as a joke, but the hoax snowballed.

Two years later, Mark Hosler, the lead singer of Negativland, met friends of David Brom's and discovered that the band's story had been regarded as absolute truth in the town of Rochester. Hosler wrote that "apparently our rumor actually made things WORSE in the town for all the punk rock misfit kids. . . . It fed into all the fears already there. Did we cross a line we now wished we hadn't? If not, did we come close?"

The Crawling Hand and the Legend of Blue Eagle

Near Loretto is a summer camp (YMCA Camp Ihduhapi, loosely translated as "Bear Your Own Burden") that has a number of creepy stories surrounding it. Legend has it that when workers were laying the foundation for cabin 13, they recovered the skeleton of a Native American chief but left one of his hands in the ground. It is said that the hand crawls across the floor in the middle of the night. People have seen the windows of this cabin glow, and I have a picture I've taken where the cabin number (13) glows, although no sun was out and the numbers were rusted over.

There is also an island in the middle of Lake Independence that is part of camp property and is home to the legend of Hatchet Jack. The story goes that there had been a gas station on the island servicing local fishermen and boats that was owned by a couple who had a troubled son. One night, the son allegedly murdered his parents with an ax and disappeared. People say that Hatchet Jack still lives on the island, waiting to lure people to their doom.

The last story is more positive. Back when the area around the camp was predominantly inhabited by the Ojibway, there was a particular tribe that held the moon as holy. One brave went on his vision quest and had a dream of a moonless night on which his tribe was attacked by a rival band of warriors. In the dream, this brave took the form of a luminescent blue eagle that rose up and took the place of the moon, bringing courage to his people and saving them from annihilation. Upon returning, he was given the name of Blue Eagle. Years passed and he became chief due to his bravery and sound leadership. One night, a dark new moon night, his people were attacked, just as in his vision quest. Blue Eagle rallied his people and led them to victory. When he died, he was buried on the (now submerged) peninsula that connected the island in the lake to the mainland. The story says that on nights when there is no moon, Blue Eagle walks the peninsula, looking for his people.–*Amy Roeder*

Profanity Above Schmidt's

Before the Schmidt Brewery started making Landmark beer and eventually closed, the letters S-C-H-M-I-D-T-'S lit up the night sky above the beautiful old building. As the legend goes, a couple of beer connoisseurs, fed up with what they deemed to be water suds brewed in enormous batches by the brewery on West Seventh Street, scaled the huge towers and managed to knock out every other letter of the huge sign (C, M, D, and S), leaving an enormous expletive above the once-proud brewery. No photos have been found to confirm this dubious claim.

Saint Paul: Not Another Siberia!

When a highbrow New York journalist visited Minnesota's capital in 1885 and dared write that Saint Paul is "another Siberia, unfit for human habitation," something had to be done. To prove that the city was in fact a winter wonderland, Saint Paul decided to build a huge ice palace. City officials knew that Montreal had built one a couple years before and was thinking about building another. But then a smallpox epidemic swept through Canada killing thousands, and building an ice palace became a low priority. "Some Montreal businessmen would just as soon have gone ahead with their winter celebration, but U.S. authorities slapped a quarantine on the province of Quebec," according to journalist Peg Meier.

So Saint Paul rounded up the Canadian architects to build a spectacular ice palace. Huge bricks of ice from a nearby lake were stacked 106 feet high to make the town's first ice castle. Saint Paulites and fellow Minnesotans took to the streets in droves—thousands more than the town's population—to see this marvel and march in the first Winter Carnival. The mercury plunged to twenty below

zero for the occasion; the number of frostbite cases was never reported. Saint Paulites assured themselves that surely Siberia must be colder.

An entire mythology was born for this winter festival, beginning with the marriage of the god of Starlight, named Astraios, to the mythical goddess of the Rosy Fingered Moon. Of their five sons—Boreas, Titan, Euros, Zephyrus, and Notos—Boreas was crowned King of the Winds. Struck by the beauty of Saint Paul and her seven hills, he commanded ten days of feasting, fun, and frolic. Every year, the envious Fire King, Vulcanus Rex, seeks to rain on the parade by sending his Vulcans to mark the women (and now the men, too) with a tarlike V on their cheeks and making them swear allegiance to Vulcanus. Thus far, King Boreas has ruled the day, but not without an annual attack of Vulcans storming the ice castle.

Saint Paul's native son F. Scott Fitzgerald wrote about this bizarre Minnesota phenomenon in a 1918 short story called *The Ice Palace*. In the story, a young woman from Georgia was engaged to a man from Saint Paul, but just when she was scheduled to meet her fiancé's family, she somehow got locked inside the ice castle. By the time she finally managed to escape, the wedding had been called off and she fled Minnesota for the southland. Obviously, she couldn't hack it. Perhaps this was autobiographical for Fitzgerald, who was more comfortable lounging in Gertrude Stein's Parisian salon and writing about the jazz age than hunkered down in the frozen northland.

Nevertheless, King Boreas's ice palaces continue to rise from ice sawed from frozen Lake Phalen. In 2004, 27,000 blocks of ice were hauled to make the 240-foot-long castle with an eight-story turret and an $8 million price tag. The temporary fortress provides welcome relief from cabin fever as well as photo ops of the multicolored ice house. At least as long as the camera doesn't freeze up.

Bootleggers' Caves

Barreling downhill into Stillwater from the Twin Cities leads right past the town's most famous caves and the many legends that accompany the dark abyss. The stories stretch back to when Tom "the Cave Man" Curtis bought the caves in 1945 and spent the next years digging and leading tours. King Neptune lived deep in the tunnels with his legions of leprechauns, Curtis would tell kids.

Then he'd show them the "bottomless pit" that goes all the way to China. No wonder no one believed the other myths that have been told about the caves.

One is that a shaft rises all the way to the parking lot many stories overhead. The Cave Man explained that Native Americans sent smoke signals through it, with puffs visible for miles along the St. Croix valley, to warn their friends.

Tourists could visit the caves on little flatbed wooden boats that were pulled by an elaborate system of cables on the ground. Curtis had flooded the caves with just enough water for the boats to keep the tourists captive so that he could spin his yarns. He stocked part of the water with trout and charged visitors a small fee to drop a line and do some fishing.

During the cold war, with impending nuclear annihilation right around the corner, the people of Stillwater asked Curtis to prepare his caves for Armageddon. Familiar with the hype required to draw in visitors, Curtis equipped the cave with emergency rations and advertised the caves as the safest place in town. "If it hadn't cost so much overtime, I'd have hired a couple of Russian pilots to drop a few test bombs to prove my point," he said. Thanks to civil-defense drills, the kids in Stillwater all knew that the local bomb shelter was the caves.

All the exaggeration puts the real (or at least the oft-told) history of the caves into question. For many years, the caves had been used by the Martin Wolf Brewery as the local suds factory. Around 1880, the Pacific Hotel was attached to the caves and became the hottest spot north of Chicago for the next fifty years. When Prohibition was signed into law, in 1919, the brewery paid it no mind and kept the beer flowing. The secret entrance to the caves was in back of the blacksmith's shop next door. Hidden rooms in the hotel led into underground spaces out of reach of the long arm of the law. Knock twice for the saloon, three times for the second-story dance hall, and show your money to enter the third-floor bordello.

Secret passages built into the caves that haven't been opened since Prohibition are still being uncovered. Recently, when the walls were being redone, a huge room that could easily seat two hundred people was discovered from Stillwater's speakeasy days. According to the owner, "We think there's one they haven't found yet that seats a hundred people."

More legends state that when an explosion blew up a section of the cave and wine leaked out of the opening, the feds got wise. A bust allegedly revealed that Al Capone was running liquor out of the back and had been trying to expand the caves with dynamite when things went awry.

Today, the caves are open for tours. Unfortunately, the kitsch Grotto Blue Dining Room with murals of the island of Capri, cobalt-blue ceilings, elegant urns, and busts of Roman legionnaires has been "updated" into a modern restaurant. Nevertheless, the beer is back. The owners have reopened the Martin Wolf Brewery and use the constant fifty-two-degree temperature to keep it fresh.

Ancient Mysteries

Minnesotans always seem to be digging up something in their fields. The most famous underground find is the Kensington Runestone, which advocates claim is proof positive that Scandinavians occupied central Minnesota more than a century before that upstart Columbus arrived on the scene. Other ancient remnants are giant beaver fossils, petroglyphs in the pipestone quarries, and some of the oldest rocks in the world.

The people who predate the Native Americans do even more to stir the imaginations of modern Minnesotans. Imagine the excitement when skeletons dug up near the glacial Lake Agassiz were found to date back six to twenty thousand years! To make the story even better, archaeologists weren't sure if these skeletons were related to modern Native Americans. Was this a different race? The missing link? No one knows for sure, but stories were quickly invented to fill in any gaps that science could not explain.

And that's just the beginning. Prehistoric glaciers, unknown ancestors, and secretive forebears have deposited all sorts of strange mementos around our state. What follows is just the tip of what's been buried under our icebergs or ancient mounds or in our own backyards.

Prehistoric Mound, at Mound Park, Laurel Minn.
Height 28 ft. Width 115 ft. One of the largest Mounds fou
built by the Prehistoric Race, called "Mound Builder

Grand Mound

Indian mounds dotted the state before pioneer farmers plowed them under without a second thought to make way for their crops. These Native-American burial sites were sometimes effigy mounds in the shape of fish, birds, and other animals. Many of the mounds are only a few hundred years old, but some date back more than two thousand years.

When European settlers found giant mounds just west of International Falls at the convergence of the Rainy and Big Fork rivers, they weren't sure exactly what they were. None of the Native Americans in the area knew the history of the large burial site, so theories raged about ancient western civilizations setting up shop in northern Minnesota. The largest hill at Grand Mound rises forty feet from its surroundings and is a whopping 325 feet in circumference. Only after four other mounds were found did the settlers realize the importance of the site. Archaeologists estimated that the mounds are at least two thousand years old. Because holes have been found in the heads of some of the excavated skeletons, archaeologists theorize that the people who built the mounds must have been brain eaters, discounting for some reason the possibility that the dead had been killed by a blow to the skull.

Archaeologists believe that the mounds were created by the ancient Laurel Indians, who were lured to the area by the promise of giant sturgeon filling the lakes. Other Native Americans also buried their dead here, making this sacred ground the largest burial mound in the upper Midwest.

Turtle Oracle Mound

In a fitting tribute to its name, mystery surrounds the Turtle Oracle Mound in Chippewa National Forest near Bemidji. The turtle effigy is actually an intaglio, or sunken impression, rather than a mound, and speculation about its creation abounds.

The twenty-five-foot-wide by thirty-foot-long effigy dates back to the eighteenth century, when it is said that the Dakota (Sioux) Indians constructed it. Exactly why they constructed it, however, is subject to speculation and debate. Some say it was created before the arrival of Europeans to the area. Others claim that European encroachment led to warfare between the Dakota and the Ojibwa, who moved into Dakota territory, and that the effigy was built to commemorate a Dakota victory. The turtle's head pointed to the northeast, the direction in which the enemy supposedly fled.

Later, however, the Ojibwa ousted the Dakota and took the turtle as its own, using it as a holy place to consult with the turtle oracle. Now, here's where the story gets interesting: Ojibwa legend says that somewhere along the way, the turtle's head and tail switched positions so that the head now points south—the way of the fleeing Dakota.

The Mystery of the Kensington Runestone

At right is the translation of old Scandinavian runes, or ancient letters, written on a huge slab of graywacke stone dug up on Olof Ohman's farm in Kensington in 1898. At last! Here was proof that Scandinavians had explored the area 130 years before Columbus!

But then the spoilsport skeptics took their turn:

1. Ohman was a Swedish immigrant to this area, so he would have had an interest in proving that his ancestors actually came to his farm five centuries before. Especially after Native Americans had been pushed off the land and subsequently participated in the Dakota Uprising of 1862—only thirty years before Ohman found the stone.

2. Settlers had been digging up all sorts of questionable objects in order to make a buck. Just two years before, in 1896, a "Petrified Man" was discovered underground in Bloomer, Minnesota, but molds for the concrete human were later discovered.

3. Ohman's neighbor and friend, the minister Sven Fogelblad, had studied runes, and Ohman was a trained stonemason. One of Ohman's neighbor's sons later reported that his father said on his deathbed that he had carved the runes.

4. The carvings can't be dated. Carbon dating is impossible on stone.

5. In 2003, the runestone went for further analysis at the National Historical Museum of Stockholm, Sweden. The runes were found to be so similar to a secret trade language used in Scandinavia in the 1800s that the stone was deemed a fake. Scholars assumed that Ohman and

EIGHT GOTHS AND 22 NORWEGIANS ON AN EXPLORATION JOURNEY FROM VINLAND TO THE WEST. WE HAD CAMP BY 2 SKERRIES ONE DAY'S JOURNEY NORTH FROM THIS STONE. WE WERE TO FISH ONE DAY AFTER WE CAME HOME FOUND 10 MEN RED OF BLOOD AND DEAD AVM [Ave Maria].
[On the side of the stone] WE HAVE 10 MEN BY THE SEA TO LOOK AFTER OUR SHIPS 14 DAYS' TRAVEL FROM THIS ISLAND YEAR 1362.

Fogelblad knew this version of runes and had used it to carve the stone.

Ohman stood by his story, however, and advocates for the stone stated their case:

1. The writing on the stone wasn't translated by Ohman or Fogelblad; they simply recognized that the runes were similar to what they'd seen in books back in Sweden. Not until nine years after the stone's discovery was the cryptic text finally unraveled, revealing that Norse explorers had supposedly beaten Columbus to the New World.

2. Ohman never became rich off the stone, compared with owners of other hoaxes. He sold the slab for $10. Ohman was mocked, ridiculed, and publicly humiliated for his stone. Why wouldn't he just admit that he had played a fantastic trick and take credit for fooling the world rather than stick to his story?

3. The graywacke stone was found intertwined in the roots of a large aspen tree that Ohman and his son were clearing from the field. Assuming that this is true, it shows that Ohman simply couldn't have buried the stone to find it again.

4. The "mistakes" of grammar in the runes are probably the result of the explorers' having been only somewhat educated. The old runestones back in Scandinavia, on the other hand, were probably carved by expert masons and scholars.

Even so, professor Erik Wahlgren, an expert in the Norwegian language, claimed that "the Swedish on the stone was a version of that language that had never been spoken anywhere outside the American Midwest."

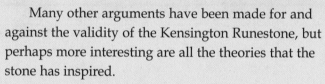

Many other arguments have been made for and against the validity of the Kensington Runestone, but perhaps more interesting are all the theories that the stone has inspired.

The translator of the stone, Hjalmar Holand, hypothesized that its tale was of an expedition led by Paul Knutson, commissioned by the evangelical Catholic king Magnus Erickson of Sweden and Norway in 1355, who had been out of touch with his colonies in Greenland and Vinland (North America). Knutson's entourage was sent to find out if the colonists were still there and had spread the word of Christ. Knutson found the settlement in Greenland deserted, so he continued on to Vinland, searching in vain for the colonists. One summer, a small party went down the Nelson River into Lake Winnipeg and on to the Red River. After a fishing trip, part of the group returned to find ten comrades had been killed, "red of blood." Holand assumed that the runestone was a memo left for the others in their party.

The rest of Knutson's followers, waiting in Hudson's

Bay, eventually returned to Norway in 1363 or 1364. The explorers in Minnesota couldn't find their way home and settled in North Dakota with the Mandan Indians. Holand speculated that this explains the Mandans' blue eyes, fair skin, and European-style villages and the runic images found on old Mandan animal bones. While this theory was a bit far-fetched, the excitement over the Kensington Runestone landed it in the hallowed halls of the Smithsonian Museum with no specific claim except "the Smithsonian Institute has appointed no commission, but states, 'Perhaps the most widely known object attributed to the Vikings is the Kensington Runestone.'"

Never mind that by 1362 the Viking era had long since ended.

In spite of all the naysayers, the myth of the runestone won't die. In 2001, author Thomas Reiersgord speculated that the "Goths" of the stone were actually Cistercian monks from the Swedish island of Gotland who were often literate stone carvers. He argues that the "red of blood" meant that the ten men had been hemorrhaging from the bubonic plague, which was ravaging Europe. Reiersgord suggested that the Dakota had carried this stone with them after the white explorers carved it. He wrote that this Dakota tribe "identified themselves as the Isanti, meaning the people who possessed 'isan,' the cut stone," or the runestone. The

Isanti buried this sacred stone according to tradition, with a new aspen sapling above it, which was the tree Olof Ohman uprooted a century later.

The possibility that Ohman's stone is valid helped fuel Scandinavian fervor across the state and created a few more tourist attractions. Walker, Minnesota, has a huge Viking ship mural on a downtown building, and Spring Grove has a replica of a Viking ship perched on a hill, along with a bronze Viking statue in town called *The Quest,* sculpted by Craig Bergsgaard. Statues of Leif Erikson have popped up all over the state. Duluth has a Viking in Leif Erikson Park; Saint Paul even has Leif Erikson next to the capitol building as though he were one of the state's founders.

Minnesota's Saint

Amid the fertile fields of central Minnesota is a hallowed skeleton from, of all places, ancient Rome. Minnesota's only saint, or relic of a saint, lies in the reliquary chapel of St. John's Abbey at Collegeville. He is called St. Peregrine, and the story of how he wound up in Minnesota is strange indeed.

In 192 A.D., the Roman emperor Commodus sent out a proclamation that citizens of Rome should come to celebrate his birthday by admiring him in his new birthday suit: a revealing lion skin. To flaunt his masculinity, Commodus strode into the Colosseum and bludgeoned some weakened gladiators to death in a fixed match. Those about to die saluted him; the crowd cheered. Their mighty leader stood over the vanquished corpses of the prisoner warriors.

Along with three other Christians—Eusebius, Vincent, and Pontian—Peregrinus ran through the streets of Rome denouncing the vanity of Commodus and his decadent gods. The Praetorian guard easily snatched up the unarmed Christians and gave them a good flogging before the official Roman torturers used their own devices to teach them a lesson.

The seeds had been sown, however. One of the guards witnessed an angel swoop down to protect one of the Christians from the flames of the fire set at his feet. The guard gave his notice and ran off to be baptized. Visitors to the condemned Christian prisoners came away born again. The blind priest Lupulus, a devotee of the Roman god Jupiter, came to try to show the Christians the error of their ways. Instead, Lupulus was miraculously cured of his blindness just by being near the martyrs.

ST. PEREGRIN

Peregrinus was secretly buried in the catacombs of Rome. In 1731, his bones were taken by abbot Kilian Kneuer and brought back to his Benedictine monastery in Neustadt-am-Main, Germany. Later, during the Napoleonic Wars, Prince Löwenstein declared the holy relics his own and took them, much to the monks' dismay.

By 1895, the Benedictines were demanding their bones back. Later Löwensteins, seeing the error of the ways of their ancestors, finally agreed to give up the bones of the boy martyr, who by now had been canonized. In 1927, St. Peregrine was shipped to his new home in Collegeville.

Commodus died the same year that he had killed the four defiant Christians. The Caesars' tyranny worked for a century more to keep Christianity down, until another emperor, Constantine, made Rome a Christian state.

Now, more than twenty centuries after Peregrine's death in ancient Rome, his holy bones lie in a small town in Minnesota.

ROCKS

Rainbow Rock

Morton, Minnesota, and the surrounding Minnesota River Valley are home to something very ancient—a type of metamorphic rock called the Morton Gneiss. Pink, white, and red lines give the rock, which is quarried for use in buildings and monuments, the nickname Rainbow Rock. More than just a pretty face, though, this is the oldest rock in the world, dating back approximately 3.8 billion years on an earth that is only 4.5 billion years old. If you don't feel like digging around the outskirts of Morton, you can see a bit of this rock for yourself near Granite Falls, where a piece is on display at the Yellow Medicine County Historical Museum. It's a rock that will outlast all of us, since human existence is just a blip on the chart of its lengthy life.

Pipestone Quarry and Petroglyphs

One of the most sacred Native American sites in Minnesota used to be held in common by all of the tribes across the continent. Pipestone National Monument was considered too precious for any one tribe to claim ownership. Artist George Catlin transcribed the legend of the origin of Pipestone from a Dakota storyteller in 1835: "At an ancient time, the Great Spirit, in the form of a large bird, stood upon the wall of rock and called all the tribes around him, and breaking out a piece of red stone formed it into a pipe and smoked it, the smoke rolling over the whole multitude."

The soft red pipestone, sometimes called catlinite, after Catlin, is easily carved into figurines, effigies, and pipes. According to explorer John Wesley Powell, who also came to the area in the 1800s, "It is not too much to say that the great pipestone quarry was the most important single locality in aboriginal geography and lore."

In Native American times, tobacco smoking was for special occasions, not the everyday habit many people came to practice after Sir Walter Raleigh brought it back to England. Instead, smoking tobacco through a pipestone pipe was intended to honor the Great Spirit, as the smoke rose like a ghost from the bowl. Smoking ceremonies were reserved for healings, councils among leaders, preparation for war, and other solemn events.

Catlin continued his retelling of the legend of pipestone: "[The Great Spirit] then told his red children that this red stone was their flesh, that they were made from it, that they must all smoke to him through it, that they must use it for nothing but pipes and as it belonged alike to all the tribes, the ground was sacred, and no weapons must be used or brought upon it." In spite of the common ownership of the quarries, the

Dakota controlled it by the time George Catlin and Joseph Nicollet visited them in the 1830s.

Henry Wadsworth Longfellow chimed in on this special site as well, even though he'd never visited the state. His *Song of Hiawatha* begins with the lines, "On the mountains of the prairie, on the great Red Pipestone Quarry."

Much effort has been made to preserve the pipestone petroglyphs found at the base of the three boulders—nicknamed the Three Sisters—in spite of white explorers' attempts to pillage these sacred objects. Since 1937, when the pipestone quarry was declared a national monument, only Native Americans may quarry the smooth red stone, and Dakota artisans use it to carve pipes and other figures.

Splitting Mountains

In 1766, explorer Jonathan Carver climbed the 343-foot Barn Bluff above the Mississippi River and wrote that the view was "the most beautiful prospect that imagination can form. . . . But above all, reaching as far as the eye can extend, is the majestic, softly flowing river." His words inspired Henry David Thoreau to amble up the steep overlook when away from his calm Walden.

Little did they know that they were only the latest in a long line of admirers. Native Americans told ancient legends of this giant bluff left over from the glaciers. According to the legends, two Dakota tribes fought continuously over the hulking mountain along the Mississippi, and the Great Spirit was not pleased. Rather than award the mountain to the more noble or brave tribe, the Great Spirit split the mountain in two—just as Solomon would have divided a baby. One half of the mountain remained on the south side of present-day Red Wing and was later named Barn Bluff for its shape.

The other half was sent to where the town of Winona now stands and was named Sugar Loaf. The shape of this half of the mountain inspired myths that it was Chief Wabasha's red cap, given to him by an officer of the British army, the redcoats. Part of this four-hundred-and-fifty-foot-tall limestone precipice was later quarried to make Winona's sidewalks. No word on what the Great Spirit thought of that desecration.

Stonehenge in Minnesota

Buffalo can roam and hide among the tall bluestem grasses. Quartzite, produced more than a billion years ago when this area was sea bottom, sticks up from the ground; it was also used as a buffalo jump by Native American hunters. This is Blue Mounds State Park, in the far southwest corner of the state near Luverne.

The most mysterious section of the park lies in its south end, however, where a pile of rocks stretch 1,250 feet in a perfect line from east to west. The only explanation is that the rock mound was an early sundial used by ancestors of the Native Americans to mark the passing of time. On the two equinoxes—the first day of spring and the first day of fall—the line of stones is perfectly synchronized with sunrise and sunset. No one knows how these early mathematicians aligned their sundial so perfectly.

Earliest Minnesotans

Not much is known about the earliest people who came to Minnesota, sometimes called the Paleo-Indians or Big Game Hunters. They left few clues, mostly in the form of arrowheads and skeletons. Twelve thousand years ago, glaciers covered northern Minnesota, and life flourished on their edges. During this Pleistocene period, more than 9,500 years ago, the melting glaciers filled the Mississippi Valley with water. Mastodons, woolly mammoths, and giant beavers provided game for hunters, who used fluted spearheads to bring down the ancient elephants. While mastodons surely existed across Minnesota, the melting glaciers are probably what washed away all evidence of them, leaving the state not as rich in fossil record as North or South Dakota.

Archaeologists guess that the early Paleo-Indians traveled in tribes of about two dozen people and rarely settled for long. The ancient mystery surrounding these people will remain unsolved until further clues are unearthed. One thing is clear, however: These early inhabitants feasted on the now-extinct six-foot-long giant beaver.

Minnesota Woman

In 1931 road construction crews digging up soil to make way for Route 59 came upon an unexpected find: a cache of ancient bones. The Minnesota Man was heralded as the oldest skeleton in the state—possibly ten to twenty thousand years old.

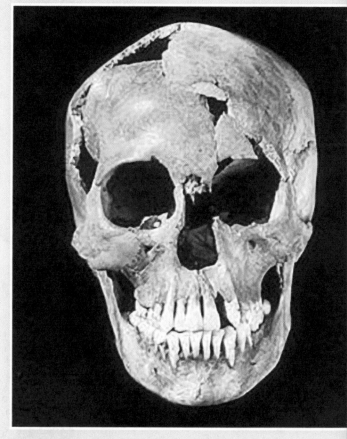

After a bit of research, archaeologists soon realized that the man was actually a woman, a young girl of about fifteen years old. Newspapers renamed her Miss Minnesota, Minnesota Minnie, and Lady of the Lake—since she had probably drowned in Lake Pelican, which was part of the ancient glacial Lake Agassiz. This huge body of water covered most of Minnesota during the last Ice Age. In one bony hand, the girl held an elk-antler dagger, leading scientists to conclude that elk were much more prevalent in Minnesota thousands of years ago. In her other hand, she clasped a conch shell from the ocean, which meant that early trade had extended to the coasts.

Her skeleton is older than other Indian and Eskimo skeletons that have been found, and it is perhaps the oldest female skeleton in America. Her bones were eventually turned over to the Dakota Indians (even though archaeologists doubt that she was an ancestor) and buried in South Dakota.

Browns Valley Man

Two years after the Minnesota Woman was uncovered, archaeologist William Jensen found the skeleton of a man buried in the gravel of the ancient glacial Lake Agassiz. The Browns Valley Man held in his hand a knife with a handle made of chalcedony, a type of quartz that is sometimes viewed as a gem. His bones date back eight to ten thousand years, which means that he is older than all of the Native American mounds in the state, even the ancient Grand Mound near International Falls.

Petrified Man

French voyagers were the first Europeans to have a real presence in Minnesota, in the 1600s. So when a rocklike human figure was unearthed in 1896 in tiny Bloomer, residents assumed that this was a petrified Frenchman. Peter Bergo dropped $175 for the now-famous Petrified Man of Bloomer and put him on exhibit. Theories of his origins blossomed, and Bergo made a small fortune on admission fees. He eventually sold the Man for $1,000, making a good profit.

But was the Petrified Man Bergo's to sell? Other northwestern Minnesotans laid claim to the fossilized creature. One couple said that they owned the land on which he was found. Others said that they owned the mineral rights to the land and that the Petrified Man was theirs because he had been found underground.

To prevent the Petrified Man from being stolen by any of the interested parties, the sheriff of Grand Forks locked him up in jail until a judge could decide his fate. Suddenly, claims were dropped, as molds for the cement man were discovered outside of Crookston. Petrified Man was just a profitable phony.

Captured Undead

Minnesota is home to two mummies with questionable pedigrees. The most authentic is now in the Science Museum of Minnesota. Any world-class museum must have its own Egyptian mummy, so loyal Saint Paulite Simon Percy Crosby searched high and low for the genuine article for his hometown museum. He finally sneaked one into town in 1925, thanks to a shady Egyptologist. Crosby donated the thirty-five-hundred-year-old mummy to the St. Paul Institute, but the poor wrapped body was without its sarcophagus. Egyptologists studied the mummy and found that his brain had been removed—the sign of a high priest. The museum painted a 1930s WPA-style sarcophagus to house its Egyptian guest and proudly put him on display.

A more questionable, but much more gruesome, mummy is housed in Hutchinson, in central Minnesota. Is it one of the corpses from the Mount Vesuvius eruption that destroyed Pompeii? Perhaps it's one of the hundred-and-fifty-year-old mummies from Guanajuato, Mexico. Did someone simply wrap an earlier settler or a Native American in bandages before he died?

The Hutchinson mummy traveled across the country as the mummy of various outlaws or perhaps of John Wilkes Booth; the stories vary. The waist-length black hair of the creature was explained by the fact that the mummy was still alive in a way—just as fingernails on corpses continue to grow. Theories abound, but the fact that the undead corpse is made of papier-mâché strips it of any credibility. The curator at the McLeod County Historical Society explained, "Well, it's not a real, authentic mummy, you know." Which raises the question as to why they need to keep it under glass.

Fabled People and Places

Minnesota is rife with storied places and offbeat characters whose reputations precede them. Some of the people were living, breathing souls who caused quite a stir in their day. Some of the places were, and are, real and are still celebrated. But some of the most famous Minnesotans never actually existed (good grief!). They may be characters who live only in a black-and-white comic strip by a Saint Paul native and self-described high school failure. Or they may be that famous brunette who threw her hat up in delight along Nicollet Mall—and then fled to Hollywood to film sitcom episodes supposedly set in Minneapolis. Not only is Minnesota full of nonexistent people (and Finnish saints); some of our most well-known places can't even be found on a map! Garrison Keillor's Lake Wobegon was, according to the author, left off the state map by a cartographer's error. Sinclair Lewis's Gopher Prairie never even came that close to being real. We're a state best known for towns and people that never existed.

These fabled places and legendary characters might just be the product of an overly imaginative populace with too much free time during the frozen winter. But, they stand as a testament to Minnesota's history, state pride, and, more often than not, sense of humor.

INDIAN LEGENDS

Na-Na-Nanabojo

Chief Bemidji, or Shaynowishkung, watches over Lake Bemidji and is honored for having helped the early European settlers survive the brutal winters of the north woods. Perhaps this statue is now a bit envious of that newcomer celebrity lumberjack Paul Bunyan, who all the tourists stop to photograph.

An Ojibwa story tells of Nanabojo the trickster, who challenged the mighty Paul Bunyan to a duel after the Indian hero saw the lumberjack greedily strip the forest of trees. The battle lasted for weeks, and the northland shook with the wrestling match. The tall tale says that Nanabojo beat the lumberjack silly with a giant fish.

Jumping Maiden, Lake Pepin

In times past, when the Minnesota woods were deep and dark and ruled by the native people, there was a mighty chief, Chief Wahpesha. He was determined that his beautiful daughter, Wenonah, marry another chief, Black Hawk. Wenonah was already in love with a man she called Great Heart. He wasn't a mighty chief and couldn't promise Wahpesha the power that Black Hawk could, so their romance was doomed.

Wenonah and Great Heart left their village, Keoxa, in a canoe before the sun rose on the day of her wedding. Just when they thought they had safely escaped, they heard wild screaming and drums as the villagers and Chief Wahpesha gave chase. Wenonah and her lover paddled furiously upstream but finally had to land the canoe and run through the forest on foot. They climbed a desolate ledge on the side of the river across from the village and watched Chief Wahpesha and his warriors approach. Wahpesha readied an arrow on his bow and aimed it toward the ledge to strike Great Heart in the chest. Wenonah knew that her father's aim was true, so she stepped in front of her lover.

Her father hesitated, and Wenonah told him that she would not marry Black Hawk and could love only Great Heart. Her father scoffed. With that, Wenonah and her lover leaped from the cliff to their death. Her father and the villagers looked on in horror at the tragedy that had befallen their village.

Ever since, the precipice on the east shore of Lake Pepin has been known as Maiden Rock (not the oft-confused Sugar Loaf, in Winona) for the leaping Indian princess.

Mark Twain wasn't convinced. In *Life on the Mississippi,* one of his characters calls the story of Maiden Rock "perhaps the most celebrated, as well as the most pathetic, of all legends of the Mississippi." He wrote that if all the myths of Indian princesses jumping off cliffs up and down the Mississippi were true, there would be piles of princess bones at the bottom of each cliff. Twain hypothesized, through his characters, that Wenonah threw herself onto her parents, who happened to be passing by below the rock. While her parents were crushed, she survived and ran away with her beloved.

Minnehaha Meets Hiawatha

According to artist George Catlin, in 1835 the Fashionable Tour of Minneapolis for Easterners was to ride the steamboat to Fort Snelling and then take day trips up to the Falls of St. Anthony and Little Falls, also known as Brown Falls or Minnehaha Falls.

For centuries, Minnehaha Falls had been a sacred spot for Native Americans. Then, chic New Englanders in top hats and hoop dresses came here for picnics. In 1857, writer Harriet Bishop waxed poetic about the Falls's "melody of waters" and the "wild, wild laugh you hear. . . . We part the foliage, and, standing upon the brink of a chasm . . . we behold the laughing waters, the whole width of the stream, making the bold leap. Nature speaks, and you are silent; but admiration is enthroned on the delighted countenance. . . ."

Bishop's words were overshadowed by poet Henry Wadsworth Longfellow's famous poem *The Song of Hiawatha.* Longfellow had never actually visited the Falls but saw a daguerreotype in 1849. Many readers took Longfellow's story to be true, but no Native American legend about Minnehaha has been found. Longfellow was simply intrigued by the name and said his poem was "founded on a tradition prevalent among the North American Indians, of a personage of miraculous birth, who was sent among them to clear their rivers, forests, and fishing grounds, and to teach them the arts of peace."

In other words, he made it up. But Longfellow had read Henry Schoolcraft's writings about an eastern tribe Indian chief named Hiawatha, who founded the famous Iroquois Confederacy.

Longfellow wrote that Hiawatha was traveling through the "land of the Dacotahs . . . Where the Falls of Minnehaha/Flash and gleam among the oak-trees/

Many readers took Longfellow's story to be true, but no Native American legend about Minnehaha has been found.

Laugh and leap into the valley." Hiawatha had been looking for arrowheads at the Falls and fell in love with the arrowmaker's "dark-eyed daughter":

> *With her moods of shade and sunshine,*
> *Eyes that smiled and frowned alternate,*
> *Feet as rapid as the river,*
> *Tresses flowing like the water,*
> *And as musical a laughter;*
> *And he named her from the river,*
> *From the water-fall he named her*
> *Minnehaha, Laughing Water.*

Hiawatha asked for Minnehaha's hand and carried her over the creek, risking the fifty-three-foot drop of the falls to carry her back to "the land of the Ojibways."

To honor the famous poem, the neighborhood north of the Falls carries Longfellow's name, and parallel streets—Minnehaha and Hiawatha—travel diagonally to the Falls. In 1911, schoolchildren in Minneapolis raised more than $1,000 in pennies to bring Longfellow's story to life by hiring Norwegian sculptor Jacob Fjelde to erect a statue of Hiawatha carrying Minnehaha over the creek above the Falls.

FABLED PLACES

Utopia on Lake Constance

Frans Herman Widstrand was a late 1870s visionary who dreamed of forming a utopian commune on his property at Lake Constance that would grant every member two furnished rooms and a chance for meditation. Everyone in his community would have work to do, and the bulk purchase of food would save time and money. Neither the majority nor the strongest would rule the colony; rather, everyone would obey "the rule of right."

Right off the bat, Widstrand ran into trouble. His dream was compared to communist Bolshevism. He rebutted that it was nothing like "communism in the vulgar sense of that word." Others dubbed his idea a sexual perversion and compared it to the free-love Oneida colony in upstate New York. Widstrand's goal was nearly the opposite, however. He wanted his colony to be a place of enlightenment, not of new families. "Marriage tames the Democrat," he warned, saying that it bogs down upstanding folk with the toils of raising a family rather than becoming better people themselves. Love was to be viewed suspiciously as an inexplicable sort of "craziness induced by education of fashion."

According to Helen White in *The Tale of a Comet,* "Rather than reproducing themselves, members of his colony could adopt poor children and soldiers' orphans. Until mankind became fully happy, no other children ought to be brought into the world; there would be no marriages in his colony until that day."

Widstrand wouldn't allow any tobacco or alcohol, and meat would be eaten only as a last resort. He studied Benjamin Franklin's theory that meat makes us cruel and wastes our money. Widstrand noted that if everyone "had to butcher . . . there would not be so much meat eating."

Things progressed slowly. Widstrand was able to attract only eight people to his community, to help plant his crops and search for enlightenment. But all the colonists agreed to abstain from alcohol, tobacco, and producing babies. Widstrand finally had his utopian commune, but like so many dreams, it didn't turn out as he'd envisioned. He found himself bothered by all the people milling around and distracting him from writing for his newspaper, *Agathocrat.* To get away from the hubbub, he moved to Kansas for the winter and stayed with a friend. As soon as the intrepid leader wasn't around to crack the whip, the colonists began to sell off that year's crops to buy booze.

Widstrand got wind that moral corruption was sneaking into his dream, but by the time he returned in the spring, only one couple was left. The husband was drunk and met Widstrand with a shotgun. The hysterical wife threatened to drown herself in the lake. On top of it all, Widstrand received a $175 bill that the husband had sent for failure to pay for labor. No lawyer in town would represent the utopian dreamer against his colonists. To add to his troubles, Widstrand hadn't paid one tax installment on his property, so he lost his land to drunken squatters.

All Along the Witch's Tower

Around the turn of the last century, a wooden mold of a tower was built on the tallest hill in Minneapolis. Heavy concrete was lugged up the many steps and poured into the mold, and a medieval-looking spire was formed beneath the frame. By 1913, the tallest tower in the Twin Cities was finished, a *château d'eau*, or water tower. Architect F. W. Cappelen added a lookout on the very top, covered by a Spanish-tile roof ending in a point, which gave the water tower the name Witch's Hat, or sometimes simply Witch's Tower.

The tower, located in the Prospect Park neighborhood, originally contained a small band shell to give concertgoers a fantastic view of the Cities while listening to big bands on summer evenings. Legend has it that the first band scheduled to play in the band shell was so winded by the time they climbed all of the Tower's circular steps that they couldn't perform. The witch's curse had begun.

It struck again when lightning hit the water tower in 1954 and rendered it useless. Over the years, it fell into disrepair and almost disappeared. Interstate 94 was scheduled to bulldoze the neighborhood, but Witch's Hat and a Frank Lloyd Wright house were reason enough for city planners to give the area a pass. In 1986, the residents around Tower Hill convinced the Minneapolis City Council to renovate Witch's Tower to its former grandeur.

Local legend states that Bob Dylan penned his song "All Along the Watchtower" after hanging out under Witch's Hat when he lived in Dinkytown and would cut classes to strum his six-string. These days, the top of the tower is open only once a year, during the neighborhood ice cream social in June. Some people say that one too many university students has taken a leap from the top of the tower.

Does Wabasha Hide Lost Land Deed?

A rumor I heard while growing up is that somewhere in Minnesota, a deed is buried that proves ownership of large sections of Minnesota and Wisconsin, including the Minneapolis/Saint Paul metro area, by one family. I don't remember which family is the alleged owner of the deed, but I think the town of Wabasha, Minnesota, has something to do with it. –*Scott Graupner*

FAMOUS NONEXISTENT MINNESOTANS

Charlie Brown

When Charles Schulz came home to Saint Paul for his high school reunion, nobody believed he was the creator of *Peanuts*—"At our 25th reunion, I was on the list of people nobody knew what happened to," he recalled. Even when he attended Central High School, his drawings for the high school yearbook were always rejected. When he returned for the reunion, he had to sketch a portrait of Charlie Brown before anyone believed that Schulz was who he claimed to be.

"I don't know which was worse—the Army or Central High School," he told Curt Brown of the *Star Tribune* in 1997. "I was a bland, stupid-looking kid who started off bad and failed everything and hated the whole time."

Postwar, Schulz managed to persuade the *Saint Paul Pioneer Press* to publish his cartoon *Li'l Folks* for a couple years. Then, the paper decided that $10 a week for Schulz drawings was excessive. Schulz sold his strip to the United Feature Syndicate, which changed the name to *Peanuts*, a name he never liked because it made the characters sound unimportant. Schulz eventually got revenge on his hometown paper, when he refused to let them run his strip. He gave that honor to *The Minneapolis Tribune* (later the *Star Tribune*).

While Saint Paul claims Schulz as its own, he was, in fact, born on Chicago Avenue in Minneapolis. The landmarks and characters of his strip, however, are found almost entirely in the capital city. Charlie Brown's dad's barbershop was modeled on Schulz's own father's shop at Selby and Snelling, where O'Gara's now stands. Most of the *Peanuts* characters were real people (or dogs) in Schulz's life. Snoopy was his wild, untamable beagle. The Little Red-Haired Girl was Donna Johnson

"I was a bland, stupid-looking kid who started off bad and failed everything and hated the whole time."

Wold, whose mother told her that Schulz would never amount to much, so she chose a fireman. Schulz went on to become the most successful cartoonist ever (well, maybe after Walt Disney), making $20 million a year.

Saint Paul has finally recognized its native cartoonist. Polyurethane statues of Snoopy, his doghouse, Charlie Brown, and Lucy and Linus Van Pelt number in the hundreds across town. Each one was sponsored by a different organization and painted by a different artist. Bronze statues of the cartoon characters stand next to the Landmark Center downtown.

Charles Schulz died on February 12, 2000, the day his last Sunday strip ran in 2,600 newspapers worldwide, read by two hundred million readers.

Stoic Swedes

In the Swedish burg of Lindström, two statues stand in front of the Chisago *County Press* office in honor of the early settlers of the region. Karl Oskar and Kristina never existed, however, beyond the imagination of Swedish writer Vilhelm Moberg, who featured them in his books *The Emigrants, Unto a Good Land,* and *The Last Letter Home.* Identical statues stand in Karlshamn, Sweden.

Some locals joke that these rigid statues are the perfect representation of the stoic Scandinavian character. Nevertheless, the rugged settlers succeeded in making and keeping Lindström a prosperous, bustling small town, and the statues used to be carried proudly on floats down Main Street for the town festival.

Han Ola og Han Per

In 1878, Peter Rosendahl was born in Spring Grove, the oldest Norwegian town in Minnesota. He grew up speaking Norwegian and used his native dialect for characters in his comic strip featuring Han Ola og Han Per. Just south of the border in another Norwegian town in Iowa, *The Decorah Post* ran Rosendahl's cartoons in its Norwegian-language newspaper. *Han Ola og Han Per* became the only continuous Norwegian-American cartoon printed in the United States. Because comics use actual speech patterns and slang that books rarely contain, many scholars now look to Rosendahl's cartoons for clues about many of the old Norwegian dialects that have fallen out of use.

Saint Urho

In 1975, Minnesota was the first state in the Union to officially recognize the patron saint of Finland by declaring March 16 Saint Urho's Day. By the 1980s, all fifty states followed Minnesota's lead, honoring the Finnish immigrants living in their midst.

The only problem was that St. Urho never existed. Finns in northern Minnesota were so tired of all the hoopla over St. Patrick on March 17 that they decided to steal the Irish's thunder by celebrating a holiday the day before and wearing royal purple rather than garish green.

Then came the task of creating the legend of St. Urho. *"Heinasirkka, heinasirkka, menetaalta hiiteen!"* ("Grasshopper, grasshopper, go away!") chanted Urho as he rid Finland of the grasshopper plague and saved the grape harvest. The insects were so frightened by the giant Urho with his menacing pitchfork that they leaped into the frigid Baltic Sea (so the tall tale goes).

Another version states that the young priest Urho rid his native Suomi of poisonous frogs that were threatening the sacred grape crop and subsequent wine festivals. The mathematically inclined Urho figured out the exact height that the hoppers jumped and rigged a sluiceway right into ships waiting at port. Once the ships' holds were bursting with frogs, the anchors were lifted. On the cold Baltic Sea, the frogs were quickly frozen (which later earned Urho the title of the patron saint of refrigeration). The boats were going to drop the frogs in the Atlantic, but Urho and his sailors decided to stop in France before going to the middle of the ocean. While at port, the hungry French peeked into the Finnish fleet and found lunch. With a dash of basil and a squirt of olive oil, the frogs were sautéed to perfection and became the French national dish. Urho, who was hailed as a hero, brought back fancy French wine as payment.

In honor of the ancient holy man, in 1975 Menahga erected an enormous wooden statue of the saint with his pitchfork impaling one of the troublesome grasshoppers. Seven years later, a fiberglass version replaced it. The headline THE ERECTION OF ST. URHO ran on March 19, 1982, in the publication *A History of St. Urho,* marking the historic day that the saint honored by inventive Finns got his own permanent memorial.

Hermann the German

The highest object in New Ulm, Hermann the Cheruscan stands atop a cupola with his copper sword held aloft. In 9 A.D., Hermann is said to have united most of Germany and to have kept those pesky Romans on their own side of the Rhine. Some locals claim that the figure honoring him is the tallest statue in the state since the tip of his sword is 102 feet above the ground.

Hermann the Cheruscan may be tall, but unfortunately, he may not be real. Some historians believe that he may be a composite character whose actual deeds don't live up to the legends perpetrated by his beer-stein-raising admirers. Don't mention this in New Ulm, however, as the German town has already had enough problems: It withstood being ransacked by angry Dakota in 1862 and was viewed with suspicion during World War I *and* World War II.

Nowadays, however, the town's Teutonic heritage is celebrated proudly and raucously with lederhosen, accordions, and Schell's beer during Fasching, Heritagefest, and Oktoberfest. Revelers can sober up by mounting the three flights of stairs to pay homage to Hermann the German and enjoy the breathtaking view of the city.

Ex-governor Jesse Ventura wasn't quite so taken with Hermann. Ventura claimed he entered statewide politics because he wanted to stop pork-barrel projects like the expensive renovation of New Ulm's famous statue, after it was damaged in a storm. Ventura lost the battle but won the war. Hermann was restored to his previous grandeur, and Ventura got elected governor.

Who Can Turn the World On with Her Smile?

A few of the opening shots of the hit TV series *The Mary Tyler Moore Show* were shot in Minneapolis, but no episodes of the actual show were ever filmed here. Nevertheless, the show's main character, Mary Richards, has become one of the city's most famous noncitizens.

"Who can turn the world on with her smile," twinkles the theme song as Mary walks around Lake of the Isles, feeds the ducks in Loring Park, and eats some chow at Basil's Restaurant. Mary Richards originally lived in a Kenwood studio apartment, but the show was forced to move her to a high-rise at Cedar Riverside Plaza when the owners of the studio put an IMPEACH NIXON sign in their window.

The show inspired local punk rockers Hüsker Dü to cover the theme song live on *Good Morning America* when the program did a special broadcast from Minneapolis. A spoof of the show, *Mary Tyler Marx,* used video footage from the series but changed the dialogue to show Mary's boss, Lou, as a Machiavellian slave ship captain, her colleague Murray as a proletarian temp trying to learn WordPerfect to earn an extra fifty cents an hour, and news anchor Ted dosing up as part of the Second Great Depression, preaching, "Sickness unto death is now treated with Prozac!"

Mary Richards's Minneapolis legacy was made permanent in 2002. At a cost of $125,000, a bronze hat-tossing Mary was erected in front of Marshall Field's (formerly Dayton's and soon to be Macy's) on Nicollet Mall, where she used to throw her beret in the air.

Betty Crocker

"Every morning before breakfast, comb hair, apply make-up, a dash of cologne, and perhaps some simple earrings. Does wonders for your morale! Harbor pleasant thoughts while working. It'll make every task lighter and pleasanter [sic]. Notice humorous and interesting incidents to relate at dinnertime when family is together."

This was Betty Crocker's advice to the women of America for keeping them and their families chipper. Betty was invented by the Washburn Crosby Company (later General Mills) as a friend to homemakers trying to make good grub on a budget. Sam Gale, the company's vice president, is credited with having given birth to Betty Crocker. Betty, an all-American-sounding first name, was chosen, and the company's director, William Crocker, added his own last name.

Betty began as a mere advertising campaign, with down-home recipes and advice on how busy housewives could save time. As her popularity grew, she was awarded her very own national radio program. The always polite Betty, played by Blanche Ingersoll, introduced herself to the world this way: "Good morning. This is a very happy morning for me because at last I have an opportunity to really talk to you. To those of you who are my friends through correspondence, I wish to extend most cordial greetings and good wishes."

Betty not only gave cooking advice but soon also became a matchmaker, showing women what men really want (not what you think!). Bachelors who worked different jobs were interviewed to find out how they envisioned the perfect woman. Topics included: "The Mechanic Wants a Smiling Wife," "The Girl the Farmer Dreams Of," and "The Young Doctor Describes the Wife He Wants."

Letters stuffed Betty's mailbox at General Mills— sometimes five thousand a day. Suddenly, the real identity — or lack of one—of Betty Crocker had to remain absolutely secret. An exposé could prove disastrous. Only company insiders and the actress could know the true story. However, leaks revealed that she lived in Minneapolis and was "an ageless thirty-two."

By 1945, Betty Crocker was dubbed "America's First Lady of Food" after a *Fortune* magazine poll found her to be the second most popular woman in the country, after Eleanor Roosevelt. *Betty Crocker's Picture Cookbook* hit bookstore shelves in 1950 and was an instant best seller.

Over the years, Betty's 1950s innocence lost some of its appeal, but she continued to be an icon for the company. To keep up with the changing times, her image has been updated every twenty or so years. Her 1986 look caused clever journalist Colin Covert of the *Star Tribune* to note that Betty was a "dead ringer for Mary Tyler Moore."

Some weren't quite so taken with Betty's white-bread image of the happy housewife. NOW, the National Organization of Women, filed a class-action complaint against General Mills saying that "Betty Crocker's portrait was both racist and sexist." The case didn't stick, but NOW's lawyer contended, "Betty Crocker is not an image that many women can identify with."

A more recent update, however, might give women a reason to celebrate. Her newest face—with darker skin and brown eyes—was composed by morphing together images of seventy-five women of different racial backgrounds, so now she's a bit more multicultural. Whatever her image, however, Betty is a Minnesota persona who, like most Minnesotans, will continue to persevere.

FAMOUS BUT NONEXISTENT PLACES

Frostbite Falls

Cartoon characters Rocky and Bullwinkle hail from a place called Frostbite Falls, a town supposedly somewhere in Minnesota. Some assumed this was Duluth, the "air-conditioned city," or perhaps Embarrass, "the coldest spot in the lower forty-eight." No one knows exactly what (or where) the creator of the show had in mind, but International Falls has claimed the name as its own.

Rather than run from winter, International Falls, on the Canadian border, has proclaimed itself the Nation's Icebox and raised a twenty-two-foot-high thermometer to chart its chilly temperatures. At the end of January, International Falls celebrates its nickname by hosting the Frostbite Falls Frozen Foot Broomball Tournament as part of Icebox Days. Outdoor chess matches are tests of endurance to see which team can withstand frostbite before checkmate. Perhaps this was the town Rocky and Bullwinkle meant after all.

Lake Wobegon

According to writer Garrison Keillor, Lake Wobegon is not on any map because "when the state map was drawn after the Civil War, teams of surveyors worked their way in from the four outer corners and, arriving at the center, found they had surveyed more of Minnesota than there was room for between Wisconsin and the Dakotas, and so the corners had to be overlapped in the middle, and Lake Wobegon wound up on the bottom flap."

On his radio show, *A Prairie Home Companion,* Keillor describes the buildings in town: Our Lady of Perpetual Responsibility Church, Ralph's Pretty Good Grocery ("If you can't find it at Ralph's, you can probably do without it"), Art's Bait & Night O' Rest Motel, the Chatterbox Café, and the Sidetrack Tap.

Since the name of his radio show could be traced to the Prairie Home Cemetery in the center of Moorhead, listeners assumed that they knew where the real Lake Wobegon was located. Anoka claimed the title because Keillor grew up in town and graduated from Anoka High School in 1960, although he lived in Brooklyn Park. Freeport claimed that it must be Lake Wobegon because Charlie's Café is surely the inspiration for the Chatterbox Café, and Keillor had lived in Freeport with his first wife.

Listeners searched for clues. The town, which was revealed to be situated on the western shore of a lake, affording beautiful sunrises, had a population of 942. That could be anywhere!

Keillor was careful not to make the same mistake Sinclair Lewis had made with Gopher Prairie by only thinly veiling (and mocking) his hometown and its residents. Instead, Keillor jumped into the debate with his book *In Search of Lake Wobegon.* He places the town firmly in Stearns County, where he lived in "a big brick house on the Hoppe farm in Oak Township . . . [and] the cemetery behind it where people named Schrupps, Wendelschafer, Frauendienst, Schoppenhorst, and Stuedemann lay shoulder to shoulder." There weren't many Norwegians in the area, so he "bused them in" for his stories.

He claims that the name of Lake Wobegon comes "from an Ojibwa word that means 'the place where we waited all day for you in the rain.'" Finally, he revealed Lake Wobegon's location: "The town is in central Minnesota, near Stearns County, up around Holdingford, not far from St. Rosa and Albany and Freeport, which is sort of the truth, I guess." But why should Anoka, Moorhead, or anyone else believe Keillor when he calls himself a "professional liar"?

Gopher Prairie

Carol Kennicott, a hopeful new bride, left her exciting job at the Saint Paul Public Library and went north with her doctor husband to his hometown of Gopher Prairie, Minnesota. Taking the train across the prairie, she was instantly distressed by the "peasantry." "They're so provincial. No, that isn't what I mean. They're—oh, so sunk in the mud," she said. "Life seems so hard for them—these lonely farms and this gritty train. . . . If it's these towns we've been passing that the farmers run to for relief from their bleakness—can't you understand? Just look at them! . . . They're so ugly!"

Written by Sinclair Lewis in *Main Street,* this was hardly a glowing review of small-town Minnesota. The train finally arrives at Carol's new home, and she gamely settles in, trying to change the town's backward ways. But she's endlessly backstabbed and beaten down by gossip and small-mindedness.

When friends and neighbors from Lewis's hometown of Sauk Centre read *Main Street,* they had a sneaking suspicion that it wasn't fiction. The thinly veiled nickname involving the state rodent and the fields of western Minnesota couldn't cover up the cast of recognizable characters from Sauk Centre. Lewis always wanted to leave his hometown for the big city of Saint Paul (which, ironically, F. Scott Fitzgerald wanted to leave for Paris and New York). Lewis felt at home on Saint Paul's majestic Summit Avenue, just down the block from Fitzgerald's row house.

Lewis had worked as a clerk at the Palmer House Hotel in Sauk Centre but was fired for spending his time reading books, writing, and daydreaming. When *Main Street* was published, the owners of the hotel realized what he had been writing— he had been taking notes about them.

While Sauk Centre took offense at Lewis's *Main Street,* the Alexandria Public Library banned it outright because it assumed that Alexandria was the town being satirized. The *St. Cloud Journal-Press* mocked this move in a 1921 article:

"'Main Street,' which eminent literary judges decided was the best contribution to letters of last year and which brought Sinclair Lewis the Pulitzer prize of a couple thousand dollars, has been ousted from the public library of Alexandria, Minnesota. Possibly somebody up that way read the book and came to the passage where Gopher Prairie was located a day's journey for an ox team from Sauk Centre, which might fit Alexandria. The library board of that city is taking itself too seriously, and there is always humor in asinine solemnity."

Lewis went on to publish a total of twenty-three novels, including *Babbitt* (1922), *Arrowsmith* (1925), and *Dodsworth* (1929). When he won the Nobel Prize, in 1930, the residents of Sauk Centre began to realize that maybe he wasn't such a bad fellow and perhaps even a hometown treasure. Eventually, street signs boasted THE ORIGINAL MAIN STREET, the high school football team changed its name to the Mainstreeters, and the town park was renamed Sinclair Lewis City Park. Lewis never moved home to "Gopher Prairie," however. He died in Rome in 1951.

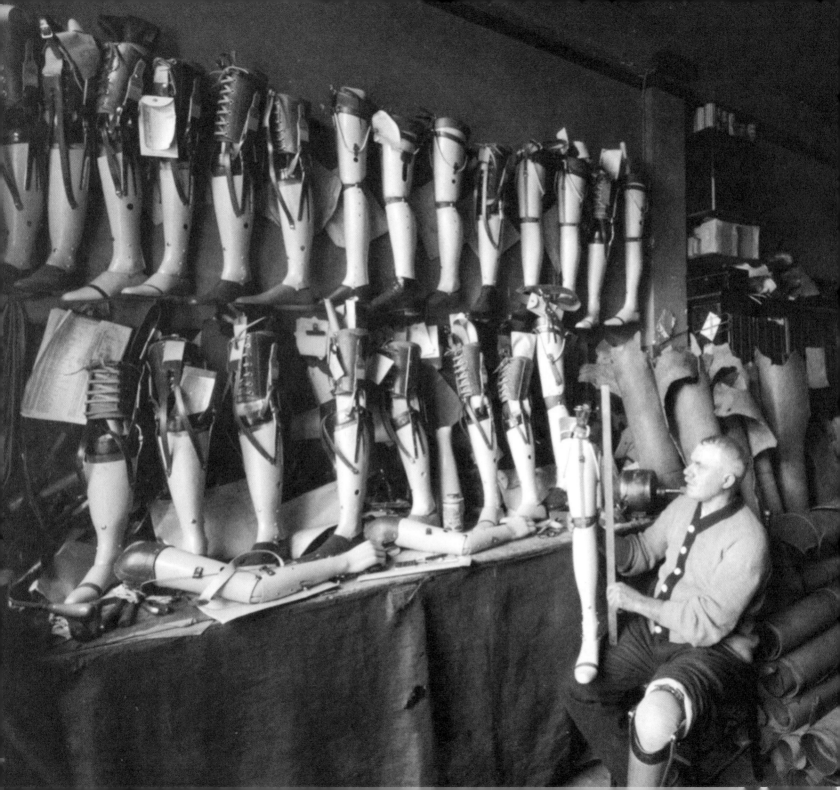

We *Minnesotans* tend to view ourselves as tame while the rest of the world is cuckoo. This chapter proves otherwise. Our fair state is full of baffling events and even more baffling behavior. It was one of our citizens, for example, who decided that the best way to make food more digestible is to blow it up with a cannon. And it was right here in Minnesota that a governor tried to banish a plague of grasshoppers with a statewide day of prayer. Even more strange: It worked!

People left to their own devices can get, well, weird. Read on to learn about the odd things that happen all the time in mysterious Minnesota.

Unexplained Phenomena and Curious Occurrences

Ghost House of Clamshell Lake

The kitchen table is still set, the beds are made, and the furniture is all in place. The only problem is that no one has lived here for years, maybe decades. The residents fled in such a hurry that they didn't even pack up their personal belongings.

While most of the other cabins are clustered around the lake, this little ghost house stands four hundred yards from the shore, deep in the forest. The air surrounding the house is strangely dead even when storms swirl angrily overhead. The dirt road stems off Clamshell Boulevard but has no name of its own. The lengthy driveway is more of a dirt rut than a road, and a giant pile of dumped leaves, along with poison ivy and stinging nettle, now fills the muddy path to the house, blocking access to everyone but the truly determined.

In 2005, a couple kids ignored the NO TRESPASSING signs, risked the weeds, and made their way past the old refrigerator out front. Then they sneaked into the house, whose windows were broken. Back outside, they looked into the abandoned Airstream camper next door, which would have been a valuable find if animals weren't having their way with its insides. Out of nowhere, a caretaker appeared and threatened to throw the little trespassers in jail. The kids ran home terrified but never heard anything more from the caretaker.

The house has since been boarded up, but a peek behind the wooden planks reveals that everything is still set up inside, waiting for someone to come home to the ghost house of Clamshell Lake.

UFOs Over Duluth

Duluth, which looks out onto the seemingly endless Lake Superior, is prime UFO-spotting territory. Over the years, there have been many reports here of spacey visitors. A Duluthian named Jim agreed to share three of his sightings with us.

The first incident may have been more of an unexplained weather phenomenon, which took place in the winter of 1974 at about two a.m. "I'd been out drinking that night and took a beer and went out on the deck for a smoke," Jim remembers. "It was a cloudy night—overcast, dark. The only light was some downtown lights. One mile out [on the lake] toward the east [was] a black column, darker than dark, kind of like antimatter. Maybe a black hole? I don't know. I learned in the Army to look away and look again in your peripheral vision. There was just this perfectly straight-up column going right up into the clouds. I stared at it for forty-five minutes before I went to bed."

Jim's second sighting took place in August 1988 while he was distributing *USA Today.* It was early in the morning, between 3:30 and 5:30, and he was driving onto the ramp at 27th Avenue West when he noticed that it was still dark in the west and that just a faint orange glowed low in the east: "Then it came forty-five degrees down from the right, about a quarter mile in front of me over west Duluth. It was an ovular, oblong disk that went so fast, I can't recall." He argued that it couldn't have been a Cessna or a single-engine helicopter. "It had a hot white light, the kind you remember, and different colors: orange and blue. It took two seconds, then I lost sight of it over the Spur Station." Afterward, at the gas station, he saw a "fairly large sheriff's deputy, whom I asked, 'So you've been getting a lot of calls tonight?' He said, 'You got it! Jesus Christ, you can't believe it. The switchboard lit up like a Christmas tree!'

Jim's final sighting occurred on the evening of November 1994: "I was delivering Fantasy Football . . . to the Sunset Lounge at Airport Road and Haines. I saw a bank of clouds about a half mile east of the airport. Over the cloud bank, I saw a light just above the horizon that moved thirty miles in the count of three. Nothing man-made can cover that much ground! It couldn't be a plane—not that low to the ground. A plane would take three to four minutes for what took the light three to four seconds."

SCIENTISTS GONE WILD

Shooting Rice Through Cannons

Digestive geniuses C. W. Post and Will Keith Kellogg proclaimed at their Michigan health spas that their breakfast cereals (followed by a refreshing enema) would cure all the nation's health problems. However, Alexander Anderson of Red Wing couldn't digest all that grain. His solution lay in ballistics.

Working as a scientist for the New York Botanical Garden, Anderson took a bit of rice and cooked it in an airtight test tube. When he pulled the tube out of the oven, the rice had expanded to nearly ten times its original size. The bloated rice turned out to be soft and much easier on his constitution. In 1901, he wrote to his friends back in the mill city of Minneapolis and told them about his experiment. Sensing money was to be made here from the gastronomically challenged, his friends set him up in a laboratory to refine his discovery. Explosions rocked the lab as Anderson tried to expand rice to its puffiest. "It's a wonder he doesn't blow himself up with the rice!" a coworker said.

Word of Anderson's madcap experiments spread to the Quaker Oats company in Chicago, who bought up all his patents in hopes of giving Post and Kellogg a serious

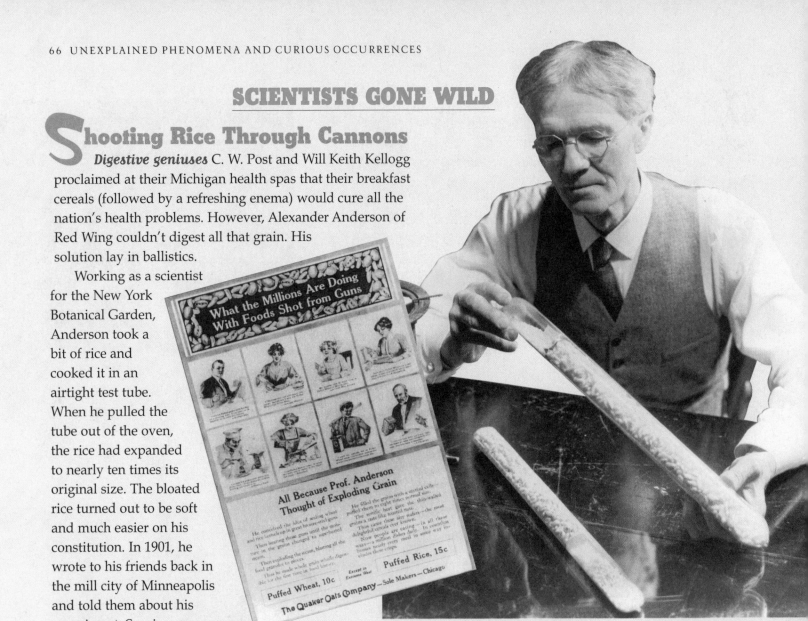

challenge for the cereal market. Anderson went to work for Quaker and built a puffing cannon that shot both rice and wheat. He awed the crowds at the 1904 World's Fair in St. Louis with his transformation of a simple grain into a soft, edible breakfast delight. The spectators were skeptical, however, and required Anderson to demonstrate that eating cannon fodder was indeed safe.

Starvation Study

Below Gate 27 of the old Memorial Stadium at the University of Minnesota, Ancel Keys, a professor of physiology, was busy denying his patients food. The U.S. had just entered World War II, and the government was worried about the starved people in Europe who would emerge from the rubble and concentration camps after the war. Keys was tapped to conduct the now-famous "starvation study" to determine the effects of lack of food on health and mental functioning.

First, though, he had to find some human guinea pigs whom he could starve. Since conscientious objectors refused to fight, they were chosen to volunteer to undergo food deprivation. (Max Kampelman, one of the subjects of the study, went on to become the chief U.S.

nuclear-arms-reduction negotiator with the Soviet Union, for which he was awarded the Presidential Citizens Medal and the Presidential Medal of Freedom.)

Keys's starvation study yielded useful results. The professor also developed K rations (the K stood for "Keys"), which provided healthy sustenance to countless soldiers and civilians during wartime. After the war, he was the first to link diet and cholesterol with heart disease. He popularized the Mediterranean Diet of low fat and lots of fruits and vegetables, which landed him on the cover of *Time* magazine. "People should know the facts," he told *Time*. "Then if they want to eat themselves to death, let them." He took his own advice and lived to be a hundred years old.

Prosthetics Capital of the World

St. Anthony Falls in Minneapolis provided so much waterpower that sawmills were run constantly by the steady flow of the Mississippi, which also brought the logs right to the mill. Logjams in the rivers sometimes required lumberjacks to hop on dangerously slippery floating timber. Less-nimble woodsmen might lose a limb on the churning river or in the sawmill, with its sharp blades whisking to and fro. When flour mills set up shop at the falls, the dangerous grindstones also claimed the limbs of unlucky workers. Then came the booming new railroads, with more pumping and spinning machinery and yet another set of hazards to wayward arms and legs.

With this critical mass of dangerous machinery, the market for prosthetics was hot. The Minneapolis Artificial Limb Company, along with others, established themselves in the warehouse district nearby. Organizations were set up to help supply prosthetics in case of an accident in one of the mills.

Soon, the city became known as the artificial limb capital of the world. The Minneapolis Artificial Limb Company took a booth at the Minnesota State Fair in 1918, boasting that their "Locktite Hook takes place of human hands. . . . Fits any arm. . . . Price $25.00 . . . Take one home. . . . If you have any friends in need of our products, please leave their name and address."

As new safety measures came into place, fewer prosthetics were needed, and some of the artificial limb companies went belly-up in the 1980s. Old stock from the prosthetics companies that was deemed impossible to sell was thrown in the trash. Punk rockers and artists living in the city's old warehouses raided the dumpsters and used the limbs to create bizarre art installations that would make the many-armed Indian goddess Shiva proud.

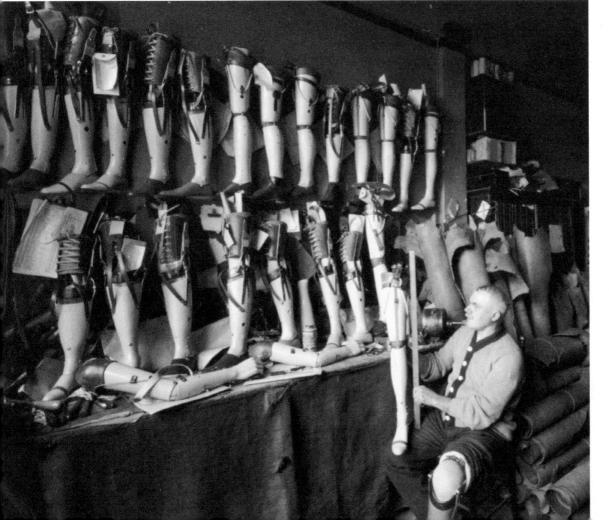

The Rainmaker

Before the development of cloud seeding (dropping dry ice into clouds to produce rain), Charles Hatfield gained notoriety around the country as the Rainmaker. Born in Minnesota in 1876, Hatfield soon realized that his curious talent was more sought after in the dry climes of the Southwest.

When Los Angeles was in the midst of a drought in 1905, Hatfield was hired for $1,000 to bring the rain. He stirred up a batch of mysterious chemicals and let them evaporate through an enormous tower up into the sky, and the rains came. And came. The angelic city's thirst was quenched as L.A.'s water reservoirs rose eighteen inches.

Newspapers reported that Hatfield had performed his chemical rain dance five hundred times for drought-stricken areas. His most notorious miracle, however, took place when he was hired by the city of San Diego for $10,000. Once again, he raised his tower and sent his chemicals into the cloudless sky. Nothing happened. City officials were furious. Hatfield and his brother quickly mixed up another brew of their chemical formula (known only to them), and finally, the rains came. In fact, it stormed for two weeks. Rivers spilled over their banks, streets were flooded, dams crumpled under the weight of the water. Fifteen inches of rain fell, and several people were killed by the disaster. Although Hatfield the Rainmaker became a household name due to the event, he was stiffed by the city of San Diego, as it was sued by its citizens for millions of dollars.

Hatfield's rain washes away the Lower Otay Dam in San Diego

BIZARRE BEHAVIOR

Duck and Cover!

When Russia exploded its first atomic bomb, on August 29, 1949, Americans panicked. Civil defense plans were laid, and a nuclear confrontation with the Soviets seemed just a matter of time. Children were taught to hide under their desks when they saw a flash or to drop from their bicycles and cover their eyes. Colleges such as Macalester outfitted bomb shelters with survival rations that lasted until they were discovered by students in the 1980s.

The caves on the south side of Stillwater that were supposedly used by Al Capone for storing moonshine were advertised by Tom "The Cave Man" Curtis as a bomb shelter in the 1950s. Curtis equipped the caves with emergency rations and advertised them as the safest places in town. "If it hadn't cost so much overtime, I'd have hired a couple of Russian pilots to drop a few test bombs to prove my point," he's been quoted as saying.

Revolutionary Anarchist Bowling League

The Revolutionary Anarchist Bowling League, or RABL (pronounced *rab-ble*) chucked bowling balls through the window of a military recruiting station to protest U.S. imperialism. What policeman would want to meet a group of anarchists rolling bowling balls down the street? This *RABL Rouser* newspaper was an early political zine promoting the league's politics.

Panty Raids and Streakers

Here's proof that panty raids did indeed exist. At the University of Minnesota in 1952, a photographer accompanied a group of ne'er-do-well students on a nighttime foray to the women's dorms as they gleefully captured their booty.

In the 1950s, the tomfoolery didn't end with panty raids, however. At Gopher football games in Memorial Stadium, streakers (now called exhibitionists) were a regular sight at halftime, usually followed onto the field by a couple of wheezy policemen.

Another bizarre campus prank was played by a group of students in janitorial jumpsuits and armed with a ladder: They went from building to building on campus and took all the clocks. Watches weren't so common back then, so many professors and students didn't know when to begin or end classes.

A former fraternity brother from Sigma Alpha Epsilon on University Avenue recalls rigging his rear-engine Volkswagen Beetle with a keg in the front compartment and a line of cold beer in the glove box. (Today, this is called DUI.) For a special beach party at his fraternity house, he and his brothers lined the basement with plastic and called in the fire department to fill it up with water. Guests brought their swimming trunks— or didn't—and went swimming (or skinny-dipping, as the case may be). Never mind the electrical outlets. "The next day, when the party was all over, the fire department came over and pumped out all the water," remembers the SAE brother.

Sheet People

When the Finns settled in the Iron Range, many of the other settlers weren't too sure about the bizarre practices of these northern people. In Esko, a farmer reported that the Finns were running around in the middle of winter with just white sheets covering their bodies. He warned the rest of the town that they were performing some bizarre pagan rituals: They'd gather in their sheets in a square building and worship the Nordic gods and wish death and destruction upon their neighbors. The locals soon set the man straight and explained that his neighbors were simply taking a sauna, continuing their Finnish customs here in Minnesota. Whether or not Norse gods were involved, only the saunaers can say.

Bombing with a Smile

Less than a year after the September 11 attacks, eighteen pipe bombs went off in mailboxes across Nebraska, Colorado, Texas, Illinois, and Iowa. When four mail carriers and two people opening their mailboxes were injured—on top of the anthrax scare—the nation panicked. When the bombings were pinpointed on a map, the FBI was perplexed. Could the bomber be making a giant smiley face?

The bomber turned out to be Lucas Helder, of our own Pine Island. A student at the University of Wisconsin-Stout, he had become fascinated by astral projection and wrote to his school newspaper, the *Badger Herald,* that "there is no such thing as death." Helder left college to go on the bombing spree and was finally nabbed in Nevada. He admitted to Lt. Thom Bjerke of the Pershing County, Nevada, Sheriff's Department that he was indeed trying to make an enormous smiley face to protest the U.S. government's laws against marijuana.

Some of the media blamed rock 'n' roll, since Helder was wearing a Nirvana T-shirt when he was arrested and had played in a three-piece grunge band called Apathy. The judge ruled that he wasn't competent to stand trial. Helder is being held in Rochester at a federal medical center. Meanwhile, the price of his band's only CD, *Sacks of People,* skyrocketed to $200 on eBay.

STRANGE DISASTERS

Meteor Falling!

When I was a kid, my dad would take us on an annual pilgrimage through the poison ivy to see the "meteor" located near Pequot Lakes, across from Blueberry Acres. The story goes that the meteor fell from the skies in 1939 and "burned the forests for months on end." Ben Knaeble lived in an old farmhouse near where Blueberry Acres is now, and his mother set up a turnstile in the mid-1940s and charged admission to see the giant rock that is easily thirty feet in diameter.

In elementary school science class, we learned that technically, a stone is called a meteoroid when it's still in space and a meteor or shooting star when it enters the earth's atmosphere; what's left—what doesn't burn up—is a meteorite.

I asked an astronomer at the old planetarium in Minneapolis his opinion of the meteorite. He told me, "A meteor burns up when it enters the earth's atmosphere, and only about a tenth of it sometimes survives to hit the ground. Therefore, if the 'meteorite' is about fifteen feet by thirty feet, the original meteor would have been enormous and would have left a crater the size of most of northern Minnesota."

Okay, that's not very likely. But then I discovered an old Brainerd newspaper from March 2, 1939, that backed up the original story: Under the headline COMET SEEN NORTH OF PEQUOT, the article includes a description of a forest fire. The Pequot Lakes Chamber of Commerce stands by the old meteor story too. The receptionist told me, "A man was in here a couple of years ago and swears that it's a meteor that he saw fall from the sky—but he's long dead now."

At some point, someone wedged dynamite into a crack in the giant meteorite, perhaps in hopes of discovering

some precious gems deep inside or to prove definitively that it was from outer space. The big rock barely budged, but the TNT did cause a split down the middle. A little tunnel was formed underneath, where a bobcat had a den for a number of years.

The forest was clear-cut in the early 1990s, so the meteorite was very visible from Highway 16. The remaining stumps and debris make for tiger traps, and the forest—poison ivy, raspberries, moss—has taken over again.

In 2004, "A St. Cloud professor came to study it and take samples of the rock," according to a journalist at the *Pequot Lakes Echo.* "He claimed it goes forty-five feet into the ground." The myth grows. Most likely, he claimed, the giant stone, which sits on private property, is an isolate of low-grade granite left over from the glaciers.

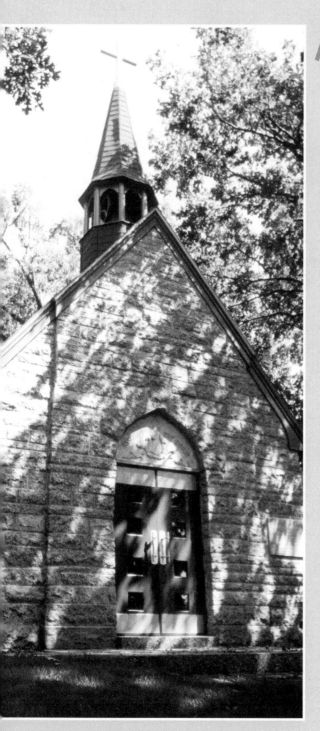

Attack of the Killer Grasshoppers

The grasshoppers munching on the crops sounded like "hundreds of hogs turned into the fields," according to farmers that spring in 1876. A scourge of the big green insects had attacked the state. They were everywhere, dead and alive, piled up in the fields and along the roads to a depth of two feet.

At first, Minnesotans thought the approaching clouds they saw were just a spring storm. "It gradually darkened," says one survivor. "The men hastily went out to see if anything should be brought in before the storm. What a sight when we opened the door! The sky darkened by myriad grasshoppers, and no green thing could be seen."

Clothes were eaten right off the lines, leaving only buttons on the ground. A hundred grasshoppers would attack a single stack of wheat, eat everything, and move on to the next one. Some cows even died as a result of blood poisoning from the grasshoppers.

After the insect scourge of 1876, farmers hoped the worst was over. Then, the state entomologist announced that because of the inundation the previous year, two thirds of the state was covered with grasshopper eggs ready to hatch in the spring of 1877. What they'd seen had just been a warm-up.

Governor John S. Pillsbury was called upon to do something. With no practical options in sight, Pillsbury called for a statewide "Day of Prayer." His gubernatorial proclamation said that all businesses should close up on April 26, 1877, for "a day of fasting, humiliation and prayer in view of the threatened continuation of the grasshopper scourge."

Skeptics scoffed at this do-nothing approach and labeled it "Pillsbury's best," a spoof on the famous brand of flour. "We hold that this belief in the power of prayer is palpably untrue, its influence pernicious, and in this day, a marked discredit to the intelligence of Minnesotans," complained the Liberal League. "From the beginning down to this day, outside of so-called Sacred History, there is not one well-authorized instance of such prayer having been answered, not one."

Father Leo Winter stood up for the governor and argued that the plague was a punishment sent by God for all the disbelievers abandoning church. He vowed to erect a chapel near Cold Spring where sinners, such as those of the Liberal League, could repent, in hopes of staving off another grasshopper plague.

The big day of prayer came. Minnesota was quiet as stores and bars closed their doors and everyone stayed home or prayed in church. The national media converged on the state for this unusual reaction to an insect plague.

Then something unexpected happened: A winter [Winter?] storm appeared out of nowhere and rained down ice on the eggs, freezing most of the grasshoppers just as they were hatching. The newspapers splashed exuberant headlines declaring Pillsbury's best a bona-fide miracle. An ecstatic New York journalist wrote, "Entomologists did not prophesy it. Editors did not expect it. Statesmen dared not hope for it. Infidels railed at the bare idea of it."

Father Winter gloated about the power of prayer and set to work building his Assumption Chapel, known as the Grasshopper Chapel, for the Virgin Mary. By 1894, pilgrimages to the little chapel near Cold Spring had waned, and a twister took the church and blew it into the trees, scattering its lumber around the hill. The angry tornado then headed north and ripped down the church at Jacob's Prairie and put a sizable dent in St. John's Abbey.

Using the beautiful granite from around Cold Spring, a new Grasshopper Chapel was erected in 1951, with kneeling grasshoppers carved at the feet of the Virgin Mary above the door. No grasshopper plague has struck Minnesota since that fateful spring in 1876.

Black Hole in the Lake

Lakes in Minnesota generally freeze from December to March, with ice so thick that pickup trucks can safely drive across. When a two-acre patch of North Long Lake near Brainerd refused to freeze, locals were left scratching their collective heads. *The Brainerd Dispatch* reported in 2002 that a dozen ATVs and snowmobiles had plunged into the hole and that one person had died.

Warning signs were placed around the lake when the hole showed no sign of closing up and perhaps even of expanding. A diver was sent down to find out if seismic activity had somehow opened up the ice. The *Dispatch* reported that all the diver found was "an ordinary lake bottom." The newspaper asked, "What caused the hole to appear? Distant earthquakes? New thermal springs on the lake bottom? Sabotage by unknown enemies?"

The mysterious hole returned the following winter and became something of a celebrity. Statewide, if not national, attention was focused on Brainerd's lake. Tourists ventured out on the ice just to look at the patch of water. Scientists and more divers were sent to the bottom of the lake but were stumped by the phenomenon. Everyone had a theory—aliens, backed-up septic tanks, faraway volcanoes—but no one had an answer. Then, one day, when the weather rose to forty degrees, well above freezing, the hole closed up. All bets were off. The next day, when the temperature dropped, the hole opened up again.

Bizarre Beasts

Every *Minnesotan* knows about Babe the Blue Ox, the enormous bovine who formed the lakes of Minnesota by wrestling with his buddy Paul Bunyan. But not all lumberjack beasts enjoyed such fun and games with their masters. Legend says that some came to a fiery end, victims of the curses of those very woodsmen. Hodags, the undead monsters that rose from the oxen's ashes, tormented lumberjacks with their trickery in the dark north woods.

Escaping these monsters should be easy— just hop in the nearest lake. But wait! Isn't that a ten-foot-long leech? Or maybe it's yet another world's largest tiger muskie, hungry for a swimmer's toes.

These odd critters and more roam Minnesota's dark forests and swim the depths of its many lakes. So watch out, for while some of these strange creatures are nothing more than myth, superstition, and imagination—others are all too real.

Superior Sea Serpents!

A *treacherous beast* swims beneath the surface of Sea Serpent Lake in Crosby. Locals tell of Kanabec, the mythical snake, which gives the lake its name and slithers from its underwater lair to nibble at unsuspecting vacationers. More likely, however, is that the S shape of the lake inspired its name and the alliteration.

The world's largest sea serpent may seem unlikely in these times of supposed enlightenment, but when the first Europeans ventured inland, they didn't know what sorts of creatures to expect. The legends told by Native Americans were often taken as fact, unleashing the imaginations of the early explorers.

Many sailors swore that they'd witnessed sea serpents in the vastness of Lake Superior. Upon returning to port, seamen told of their brave fights against these creatures of the deep, and the newspapers of the day often reported them verbatim. The *Oswego Palladium* flashed this headline in September 1821: THE SEA SERPENT NAVIGATING THE WESTERN LAKES. Perhaps this was a ploy to keep competing businessmen off their turf, but the sailors' yarn goes into such detail that it's hard not to get caught up in the drama:

> We discovered at the distance of five or six hundred yards a large body floating on the surface of the water, very much like a burnt log from 20 to 25 feet length; but on approaching it three or four hundred yards closer, it proved to be an animal motionless and apparently asleep. We continued to advance towards it until within 30 yards, when the animal raised its head about 10 feet out of the water, looking around him in the most awful and ferocious manner, and darting forward with great velocity, making the water fly in every direction, and throwing columns of it at a vertical height of seven or eight feet with his tail…we then resolved to attack him, and accordingly loaded our guns for this purpose. [The monster] is covered with black scales [and has] a tremendous head and similar to that of a common snake—frequently thrusting from his mouth a large red and venomous looking tongue.

The *Boston Gazette* issued a reward of $10,000, an enormous amount at the time, for the capture of this creature, dead or alive. Perhaps the publisher knew the story was a lark, but that didn't mean it wouldn't sell a lot of newspapers.

Bostonians never got their beast, but that didn't stop the *Oswego Palladium* from publishing more fantastical stories about the sea serpent. In July 1833, the paper reported, Captain Abijah Kellogg of the *Polythermus* swore that he saw the monster from the deep:

> He saw something lying still on the weather bow that looked like the mast of a vessel. Observing it more attentively, he was surprised and alarmed to see it in motion, and steering towards the schooner. . . . The serpent, for it was no other than an immense snake, neared the vessel fast and passed immediately under her stern, taking no notice whatever of the schooner or those on board, but affording to everybody an ample opportunity to observe and note his monstrous dimensions. In length he was about 175 feet, of a dark blue color, spotted brown; towards either end he tapered off, but with the middle his body was of the circumference of a flour barrel, his head was peculiarly small and could not well be distinguished but from the direction in which he moved.

A cousin of the sea serpent's near Crosby? An oversize, undiscovered relative of the muskie? History is silent.

Gigantic Blood-sucking Worms

Minnesota's third largest lake covers an old forest and incorporates possibly six different ancient lakes. Tree stumps can be seen underwater, and we can only wonder what sorts of creatures got buried in the floods that created the lake. The Ojibwa who lived here named this massive body of water after a mythical creature they believed they saw swimming in its murky depths.

Its slimy black skin seemed to slide through the water effortlessly, and different accounts put its length at anywhere from ten to a hundred feet long. Unfortunately, the enormous beast was sighted in prephotography times, so no Loch Ness Monster snapshots could be taken of this distant relative. The Ojibwa deemed the monster a giant leech and named the water Leech Lake for its colossal blood-sucking worm.

Babe: The Legendary Blue Ox

On Paul Bunyan's first birthday, the story goes, his father gave him a baby blue ox who rivaled Paul in how fast he grew. (Another story says that Paul found a frozen ox stuck in a snowdrift during the Year of Two Winters. Paul warmed up the big ox, who was miraculously resurrected but had turned blue by the cold of Jack Frost.)

Babe munched down thirty bales of hay at each little snack and even digested the baling wire. In no time, he grew to be seven ax handles and a plug of tobacco wide between the eyes.

Paul and Babe wrestled for fun, and each time they fell, another big lake was carved out of the earth. Minnesota's ten thousand lakes are testament to their hardy wrestling tradition.

One day, while Babe was lugging a load of water back to the lumber camp, he accidentally tipped the giant water tank, and the flow went all the way to New Orleans, creating the Mississippi River. Itasca State Park, headwaters of the Mississippi, has the wheelbarrow that Babe dumped to prove it. Once, when straw boss Chris Crosshaul let the wrong logs float down the Mississippi, Paul asked Babe to bring the wood back simply by taking a swig of the river and reversing its flow.

Babe lugged more loads of timber out of the north woods and down to the lumber mills than any other ox. But he refused to haul logs over mud roads in the summer because the snow made moving the wood so much easier. Paul put one over on his bovine friend by quickly whitewashing the logging roads so that Babe thought they were covered in slick snow.

When Paul died, he was laid to rest in Kelliher, Minnesota. Babe spent his golden years in South Dakota and was buried in the western part of the state, forming the Black Hills.

Hot Dog, a Hodag!

While Babe the Blue Ox and Paul Bunyan got on like a woods on fire, many of the poor oxen that worked in the north woods lumber camps weren't quite so loved. These poor beasts of burden were lucky if they lived five years before dropping dead from the stress of hauling timber. Lumberjacks cursed the slow beasts with blasphemies that would make a sailor blush. To prevent the souls of the oxen from forever haunting their profane owners, lumberjacks had to burn the oxen's corpses for seven years to cleanse their spirits of the profanities. If a body wasn't sufficiently charred, a brutal monster scientifically named *Bovine spirituallis* would rise from the ashes. Lumberjacks nicknamed this beast a hodag (horse meets dog) and feared that it would inflict years of mistreatment.

Smelling like a cross between a buzzard and a skunk, the hodag retained the ox's head with a menacing smirk and bulging canine teeth. If the hodag opened its black lips, a deadly halitosis emanated that could knock a lumberjack dead from ten feet away. Hodags ran on strong, stubby legs and wagged dangerous spiked tails as long as their whole bodies.

Lumberjacks told of trying to trap hodags, but most weapons were useless against them. The beasts devoured dogs, and bullets bounced off them. The only effective weapon, according to a newspaper story from 1893, was dynamite. A hunter, Eugene Shepard, brought back into town a pile of bones with tales of a fantastic fight. Shepard told of the hodag's escaping snares and thrashing for nine hours even after Shepard had blasted it with dynamite.

He became an expert on hodags and reported that they usually were black from being burned but sometimes were red or green. In 1896, he shot a photo of a small hodag in the forests of northern Wisconsin. The new species was confirmed, and the photo was printed on the front page of newspapers across the country. Groups of hunters set out into the north woods in search of this exotic new game.

Strangely, Shepard and his comrades were the only ones who returned with reports of the beast. In his column in the *New North,* Shepard wrote that, to silence skeptics, he would now attempt to capture a hodag alive, using a rag doused with chloroform held on a long pole. He did succeed in catching the first live hodag, and people paid a dime to see the jailed creature at the Oneida County Fair. The seven-foot-long beast was visible in a dark cave through a thin curtain. Shepard warned fairgoers not to get too close to the dangerous animal, which he said was "the transmigrated soul of an ox used by Paul Bunyan."

A representative from the Smithsonian Institution showed up to investigate this amazing discovery. Shepard wouldn't let the museum curator get too close for fear that he'd be bait and cause the hodag to go wild again. The man from the Smithsonian dismissed the hodag as a freak-show ruse, but that didn't stop eager visitors from lining up to see the monster of the north woods.

Leaping Kangaroos

Do kangaroos roam the wilds of Minnesota (or even its suburbs)? Since at least as far back as 1899, Minnesotans have been seeing mysteriously out-of-place kangaroos jumping across the landscape from time to time. In the mid-1950s to early 1960s, sightings were especially prevalent around Coon Rapids, where several people reported seeing "big bunnies." The kangaroos are often imbued with supernatural powers or described as phantoms because those who see them can find no other explanation for how they wound up here.

As recently as 2005, the *Pine Journal* reported the following kangaroo spotting from around Cloquet Pine Knot: "The phone lines buzzed with people who had either already seen the kangaroo or who wanted to and wanted to know which alfalfa field he was in. The farming area to the west of town quickly filled with families in cars, cruising around slowly, looking for the visiting foreigner. Veterinarians were called by reporters to see if anyone had a pet kangaroo who might have escaped. The zoo is 25 miles away, but it quickly counted noses and couldn't come up one kangaroo short. The Great Kangaroo Hunt lasted until dark."

Indeed, when kangaroos are seen in the Land of Ten Thousand Lakes, they're usually wreaking havoc. Blamed for the slaughter of pets, sheep, and other animals, the wayward kangaroos are said to be between three and a half and five and a half feet tall and to harbor a hostile attitude. While proof of their presence in this state is scant, a kangaroo was recently hit by a truck in Wisconsin, a photograph of which was published in the *Wisconsin State Journal.* It is no doubt simply a matter of time before a Minnesotan captures evidence of these marsupial nomads on film and proves that this bizarre beast is more than just local legend.—*Abby Grayson*

How to Escape a Sidehill Gouger

"Beware of the Sidehill Gouger!" I was told by Jim Gilbert, the head of the YMCA in Minneapolis, the day before I was supposed to get on a bus to Camp Christmas Tree.

"Sidehill Gouger? What's that?" I'd taken the bait, as any nine-year-old would.

"They're gruesome creatures with one leg longer than the other. They live on hills and go in circles around the hill but can only run in one direction. If you see one, run up or down the hill so they can't get you."

"Really? Do you have a picture of one?" I asked.

"Picture? Do you think anyone would wait around to pull out a camera and shoot a photo? If someone did, I'm sure they'd make a great lunch," he answered.

"Well, how will I know when I see one?"

"Oh, you'll know. Just look at the legs!"

I later learned that there are two varieties of Sidehill Gouger: left-handed and right-handed. One walks clockwise around hills and the other counterclockwise. Their name derives from their hooves gouging a round path in a circle. Luckily, Minnesota is relatively flat, so Sidehill Gougers are rare. Still, my mind wasn't laid to rest.

"Every year, the Sidehill Gougers get a few campers, but I don't think they've gotten any this year. They must be hungry. . . ." my counselor warned.

I did not sleep well that night. The next morning, I went to camp—but very reluctantly—and I resolved to avoid any inclines, however gentle.

Jackalopes of the Prairie

In the 1800s,
newspapers of the east splashed amazing
stories across their front pages. Strange new creatures had been
discovered in the vast American west, and the creatures, never seen or
heard of before, were something to behold. There was the camelce, for
instance. It seems that when camels were introduced to the New World,
the large humped beasts couldn't resist mating with the lusty elks
roaming the northlands. The camelce was discovered in the Black Hills
by imaginative (or perhaps gullible) journalist R. B. Davenport of the
New York Herald in 1875.

Then there were the jackalopes. Farmers and ranchers from
Minnesota to Montana swore that they saw bizarre critters hopping
above the seven-foot-tall grasses of the Great Plains. More than mere
jackrabbits jumping through the fields, these newfound mammals
sported huge horns and were feared by the pioneers.

Somehow, it seems, amorous rabbits had managed to mate with
antelopes by quickly hopping on top of the slender, hoofed animals.
Using this as an excuse for the ever-decreasing levels of their whiskey
jugs, cowboys claimed that these darn jackalopes had been lured by
their hooch. The drunken bunnies then had the audacity to mimic
perfectly their cowboy songs and tease the wranglers with warbled
versions of "Don't Fence Me In."

When the ring-necked pheasant was introduced into the United
States from China in 1881, the bird quickly spread across the plains.
According to some settlers, the randy jackalopes bred with the
pheasants, and their offspring could fly.

The Minnesota Iceman Cometh (and Goeth)

During the autumn of 1967, college zoology major Terry Cullen spotted an extraordinary exhibit in Milwaukee: the fresh, apparently authentic corpse of a hairy manlike animal. For twenty-five cents, people could see the "man left over from the Ice Age," whom exhibitor Frank Hansen kept frozen in a block of ice inside a refrigerated glass coffin.

Amazed at what he was seeing, Cullen tried unsuccessfully to get the attention of academic anthropologists. However, none were interested in pursuing something they saw as a carnival exhibit, probably a model of a fake primitive man. But although Cullen was only a student at the time, his training led him to believe that the creature was real or at least deserved further investigation. As Mark A. Hall reminds us in his book *Living Fossils:* "Some of the reasons for Cullen's avid interest in the Iceman exhibit were that he could see: plant matter in the teeth, shed skin of ekto-parasites (lice) on the skin, and unique dentition showing in the mouth where a lip was curled back."

Shut out by mainstream science, Cullen alerted Ivan T. Sanderson, a naturalist and the author of the book *Abominable Snowmen.* Following the instincts that already had allowed him to discover new creatures, Sanderson was interested.

The obvious question was, why hadn't any legitimate researcher noticed this before? After all, the body had been on public exhibit for almost two years in Minnesota, Illinois, Wisconsin, Texas, Oklahoma, and other states. Why hadn't anyone spotted it until now?

Sanderson answered such questions this way: "Just how many people with proper training in any of the biological sciences go to such shows?... The answer is: practically nobody."

After hearing from Cullen, however, Sanderson invited a colleague, noted Belgian cryptozoologist Bernard Heuvelmans, the author of *On the Track of Unknown Animals,* to accompany him. (Cryptozoology is the study of unexplained animals, in an attempt to either prove or disprove the existence of such creatures.) The two immediately set off to see firsthand what was being shown at fairs and shopping centers across the American Midwest.

For three days, Sanderson and Heuvelmans examined the creature in Frank Hansen's cramped trailer. Peering through the ice, they could hardly believe what they saw. The specimen was an adult male with large hands and feet. Its skin was covered with very dark brown hair that was three to four inches long. The creature had apparently been shot through one eye, which dangled on its face, but it also had a gaping wound and an open fracture on its left arm. Smelling putrefaction where some of the flesh had been exposed because of melting ice, the two concluded that the creature was authentic.

Heuvelmans described it this way in *Bulletin of the Royal Institute of Natural Sciences of Belgium:*

The specimen at first looks like a man, or, if you prefer, an adult human being of the male sex, of rather normal height (six feet) and proportions but excessively hairy.... The specimen is lying on its back... the left arm is twisted behind the head with the palm of the hand upward. The arm makes a strange curve, as if it were that of a sawdust doll, but this curvature is due to an open fracture midway between the wrist and the elbow where one can distinguish the broken ulna in a gaping wound. The right arm is twisted and held tightly against the flank, with the hand spread palm down over the right side of the abdomen.

Hansen wanted the discovery kept quiet. Sometimes he claimed he had killed the creature in the wilds of Minnesota or Wisconsin. But at other times, he said it had been found in a block of ice in the Sea of Japan.

The Smell of Mystery

One of the points made by many who support the reality of the Minnesota Iceman is the smell of rotting flesh, which Heuvelmans and Sanderson mentioned in their discussions. Here's how Sanderson described it: "Let me say, simply, that one look was actually enough to convince us that this was—from our point of view, at least—'the genuine article.' This was no phony Chinese trick, or 'art' work. If nothing else confirmed this, the appalling stench of rotting flesh exuding from a point in the insulation of the coffin would have been enough."

Debunkers have said that this is an old carnie illusion, wherein one puts a piece of old meat underneath the exhibit, discouraging people from staying long so that more people will pay to get in. But it's not such a simple matter with the Minnesota Iceman.

Few have stopped to note the exact situation that has caused the widely reported smell of putrefaction. The episode is well summarized in Mark Hall's book: "In the course of the inspection Heuvelmans touched a hot lamp to the top pane of glass, causing cracks in it. The result was the smell of putrefaction through the cracks." So it seems that the smell was the result of an accident during Heuvelmans's close-quarters examination.

We may never know what became of the Minnesota Iceman. Until one of these mystery primates is discovered, we may not understand the true role they should play in the history of hairy hominoid studies. But for now, we must accept that the enigma of the Minnesota Iceman remains one of the most hotly debated episodes in cryptozoology.

Nevertheless, both Heuvelmans and Sanderson had written scientific papers on it within the year. Heuvelmans named it *Homo pongoides*. Sanderson, who was a well-known nature personality on TV, mentioned the Iceman on *The Tonight Show With Johnny Carson* during Christmas week in 1968. The Iceman was out of the bag.

Then, however, the story takes a strange twist: The original body disappeared under mysterious circumstances. Hansen had exhibited it in Canada as well as the United States. He said that at some point, he had replaced the original with a model after a run-in with U.S. Customs over transporting the carcass back and forth. The original creature was now owned by a millionaire, he said, who declined to have it examined further. This switch from original to model has caused some skeptics to shelve the whole Minnesota Iceman issue as a joke, a carnival display used to fool people.

But there is evidence that there was an original body and that it was indeed replaced by a model. Thanks to photographs of the traveling exhibit taken by Mark Hall and me, Sanderson and Heuvelmans would later be able to enumerate at least fifteen technical differences between the original and the replacement. The differences were so seemingly minor level that a lay manufacturer wouldn't know that they could be seen by a biologist. But they were seen and identified.—*Loren Coleman*

Carnivorous Bigfoot

When the gigantic footprints of an unknown creature were discovered in Humboldt County, California, in 1958, it didn't take long for a Bigfoot to be spotted in the wild north woods. In 1968, a four-and-a-half-foot-tall Bigfoot was sighted ten miles north of Floodwood by Uno Keikkile, who claimed that the beast hopped out of a tree and scurried off into the forest.

A white version of Bigfoot was seen by thirteen-year-old Debby Trucano in the woods near Tower-Soudan in 1972. Critics doubted little Debby's sighting of an abominable snowman, or yeti, but four other campers in the woods soon backed up her story.

While these first two Bigfoots measured less than five feet (and probably had rather small feet), the next sightings told of an eight-and-a-half-foot monster near Duluth. In 1973, eleven-year-old Bob McGregor witnessed this beast stumble across a neighbor's garden. Five years later, Richard Johnson claimed that he'd seen the same Bigfoot wading through a swamp.

Suddenly, the Bigfoot stories weren't so easy to dismiss as those of just a frightened black bear on its hind legs. Either the boys were flat out lying, a grizzly bear had wandered into northern Minnesota, or a genuine Sasquatch was hiding in Duluth.

After northern Minnesota got reams of publicity for its Bigfoot sightings, the forest around Rochester became the beast's new home. In 1979, a woman driving outside of town slammed on her brakes to avoid hitting the creature. She watched the seven-foot-tall beast shield its eyes from the car's headlamps and run into the woods. In December of that year, Larry Hawkins saw a carnivorous Bigfoot rip apart the corpse of a rabbit. When the monster saw Larry, however, he ran into the woods to eat his bunny in peace.

Photos of Bigfoot were nonexistent in Minnesota, so skeptics wrote off these claims as untamed imagination. Then, in 1981, a set of giant tracks was discovered in a field near Red Lake River off County Road 11 near Crookston. Snapshots were taken and examined, but no one could explain the prints' origins.

A full fourteen years later, Crookston decided to cash in on the craze by declaring itself the Bigfoot Capital of the World. Newspapers took the bait, and soon media wire services transmitted the story across the country. In 1995, Crookston's Ox Cart Days parade was overtaken by two Bigfoot floats. Bigfoot burgers were bought by the dozen, and kids demanded that their parents buy them a stuffed baby Bigfoot doll. The next year, Kim Samuelson paid a taxidermist to stuff what was said to be a nine-foot-tall, three-hundred-pound Bigfoot. Samuelson wanted the prize for her RBJ's Family Restaurant on the northwest side of town. Sadly, the restaurant sold the new town symbol to a jeweler in the Twin Cities, who keeps it in a private collection, perhaps so cryptozoologists can't examine it.

CROOKSTON, MN
BIGFOOT CAPITAL OF THE WORLD

Bigfoot Creator: Curtis Christensen, Union Grove, WI

Contributor Dennis Murphy seems to have a knack for running into Bigfoots. Here are his accounts of two close encounters.

Face-to-Face with a Bigfoot Couple

It was a sunny and crisp morning in Willow River, Minnesota, in late August or early September of 1972. I was heading out to catch some fish in one of the area's shallow backwoods lakes. Back then, there was no traffic and no ATVs flying around, so I was hitting a pretty good clip at 50 mph or so on the gravel. Up ahead, in an opening to my right, there was a field about a hundred yards across and as many deep. There, just off the road, I saw two white figures standing like statues, just like deer will do if you surprise them and they hope you don't notice them. Well, the big guy had to be well over eight feet, and his head was turning slightly as I crunched ever closer to them, slowing a bit but not wanting to slide on the gravel. As I pulled within fifty yards or so, the hairy-faced smaller figure, which I assumed was the female, started to lose her nerve and turned away from me. As she did this, she sort of duckwalked in place.

The larger one's fur spiked out noticeably at the shoulder tips and above the knees. He also had a rather pronounced curl of hair running down the back of his arm and out from his elbow like a spur of hair. Really a magnificent beast—and I say "beast" reluctantly because under all that hair, he sure looked human. She, on the other hand, had a lustrous white coat like an otter's— longer and thicker. From what I could see, she was not in any way equipped to hunt and likely was an underground dweller or something. Quite a strange pair! I could not see her eyes, nose, or mouth, even though I was real close at that point. So I stared at the big guy instead, and he was staring back at me—glaring, really!

He was obviously telling me "Don't stop here," and I didn't! I left the scene. I did turn around and come back a few moments later, though. I started to get out to see if there were tracks but changed my mind, thinking that they couldn't have crossed the field in so short a time. The weeds were hip high on me, and I'm six feet tall, but before, I could see his knees plainly over them. I am willing to submit to a polygraph and have been trying for months to get anyone to administer one. These creatures really do exist!

My Bigfoot Buddy

In 2002, I reported my 1972 Bigfoot sighting at Willow River to the BFRO (Big Foot Research Organization) and took up a friendship with Curt, the BFRO guy up here. Soon, I was hooked on going out to find another one. I started to do that in March, off and on, and carried apples along to bait any spot where a track might be found. I came up empty until June 1, 2002, when I crossed over into Wisconsin and took the first road heading back over the border. There was a big muddy curve on that road, so I found a good hard spot to pull off and walked back there.

When I first saw a track, it was so big and had a couple leaves in it, so it didn't quite register. I looked all around the area for a second print, but finding no more, I went back and took the leaves away. Sure enough, the print was seventeen and a quarter inches long. I tossed the apples out along the roadside and headed into town for some plaster of paris and a camera, having left mine at home.

It was maybe an hour before I got back. I took a few pictures of the track and the area and finally decided to mix up the casting material. That was when things started jumping, quite literally. As I knelt and poured the mixture into the print, the foliage nearby started bouncing back and forth and up and down. It was not a particularly windy day, so I stood up to see what was going on. That's when the top of a tree flew up into the air as if some great weight had come off of it. It made a big whiplash, cracked, and fell to the ground. Everything was now absolutely still, and I slowly walked the ten yards or so over to it and started taking pictures. When I saw which tree it was, I remembered having taken a photo of it when it was intact just a few minutes before. So I turned my back and walked across the road to where I had stood the first time and quickly snapped another shot of the now-barren stump. I guess I spun and snapped the picture too quick for him. There he was in the photo, and he clearly was NOT in the first one!

Our meetings would be in the same spot at nearly the same time every day. He would follow me as I checked for his tracks along the roadside. He would stay twenty-five or more yards out and just behind me. I started tossing him apples. I guess we did this "I walk, he follows" game over half a dozen times. I could hear him plainly, but the foliage and his reaction time stymied my every attempt at getting a picture of him with the camcorder.

I had a great time with that Bigfoot and learned a little about his habits, food, and some surprising weaknesses to his supposed invulnerability over the next few weeks. On our last meeting, in late July or early August, it was terribly hot and humid. So rather than go through with our usual routine, I walked directly toward the sound of his footfalls, hoping to get a photo of him. Instead, he let me walk past and then stomped off angrily in the other direction. That was the last I saw or heard of him. The heat and deerflies were getting so bad, I think they were bothering him, too. The mosquitoes, on the other hand, which bled me dry, seemed not to have any effect on his activity.

I believe one reason he was so active during the day was because of the weather. With it being rainy and overcast all the time, he would have had no light to hunt by during that period at night. That is why you and I are twice as likely to smash our car into a deer on such a night. The deer's instincts tell him that no predators are about on a pitch-black night. Unfortunately, his instincts are moot about cars.

I am not pulling your leg or anyone else's about these two encounters.

Windigo

As tall as pine trees, windigos loomed large in Ojibwa and Mandan myths. An Ojibwa priest, the Reverend Peter Jones, wrote in *The History of the Ojibway Indians* in 1861 that windigos "are said to live on human flesh, and whenever they meet an Indian are sure to have a good meal; being also invulnerable to the shot of an arrow or bullet, they are the constant dread of the Indians. Persons who have been known to eat human flesh from starvation are also called waindegoos [sic], after the giants."

Most tales of the windigo say that the beast was once a human who ventured into the woods on his own and went crazy from the harsh Minnesota winter. In fact, the term windigo is synonymous with "insane" in Ojibway. The man turned monster terrorized Native American tribes and wreaked havoc on Roseau, Minnesota, in the late 1800s.

Through frequent retelling of the stories, windigos grow in height from fifteen feet with bright stars on their foreheads to Rev. Jones's tale that "they pull down and turn aside immense forests, as a man would the high grass as he passes through."

Cryptozoologists claim that the windigo was actually just Bigfoot, before that name was commonly used. Others claim that this was some sort of early gigantic race, perhaps the one that made Grand Mound outside of International Falls. In 1911, one of these human giants, covered in hair and with apelike arms, was seen by hunters in northern Minnesota. Jay Rath, in his book *The M-Files*, asks, "Could Native Americans have recalled the Neanderthal? After all, the Ojibwe and Dakota tribal memories extended far enough back to embrace the woolly mammoth."

All agree, however, that to properly kill a windigo you must rip it apart limb from limb, and all the body parts must be burned and buried. Remember that the next time you run into one.

Go, Turtle, Go!

The tortoise may have beaten the hare in the end, but boy, was he poky. Longville stages turtle races every Wednesday in the summer on a huge targetlike racetrack smack-dab in the middle of town. Traffic is diverted, and the turtles (four inches or longer, according to regulations) are raced from the center to the outer ring. For over forty years, the locals in Longville have raced turtles, causing the state legislature to declare the town the Turtle Racing Capital of the World. While Nisswa races minnows in long gutters and Worthington races turkeys, Longville could at least spice up the slow-motion turtle races by allowing a few snapping turtles on the racetrack.

A Tribute to Bugs

Since most of Minnesota's big animals are already taken, some towns have opted to adopt multilegged creatures with wings as their symbol. In other words, bugs.

The tiny town of Effie looked itself in the mirror and decided that it is most famous for the swarms of mosquitoes that converge on any warm-blooded mammal there. Not surprisingly, no other town has competed with Effie's claim to have the world's largest mosquito statue.

In September, when box elder bugs swarm the town of Minneota, local poet Bill Holm decided to have his students write poems about the harmless insect infestation. A book resulted from these odes, and the town has since ardently embraced the red-striped bug. In 1990, the town festival was named Box Elder Bug Days in honor of the clumsy insects.

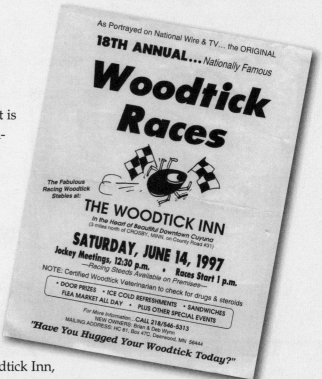

The best tribute to Minnesota insects, however, is the Woodtick Races in Cuyuna. Stop in at the Woodtick Inn and admire the old hubcaps now sprouting dangling limbs and transformed into giant wood ticks. In the height of summer, in the parking lot next to the Woodtick Inn, circular race courses are set up for these bloodsuckers. Where else in the world would anyone buy a wood tick for a dollar? Kids from Cuyuna run in the fields in their shorts to harvest the tick crop and make a quick buck. The bug races begin at one o'clock sharp, and the first tick to scurry to the edge of the ring wins. Because of foul play in this hotly contested sport, the Woodtick Inn posts strict rules outside its bar:

TEN COMMANDMENTS OF WOODTICK RACING

I. Entrants shalt not lose their woodticks.

II. Entrants shalt not be too sober to drive their woodticks.

III. Entrants shalt not wear spurs.

IV. No supercharged woodticks.

V. Thou shalt not hit, smash, or splatter thy woodtick.

VI. Woodticks shalt not "yell or fight" or die by fire.

VII. Thou shalt not steal thy opponent's woodtick.

VIII. We will not tolerate woodtick droppings on bar.

IX. He who passes out shalt feed the woodticks.

X. Thou shalt not race "big, fat dog woodticks."

Bear Attack, Downtown Duluth

On the night of August 18, 1929, a three-hundred-and-fifty-pound black bear lumbered out of the woods and down Superior Street in Duluth. He must have smelled something good, because he headed right for the Hotel Duluth and looked through the window into the cafeteria. Clearly, he wanted some service. However, since he was unable to open the door like a gentleman, he simply bashed through a giant plate-glass window and stormed the café in search of pie. The night watchman, Albert Nelson, threw chair after chair at the bear to stop the attack. The Duluth Police Department arrived on the scene but couldn't trap the hungry beast, so Sergeant Eli LeBeau took him down with one shot. The bear was promptly stuffed and put in the lobby of the hotel as proof that the food was so good that even bears come crashing in.

The now-famous bear has been moved to Grandma's Saloon & Grill in Canal Park. "It's the poor little bear on all fours," the waitress told me. "It doesn't look like much after all the stories about it. The poor little thing was probably just hungry and looking for some garbage."

Caiman Went

When I visited the house of my friend Mark in northeast Minneapolis, a round tin tub six feet in diameter filled his dining room. Cement blocks and boulders lay on top of sheets of plywood on top of the tub. I asked Mark what this was all about. "My caiman is inside," he deadpanned. "Wanna see?"

Before I could respond, he tilted up the edge of the plywood, and giant jaws snapped at his hand. The alligator-like creature splashed violently inside with its tail and struggled to escape. Mark, unfazed and with all the digits of his fingers intact for the moment, pushed the wood down and readjusted the rocks on top to keep the vicious animal inside. "That's my pet," he told me.

My heart stopped racing once I was out the door. That couldn't be legal, could it? Mark agreed that his caiman was a little too big now, but he'd grown fond of his lizard. Fond? Of a five-foot-long wild creature that would eat him if it could?

I lost touch with Mark but thought about him ten years later when I was down by the Mississippi. I was searching for entrances to the caves near the abandoned power plant in Saint Paul. A woman pulled up in an SUV and asked, "Are you here about the alligator?" Because I had a camera around my neck, she assumed I was a newspaper reporter.

"Um, alligator?" I responded nervously. "There's an alligator loose down here?"

"Oh, you must not be from the media. Never mind," she told me as she got out of her car with an enormous net and walked toward the river. I followed her at a safe distance.

The caretaker of the power plant, Randy Mann, met us and showed me a few snapshots he'd taken of an alligator down by the docks. "My guess is that it's only a couple of feet long. On the TV news, though, they'll make him look huge," he said. From the shore, he pointed to what looked like a floating log that quickly dove when we got close. "It's not the alligators that you have to worry about so much as the carp. They'll eat anything," Mann added.

A television news crew headed by a slick newsman with a cracking layer of tan foundation on his face and strangely immobile hair showed up. The little alligator disappeared into the water upon their arrival, but the disappointed anchor kept his grin in spite of the curses coming from his mouth. The woman with the net who had been hoping to snag the creature was unmoved and waited patiently on the dock. "Oh, it's probably from somebody who had a caiman and was told by their landlord that they couldn't have it anymore. At the last minute, they go to the river and decide to 'set it free'!"

John Dillinger

Local Heroes and Villains

Minnesota has more unique characters than you can shake a gopher at. The world was shocked when we voted in as governor an all-star wrestler who proclaimed he wanted to be reincarnated as a 38DD bra. (At least we didn't elect the "vampyre" who ran!) High on the list of Minnesotans we can't get out of our minds is Dr. William Mayo, who launched a world-renowned medical facility but honed his surgical skills on a stolen corpse. Then there was Ralph Samuelson, who almost drowned in Lake Pepin while trying to give the world water skis. And who can forget Tammy Faye Bakker (now Messner)—much as you might want to? It was right here in our home state that Tammy Faye first fluttered her mascaraed eyelashes at future televangelist— and embezzler—Jim Bakker.

The Minnesotans in this chapter aren't the only ones with an unusual story to tell, but theirs are some of the most bizarre. Many of them are internationally famous, while others are known only to some or have been largely forgotten as time trods on. Where else but in Minnesota would a dairy princess's bust be honored in butter?

Clockwise from left, Charles Lindbergh, Jesse Ventura, and Judy Garland with Toto.

Mind the Body

When Jesse Ventura was elected governor of Minnesota, in November 1998, he proclaimed that he had "shocked the world." Indeed he had, but the best was yet to come.

Jesse "The Body" Ventura, né James George Janos, played the bad guy in the wrestling ring. "I bleached my hair blond because people dislike blond men, especially if they know their hair's been dyed," he said in *Body Slam: The Jesse Ventura Story.* When asked to compare himself to one of the presidents, he responded, "I see myself closest to Abraham Lincoln. We're both alike in many ways. We were both wrestlers. And we're both six-foot-four."

Of his stint as a wrestling heel, he famously pronounced, "Win if you can, lose if you must, but always cheat." When he took office, however, he was breathtakingly honest. Never before in Minnesota politics had any governor spoken so candidly. The media loved it and printed every word, especially when he made off-the-cuff remarks like "if I could be reincarnated as a fabric, I would like to come back as a 38 double-D bra." And "until you've hunted man, you haven't hunted yet." (Ventura never actually saw combat while in the Navy.) He later said, "My brain is operating at such a level that I don't want to put my foot in it."

His candor also showed his integrity, though, as he strongly objected to forcing students to recite the Pledge of Allegiance, saying, "No law will make a citizen a patriot." He spoke out on gay rights by announcing, "I have two friends that have been together 41 years. If one of them becomes sick, the other one is not even allowed to be at the bedside. I don't believe government should be so hostile, so mean-spirited. . . .

Love is bigger than government."

Earlier in his political career, Ventura asked, "Who knows, you know? Four years as mayor, then maybe governor, maybe senator, or maybe, at the year 2000, Jesse the Body in the White House. Be something to think about." But in the governor's mansion, all of the publicity, negative and positive, soon wore him down, and he proved to be surprisingly thin-skinned. He refused to talk to the Minnesota media, whom he dubbed "jackals." This from a wrestler who knew that offending part of the crowd was a way to build loyalty? Wrestling fans love a bad guy, but not one who cries in his soup.

He Wanted Your Blood . . . And Your Votes!

On Friday the Thirteenth in January 2006, Jonathon "The Impaler" Sharkey proclaimed his candidacy for Minnesota governor as a member of the Vampyres, Witches and Pagans Party. He sent out an e-mail press release that described his home life: "I sink my fangs into the neck of my donor (at this time in my life, it is my wife, Julie), and drink their blood."

Jonathon the Impaler and Julie Carpenter weren't officially married, but that didn't stop Carpenter's employer at the Princeton School District from getting nervous about her driving school buses filled with kids. A self-described pagan, Carpenter was branded a witch and fired from her job. She complained bitterly that her boss couldn't tell a witch from a pagan.

Meanwhile, the Impaler was nabbed in Mille Lacs County when someone in Indiana recognized him as wrestler Rocky Flash, who had an outstanding arrest warrant in Indiana for stalking. Denying Minnesota its first vampire governor, the authorities threw the Impaler into Mille Lacs County Jail and extradited the blood-sucking politician back to Indiana. So much for the governor's house—Jonathon got the big house instead.

"Are You Now or Have You Ever Been . . ."

One Minnesotan who would never deny that he was a communist was perennial presidential candidate Gus Hall. Arvo Gus Halberg was born in Little Cherry on the Iron Range on October 8, 1910. His Finnish parents helped form the early labor group the Industrial Workers of the World and became members of the Communist Party in 1919.

Hall went to Moscow to study at the Lenin Institute, and upon his return, he founded the American Communist Party. In 1934, he was at the heart of a violent truckers' strike in downtown Minneapolis during which the National Guard was called in to stop the fighting between police and strikers. He was questioned in a court trial afterward:

"Are you willing to fight to overthrow this government?"

"Absolutely!" Hall replied.

"And you are willing to take up arms and overthrow the constituted authorities?"

Hall again said, "When the time comes, yes!"

These were not popular views. War was brewing in Europe. The Smith Act, or Alien Registration Act, was put into effect in 1940, which made advocating for the overthrow of the government illegal. Hall was indicted in 1948, but like Leon Trotsky, fled for safe haven to Mexico, where he was arrested and sent back to the States. Along with eleven other communists, he was thrown into a maximum-security prison. He spent most of the '50s in prison.

In 1957, the Supreme Court made a surprise ruling that teaching revolutionary theories was not illegal unless the perpetrator called for violent overthrow of the government.

Hall ran for president four times and never received even one percent of the vote. He died in 2000.

Samuelson's Ski Success

Ralph Samuelson walked on water. At just eighteen years old, he had a vision that he could skim across the surface of Lake Pepin if he strapped his downhill skis on his feet and grabbed a rope behind a speedboat. Samuelson may have believed his dream, but he hadn't worked out the physics yet.

This was the summer of 1922. Ralph was working on a turkey farm in nearby Mazeppa, but he knew that his destiny lay upon the waves. After many dunks into the deep, he decided that he needed more surface area for his skis, so he strapped on some curved barrel staves and took another spin. Many wipeouts later, he fashioned ever bigger skis and used his mother's wash boiler to curve the ends. And there you have it! The first pair of water skis.

Samuelson's friends agreed to give him one more tow, only too happy to watch another one of his famous crashes. The outboard motor was gunned, and Ralph held onto the rope with all his might. This time, he skimmed across the waves like a duck not quite in flight. And there, on lovely Lake Pepin, waterskiing was invented by a determined turkey farmer eager to brave the laws of nature and walk on water.

Lucky Lindy

In 1919, wealthy New York City hotel owner Raymond Orteig offered the huge sum of $25,000 to anyone who could fly nonstop from New York to Paris. Prohibition was in full sway, and Orteig thought the nation needed something to take its mind off its sober state. By 1927, no one had collected on the dare, so little-known barnstormer Charles Lindbergh, from Little Falls, Minnesota, decided to take a turn. He flew a single-engine plane—more than half its weight made up of gasoline.

When Lindbergh landed in Paris, thirty-three and a half hours after taking off, he was a worldwide hero who became known as Lucky Lindy and the Lone Eagle. Five years later, though, his luck turned sour, when his twenty-month-old son was kidnapped from his New Jersey home. The baby was later found murdered. When the press and public wouldn't give the Lindberghs any peace to mourn, they moved to Europe.

In France, Lindbergh received more accolades when he surprised the world with another first: He invented an "artificial heart," a glass perfusion that pumped in substances to keep organs alive outside the body and which would make future operations possible. But when the Lone Eagle opposed American entry into World War II, he found himself on the wrong side of a political battle. Suddenly, Lindbergh went from being an international hero to a suspected Nazi sympathizer. When the Japanese attacked Pearl Harbor and Hitler declared war on the United States, however, Lindbergh immediately dropped his noninvolvement stance. Nevertheless, his request to reenlist in the Air Force was denied. Instead, he went to the Pacific war arena as an adviser for the U.S.

GREETINGS – from – LINDBERGH'S HOME TOWN – LITTLE FALLS, MINN.

Army and Navy and flew about fifty combat missions as a civilian.

In spite of his anti-intervention stance, Lindbergh eventually came back into favor with the public. President Dwight D. Eisenhower named him a brigadier general in 1954. That same year, Lindbergh's autobiography, *The Spirit of St. Louis,* won the Pulitzer Prize.

Judy and the Stolen Slippers

Judy Garland, née Frances Gumm, had only praise to heap on her birthplace. "It's a beautiful, beautiful town," said Judy Garland of her native Grand Rapids. "We had a lovely house. . . . We lived in a white house with a garden." The Gumm house is now a museum to the toe-tapping wonder, who was born here in 1922. Poppies spring into bloom along a little yellow brick road leading to the front door.

When little Frances was two and a half years old, her ambitious father put her on the stage at his movie theater. Her big debut, however, came at the fancy opera house (near the restored old theater) in downtown Aitkin. Moving from Grand Rapids to Hollywood, the newly named Judy Garland beat out the golden-locked Shirley Temple for the role of Dorothy in *The Wizard of Oz.*

Our hometown hero has been revered ever since with the Judy Garland Museum, a children's museum, and her restored house. Murals of the happy foursome on the Yellow Brick Road in search of body organs or a ticket home are lovingly painted on the side of Grand Rapids buildings. The Judy Jubilee attracts some of the original Munchkins from the Lollipop Guild, and *Wizard of Oz* sing-alongs spontaneously pop up during this annual June festival. Judy's daughters, Liza Minelli and Lorna Luft, have attended and belted out a few classics from their mother's repertoire.

To help celebrate Grand Rapids's most famous citizen, the owner of the original ruby slippers lent them to the museum in 2005 for all to ogle and awe. Then tragedy struck: Thieves broke in and swiped the slippers! Frances Gumm had been dead for years, but suddenly, she was splashed across the front page of newspapers from coast to coast. The ruby slippers are yet to be recovered.

Like Dorothy, Judy knew that there really is no place like home. Though she rarely ventured back to her birthplace, she never forgot it. "It's a swell state, Minnesota," she said.

Dinkytown Dylan

Robert Allen Zimmerman was born in Duluth in 1941 but grew up on the Iron Range in Hibbing. At his dad's office in Hibbing, a three-year-old Bobby got his hands on an old Dictaphone and recorded his first song. When Buddy Holly and the Crickets played the Duluth Armory (before their untimely demise in an airplane accident near Clear Lake, Iowa), Bobby traveled down to see them, and his musical destiny was cemented. After high school, he moved to Dinkytown, next to the University of Minnesota campus, and changed his name to Dylan in honor of his favorite poet, Dylan Thomas. Although no one is certain exactly where Dylan lived during his brief stay in Dinkytown, popular consensus is that he moved into an apartment above the old Gray's Drug Store, at 327 Fourteenth Ave. SE. When the Loring Pasta Bar revamped the building with an appropriately bohemian atmosphere, owner Jason McLean took the door from Dylan's apartment and thoughtfully placed it at the entrance to the women's bathroom.

Stories about Dylan in Dinkytown are now legendary. He borrowed and never returned early blues and folk records from friends. He hung out at the base of the Witch's Tower in nearby Prospect Park to pen the song "All Along the Watchtower." His earliest folk gigs in Dinkytown were at the Ten O'Clock Scholar at 416 Fourteenth Ave. SE and at the Purple Onion across from his apartment.

By January 1961, he'd had enough and packed his grip for New York City, where he would perform and meet his idol, Woody Guthrie. To record his first album, Dylan was paid the paltry sum of $400. He didn't compromise his music, however, and refused at the last minute to perform on *The Ed Sullivan Show* when he heard that his "Talkin' John Birch Society Blues" would be censored.

Dylan transformed his music every few years—from electric to country to Christian. His most recent stint has been a return to his folk roots. His early "The Times They Are A-Changin'" is now mirrored by his later "Things Have Changed," which, in 2001, won him a Golden Globe and an Academy Award for Best Song.

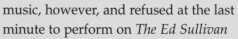

Paisley Park Purple Man

The most enigmatic Minnesotan musician is undoubtedly Prince. Rumors fly that he doesn't like to be looked in the eye, and some even claim that he should be referred to in the third person, like Caesar himself. Regardless, the mysterious Prince never ceases to surprise with original songs.

One of his earliest albums, *Dirty Mind* (1980), is true to its title, perhaps inspired by his dad's performances as a jazz pianist at downtown strip clubs. Prince became a Minneapolis staple by performing fifteen times at First Avenue and was frequently seen zooming through uptown on his purple motorcycle. His *Purple Rain* made Minneapolis a music mecca, with tourists hoping for a glimpse of the artist still in residence. *Purple Rain* boasted the top album, movie, and single all in the same week. A publicity whiz, Prince put out the *Black Album* (as a rebuttal to the Beatles' *White Album*), then immediately recalled it, causing the limited number of records released to attain instant collectibility.

Then, in a spat with Warner Bros., Prince proved that he was a force to contend with by bucking his stifling contract and changing his name to an unpronounceable symbol. The Artist Formerly Known as Prince famously wrote SLAVE across his cheek as a slap to his domineering record label. Finally free, Prince (with his name restored) kept his market sense alive with a Willy Wonka–inspired promotion of special purple tickets in his 2006 CD. Lucky winners of the—very few—tickets would get to attend a private concert at Prince's Los Angeles home.

Tourists may not be able to visit the short-lived New Power Generation store he opened and then closed in Minneapolis, nor his purple house in Chanhassen. But his giant Paisley Park Studios is the new destination for fans hoping to witness a late-night surprise concert. Just look for the little purple pyramids on top.

Saint Mudd: Home Safe Home to Gangsters

Back in the heyday of gangsters, Saint Paul became known as home safe home to Chicago mobsters who needed a place to cool down. The Mississippi was a watery highway for moonshine traveling south from Canada, and Saint Paul was the first big stop. Police chief John O'Connor reached a temporary truce with mobsters by letting them stay in Saint Paul as long as they obeyed his rules: no guns within city limits, and petty-crime statutes would be enforced to the letter of the law. And so Saint Paul became a vacation destination for the likes of Machine Gun Kelly and Baby Face Nelson.

When O'Connor retired and Prohibition was enacted, the dubious bargain backfired. The criminals who chose to hang their hats here couldn't keep their guns in their holsters, and Saint Paul was nicknamed Saint Mudd. The fuzz cracked down on the offenders, and murders, bank robberies, and shoot-outs became banner headlines in the *Pioneer Press*.

One of the most famous outlaws to make Saint Paul his temporary hideout was John Dillinger. After he broke out of the pen in Indiana in 1934, Dillinger joined up with Baby Face Nelson to knock over banks in Sioux Falls and Mason City. Then Dillinger settled back into his apartment at 93 S. Lexington Pkwy. When the truce with the cops was over, Dillinger was in trouble—his landlady tipped off the Saint Paul police. But by the time they bashed in his front door, Dillinger was already jumping out of the window. The bandit suffered a gunshot wound and fled Saint Paul. He got his comeuppance later in Chicago. After taking in a picture show with two girlfriends, Dillinger was ambushed by the FBI as he was exiting the theater. The agents shot him in the back and killed him. Apparently, one of his girlfriends tipped the feds off to his whereabouts. Maybe he should have brought just one girl to the movies that night.

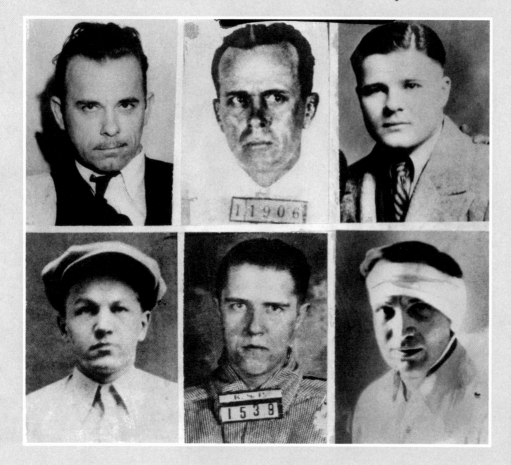

Mug shots of the FBI's most wanted criminals in 1934. Clockwise from top left: John Dillinger, Arthur Barker, Charles "Pretty Boy" Floyd, Homer van Meter, Alvin Karpis, and "Baby Face" Nelson.

Kid Cann and the Syndicate

Minneapolis's most notorious underworld kingpin got his start running moonshine from Canada to Minneapolis and Chicago during Prohibition. Isadore "Kid Cann" Blumenfeld, who supposedly acquired his nickname because he'd hide in the can whenever he heard gunshots, became the leader of the Minneapolis Syndicate, sometimes called the Minneapolis Combination. The FBI had reason to believe that Kid Cann controlled every liquor license issued in Minneapolis and Saint Paul. Bar owners paid him up to $20,000 in protection against various kinds of Mob violence.

One of Kid Cann's favorite hangouts was the Band Box diner, where he would sit and play cards for hours. Nearby, he allegedly gunned down Walter W. Liggett, editor of *The Midwest American,* for exposing his bootlegging, in one of the city's most famous gangland killings. Kid let the editor bleed to death in an alley off Nineteenth Street. He was charged with three murders over the years, but none of the charges stuck. The efforts of Minneapolis mayor Hubert Humphrey to expose the gangster only forced him underground.

Kid Cann changed his modus operandi in the 1950s. One of his most damaging exploits took place when he hooked up with Twin City Rapid Transit president Fred Ossanna to loot the remaining TCRT assets, torch the Twin Cities' trolleys, and form the American Iron & Supply Co. to cash in on the metal scrap from streetcars.

Kid Cann eventually went to jail for charges related to prostitution. After his release, he moved to Florida and teamed up with his friend Meyer Lansky, another notorious mobster. They dabbled in illegal stock trades and shady real estate deals for a while, but Kid Cann came home to die. He passed over in Minneapolis in 1981. We can only guess what was waiting for him on the other side.

Busts of Butter

Every year, the most beautiful and talented young women from Minnesota's eleven dairy regions converge on the State Fair, but only one will be crowned Princess Kay of the Milky Way. Each of these lucky ladies, however, will have her likeness meticulously carved into an eighty-five-pound mound of butter. The women sit uncomplaining in many layers of clothes in the thirty-eight-degree case for up to eight hours while their bust is done. Butter sculptures of Princess Kay and her royal court of ten dairy princesses then rotate in a giant refrigerator in the Empire Building at the Minnesota State Fair. When the fair is over, after Labor Day, each of the princesses is honored to receive her butter bust.

What do you do with eighty-five pounds of butter? Most of it is eaten by relatives or at church pancake breakfasts, but some princesses toss their bust in the freezer as an everlasting commemoration of a special day.

Atlantis Rediscovered!

"There once existed in the Atlantic Ocean, opposite the mouth of the Mediterranean Sea, a large island, which was the remnant of an Atlantic continent," wrote Ignatius Donnelly in 1882. Donnelly was Minnesota's lieutenant governor and three-term congressman, but he's perhaps best known for reviving interest in the idyllic lost continent Atlantis, which was supposedly swallowed by a catastrophe some untold eons ago.

Donnelly was respected in Minnesota but also viewed with a bit of skepticism and amusement for his outrageous endeavors. A lawyer in Philadelphia, he moved to the Midwest to form Nininger City, three and a half miles northwest of Hastings. He promoted it as a fabulous booming metropolis to easterners looking for land and opportunity out west. Nininger was "one of the great cities of the world," Donnelly exclaimed, as he boasted about his town's (future) libraries, symphonies, theaters, etc. His promotional blitz managed to lure five hundred people by 1856.

Then the steamboats decided to stop at Hastings instead. The Panic of 1857 spooked residents who fretted about potential financial ruin. By 1858, not much was left of Nininger except for Donnelly's house. (The house was torn down in 1949, and today, Nininger is a ghost town, long forgotten even on maps.)

Donnelly was undaunted, however, and went into politics to form one of the many third parties in Minnesota history: the People's Party. He was a passionate speaker and quick on his feet. When someone threw a rotten head of cabbage at him, he retorted, "Gentlemen, I only asked for your ears, but somebody has given me his whole head."

Then came his books, which postulated fantastic arguments and established Donnelly as the most famous Minnesotan of his time. In *Caesar's Column*, Donnelly predicted the demise of the U.S. by 1988. In *The Great Cryptogram*, he boldly stated that William Shakespeare was a hoax. The first chapter made clear—in all capital letters—that "WILLIAM SHAKSPERE [sic] DID NOT WRITE THE PLAYS," and another chapter claimed, "SHAKSPERE INCAPABLE OF WRITING THE PLAYS." All the genius of William Shakespeare, according to Donnelly, was, in fact, the fruit of the mind of another author of Elizabethan times, Francis Bacon. Debates raged across the country and in England about Donnelly's theory and are still kept alive today by conspiracy theorists.

His book *Atlantis: The Antediluvian World* was lauded by religious people who felt that Donnelly had proved that the Garden of Eden was a real place and that Noah's flood was a historic fact. In fact, many people heralded Donnelly's theory because it supported not only biblical writings but also many mythological ideas, wrapping them up neatly.

Today, Donnelly's theories have been mostly debunked. But the possibility that they may contain a sliver of truth and the joy of having things tidily explained keeps this Minnesotan's ideas alive.

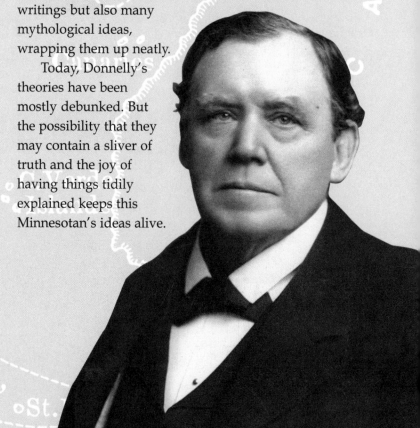

Cue the Tears!

Many may think of Tammy Faye Bakker as a Dixie lady who was once married to a Southern preacher of questionable integrity, but this mascara-smeared woman hails from one of the northernmost points in Minnesota: International Falls. One of eight children, Tammy Faye attended the local Assemblies of God church. When her mother was ousted because of her divorce, the family joined the fundamentalist Mission Covenant Church. Tammy saw the light and channeled her religious fervor as she spoke in tongues. Rumor has it that classmate Ada DeRaad taught Tammy Faye to use mascara in the girl's bathroom at International Falls High School.

Tammy Faye met Jim Bakker while attending North Central Bible College in Minneapolis. Perhaps it was her fluttering eyelashes that lured the preacher-to-be. Ironically, the couple was married on April Fool's Day. North Central Bible College wouldn't allow fellow students to marry, so the newlyweds moved south. Most of us know what happened to Tammy Faye and Jim Bakker. Tammy Faye is now known as Tammy Faye Messner.

Root Beer Lady

Dorothy Molter was the only person living on a million acres of wilderness in northern Minnesota. In 1975, when the Department of the Interior asked her to leave her cabin on Knife Lake so the Boundary Waters Canoe Area could be formed, Molter refused.

Dorothy moved to the remote area in 1930, during the Great Depression. Unable to find a job with her new nursing degree, she decided to stay with her father and stepmother at their cabins on three islands near the Canadian border. She took over the little Isle of Pines camp in 1948 and lived alone from then on. *The Saturday Evening Post* declared her the loneliest woman in America in an article describing her life snowshoeing, shooting birds for food, and felling trees.

On the side, she brewed her own secret recipe of root beer, which she shared with the almost seven thousand visitors who canoed by every year. When the feds asked her to give up her little cabin to make way for the park, she began a letter-writing campaign, drawing upon her popularity as the Root Beer Lady to corral supporters. Her thousands of visitors suddenly became a force in the push to allow her to keep her remote property.

The Department of the Interior eventually caved, letting Dorothy live out her days in the wild. Her residency was grandfathered into the new Boundary Waters Canoe Area, leaving her alone in the pristine forest for the rest of her life.

Medical Marvels of the Mayos

"I'm going to keep on driving until I get well or die," William Worrall Mayo told his wife as he headed north in a horse and wagon, trying to escape the malaria nightmares he was having in Indiana. Mayo hand-built a little white house in Le Sueur (which is now a museum) in 1859 and got to work with a microscope that would change the world.

In 1862, war with the Dakota ravaged the area around Le Sueur and left residents on both sides terrified and defeated. Thirty-eight Native Americans were hanged for their part in the uprising, making it the largest mass execution in the country. "The dead were buried in a single shallow grave near the riverfront," according to *The Sioux Uprising of 1862* by Kenneth Carley. "That night several doctors, quick to seize the rare opportunity to obtain cadavers for anatomical study, dug up the bodies. Dr. William Mayo drew that of Cut Nose and later his sons learned osteology from the Indian's skeleton."

THE NEW CLI

Mayo taught his two boys, William James and Charles, about physiology from the Dakota skeleton. The Mayo boys went on to make fantastic medical breakthroughs and formed what is arguably the most prestigious hospital in the world. In fact, when coal trains from South Dakota were scheduled to rumble near the hospital in 2006, Senator Mark Dayton loudly protested, proclaiming that the Mayo Clinic is worth more than all of South Dakota.

The wealth of this medical family can be admired at their 340-acre farm, which includes a thirty-eight-room house. The greenhouse has thousands of X-rays for windows—so that even while relaxing, the doctors could see the sun shining through body parts.

Top: William Worrall Mayo; bottom, from left: Franklin D. Roosevelt, Dr. Charles H. Mayo, and Dr. William J. Mayo, in Rochester, Minnesota, Aug. 8, 1938; inset: a 1934 postcard of the Mayo Clinic in Rochester

Saint Paul Seat of Power: The Bordello

According to reporter Fred Heaberlin, as quoted in Paul Maccabee's *John Dillinger Slept Here,* "There were three important people in St. Paul. They were James J. Hill, Archbishop John Ireland, and Nina Clifford." At around the turn of the century, Nina Clifford ran a ritzy brothel on South Washington Street, which has just been unearthed by archaeologists.

Myths abound about the notorious "dwelling house . . . and seminary," as it was described in the original building permit. Clifford supposedly could have brought down numerous Saint Paul bigwigs, since she kept records of everyone who paid her house a visit in a little black book. Unfortunately, no signs of the book turned up at the dig. The secret sex life of Saint Paul is safe.

Clifford's "sporting house" was located a few houses away from the notorious Bucket of Blood Saloon, supposedly so named because so many fights broke out there, you could get a bucket of blood any day of the week. Clifford dropped $12,000 to construct the elaborate Romanesque building designed specifically as a bordello, despite what its permit said. Clifford's brothel was just a block away from the police station, where she would allegedly make weekly payoff trips so that the cops would look the other way. A chandelier from Clifford's brothel supposedly still hangs in the office of the mayor of Saint Paul. The brothel and the Bucket of Blood Saloon once stood on the site of what is now the new Science Museum of Minnesota.

Clifford dropped $12,000 to construct the elaborate Romanesque building designed specifically as a bordello, despite what its permit said.

Thief, Scoundrel, Founder of Saint Paul

The founder of Saint Paul, according to *The History of the City of St. Paul* (written in 1876), was "a coarse, ill-looking, low-browed fellow, with only one eye, and that a sinister-looking one. He spoke execrable English. His habits were intemperate and licentious. . . . Such was the man on whom Fortune, with that blind fatuity that seems to characterize the jade, thrust the honor of being the founder of our good city!"

The very colorful writer was describing the first man of Saint Paul, Pierre Parrant—or Pig's Eye, as he was known for his ugly, bad eye. Parrant was a fur trapper and whiskey trader of whom another early visitor wrote: "Parrant . . . had only one eye that was serviceable. He had another, it is true, but such an eye! Blind, marble-hued, crooked, with a sinister white ring glaring around the pupil, giving a kind of piggish expression to his sodden, low features."

Pig's Eye Parrant was probably on the run from the law when he landed in the area of Fort Snelling sometime around 1832. Since unsavory characters like him weren't welcome at the fort, he moved on and staked a claim on Fountain Cave and the 372 feet of land where a beautiful creek flowed from the opening of the Mississippi. The site was near what is now the southern part of Saint Paul.

Pig's Eye set up a saloon just out of reach of the fort authorities but close enough to lure its soldiers and settlers from Mendota for a weekend of debauchery. Customers, it's said, would paddle to his saloon and then weave their way home on the river. Although the military authorities were none too pleased by Parrant's enterprise, his settlement was very popular with the locals. The whiskey flowed freely, and there were many other attractions to relieve the hard work and tedium of pioneer life.

Then came upright Father Lucien Galtier and several Catholic families who intended to establish a settlement nearby. Galtier built the chapel of Saint Paul in 1841 out of oak logs and with a roof of bark slabs. The location he chose proved ideal because steamboats could easily dock on the shore; his little settlement prospered and grew. The devout Catholics chose Saint Paul's Landing as the name for their new home, which was eventually shortened to Saint Paul. Galtier's chapel is long gone, but a bronze plaque attached to a granite boulder now marks its location.

As for Pig's Eye, he continued to run his saloon for a while, but then one day he simply disappeared. Some speculated that he had lost a duel, others that he drowned in the Mississippi after a drunken binge, but most likely he just moved on, tired of battling with the respectable citizens who now surrounded him. A plaque marks the spot where his saloon once yawned, just a five-minute walk south on Shepherd Road from Randolph on the river side.

Railroad Robber Baron

The best piece of land in Saint Paul sits high on Cathedral Hill on Summit Avenue, overlooking downtown. James J. Hill always insisted on the best real estate. The red sandstone mansion he built has thirty-two rooms, thirteen bathrooms, and twenty-two fireplaces. It was financed by the piles of money he made from his St. Paul, Minneapolis, & Manitoba Railroad.

Hill bought the bankrupt St. Paul & Pacific Railroad in 1879 and soon established the largest railway system in the world at the time, which eventually turned into the Great Northern Railroad. Hill opened up the west and created huge amounts of wealth for himself (some that is still distributed to artists through the Jerome Foundation), but his business style was ruthless.

When Hill charted new railroads across the state, he threatened to completely bypass settlements, leaving them ghost towns, if they failed to donate the best real estate in the area for his tracks. Wayzata, along Lake Minnetonka, was one of the towns that conceded to Hill's demands, giving its lakeshore property to the train line. Hill earned the name Empire Builder from his admirers and Robber Baron from those he pushed around.

Little Soddy on the Prairie

Laura Ingalls Wilder was born in Pepin, Wisconsin, in 1867 and homesteaded with her family in Redwood County, Minnesota. The Ingallses lived, as many homesteaders did, in a soddy, or dugout. They cut the thick prairie sod into bricks and stacked them one atop the other for ideal (but messy) insulation against the bitter winter winds and summer heat. The Ingalls's dugout site, off County Road 5, is on a private farm. Wilder writes about her experiences there in *On the Banks of Plum Creek,* set in 1873 but not published until 1937. When the grasshopper scourge descended two years in a row, the Ingallses were forced to abandon their little sod house on the banks of Plum Creek.

Last Barber Pole Producer

To earn a little extra money, barbers used to yank teeth, lance boils, and bleed their patients with leeches to "cleanse" their blood. Leeches were placed in a brass basin on top of a pole, while a white cloth, used to sop up the blood, was hung from below the bowl. The wind would twist the blood-stained bandage into a spiral, and the barber pole was born. The blue was probably thrown in for a little patriotic spirit, though some barbershop historians argue that the blue represents blood from the veins and the red, blood from the arteries.

The symbol of the trade, the barber pole was about to slip into oblivion, like the wooden Indian that used to stand outside every tobacconist's. Then, in 1950, William Marvy entered the business in an old auto repair shop on St. Clair Avenue in Saint Paul. Marvy made a pole that was "six ways better" and revived interest in the old symbol. Four other manufacturers still made barber poles at the time, but Marvy jumped in with such verve that by 1967, he'd made fifty thousand poles. When Marvy died, in 1993, he passed the business on to his son. Today, the William Marvy Company is the last remaining firm that builds barber poles in all of North and South America.

The Claw: Baron von Raschke

"You'd make a good German!" Mad Dog Vachon yelled menacingly at a bald young wrestler. "I am German!" the young man yelled back. Actually, James Raschke had only recently moved to Minnesota from Omaha, Nebraska. But from that point on, he was the Beast of Berlin: Baron von Raschke, royalty in the wrestling world.

The Baron's signature move, the claw—which would be copied by thousands of teenage boys across the country—came later. The Baron, in fact, didn't invent the move but learned it during a match with Pat O'Connor, a wrestler from New Zealand.

"I got in the ring, and we were wrestling around," he tells us. "We went about twenty-five minutes, and I was in a leg split kind of hold. He was leaning over me; I couldn't move any way but up. He leaned over me and said, 'Put the claw on my head!' I said, 'What's that?' I was pretty young in the business. He taught me how to do it right there in the ring."

The Baron's son Karl recalled that a few different wrestlers used the claw. The Funks in Texas had something deadly called the stomach claw. At some point, though, the wrestling world reached a gentleman's agreement that the claw would be the Baron's signature move. Mention it to nearly any Minnesotan, and he or she will mimic the Baron's move.

Karl Raschke remembers growing up around the strange world of wrestling. One day, while in the eighth grade, he says, "I came home and four midget wrestlers were playing video games."

His dad concurs: "I'm about as weird as anything you'll find in Minnesota."

Following his wrestling career, Baron von Raschke opened a gift shop in Lake George, to sell souvenirs and Baron memorabilia. The Great American History Theater in downtown Saint Paul is working on a production of a biographical play featuring the Beast of Berlin and written by Corey McLeod. Its title features the famous phrase the Baron blurted out to end an interview that was running too long: "The Baron: Dat is all da people need to know!"

The Sheikh of Baghdad

Adnan Al-Kaissy grew up in Iraq but now lives in a condo in Hopkins. As a teenager, he played backgammon with Saddam Hussein in a Baghdad café. Even back then, Al-Kaissy recognized that the future dictator was intelligent—and ruthless.

Al-Kaissy came to America on a football scholarship but later turned to wrestling. He went pro in the mid-'60s, wearing a Native American costume and calling himself Billy White Wolf, who trapped his competitors with the "Indian death lock."

"Then I decided to go back home, in 1969, to see my family," he tells us. "Saddam saw me on TV and sent for me. He told me, 'This is your country, and you're not going to leave now.' If he wants you to do it, you do it, because he has a lot of hit men."

Al-Kaissy became Hussein's director of youth activities and promoted his sport across the country. The Iraqis loved him, and he became a smash hit—and inadvertently, a political tool. Hussein decided that wrestling matches were the perfect diversion from his many executions.

For one match, Canadian wrestler George Gordienko was flown into Baghdad. Al-Kaissy remembers it as "probably the biggest crowd ever in the history of wrestling. The stadium in Iraq had over two hundred thousand people watching." The ring was surrounded by guards armed with submachine guns. Gordienko looked around nervously and told Al-Kaissy to be careful not to hurt himself for fear of retaliation from the crowd and the soldiers. Guess who won that match?

Hussein invited Andre the Giant to compete against Al-Kaissy in another match in Baghdad. Andre weighed almost 520 pounds and was promoted as being seven feet four inches tall, easily the biggest wrestler ever. Just before Al-Kaissy was ready to wrestle, he's quoted in the *Star Tribune* as saying, Hussein jumped into the ring and

grabbed his hand. "'If this guy beats you,' Hussein said, 'I'll send him back to De Gaulle in a pine box.'" He showed Al-Kaissy the solid gold Webley revolver that he was itching to use against the Giant.

Al-Kaissy enjoyed huge celebrity status in Iraq. He had a car, a chauffeur, and a giant palace that was built for him on the Tigris River. But he was wary of the success. "If Saddam had found out that the wrestling we were doing was a fake, you think I would be alive?" Al-Kaissy told the *Star Tribune*. When he saw the tortured body of one of his colleagues and then heard that another friend had been assassinated after having dinner with Hussein, Al-Kaissy knew he had to get out. So one night, he left his house, his friends, and whatever money he had in the bank and drove with his chauffeur to Kuwait.

In the United States, Al-Kaissy toured as a new wrestling persona, the Sheikh of Baghdad, wearing an elaborate headdress and flowing robes. When Iraq invaded Kuwait in 1990, he switched to being the Iraqi General Adnan for a bout with Sergeant Slaughter in Philadelphia. The press reported that this evil Iraqi general had brainwashed the patriotic American soldier, so the fans in Philadelphia were out for blood. After the match, stadium security barely got Al-Kaissy out with his life.

Al-Kaissy is now retired and regretful about the violence in Iraq: " Sometime, when peace is established, I hope to God I'll be able to go back. What's going to happen? We'll just have to wait and see. . . ." Until then, he's content to stay in Hopkins, where he cooks hot dogs for the town's annual Raspberry Days.

Collected Exhibitionism

Everyone collects something, but some people collect every thing. You know the type: the guy with the record collection that fills his house, but there aren't enough hours in life to listen to all that music; the woman with the shelves of precious dolls for which she spends her paycheck to buy new outfits.

What we'll be looking at here in *Weird Minnesota*, however, isn't the stuff of such relatively normal compulsions. The collections here comprise things whose enduring value might escape even the most enthusiastic aggregators among us — items like canned hams and secondhand underwear. Some are objects that can't easily be thrown away — what do you do with a fleet of old buses or trains? Open a museum!

Then there are the really odd collections, like the dangerous, and now outlawed, medical devices housed at the Science Museum of Minnesota. And for weirdest collector, we nominate Ed Krueger, who couldn't part with anything, even his dead cat Sammy, who is now the centerpiece of Krueger's museum.

Spam Museum

TV superstars turn out in force for the annual Spam Jam in Austin each June. Marion Ross, Barb Billingsley, and Tom Brokaw are among the celebrities who have promoted the wonders of the processed-pork product dear to the hearts of World War II soldiers. While festivalgoers munch free Spamburgers, teeny-boppers bounce to the sounds of former Gear Daddy Martin Zellar, who was raised on the hometown meat. Kids at the pork-related amusement park scramble up the soaped-down slide of the Spam Suds Crawl while the line grows ever longer to buy Spam boxer shorts, Spam key chains, Spam license-plate holders, and anything else that can be emblazoned with this four-letter word.

Spam Jam is an occasion for visitors from far and wide to tour the new $8 million Spam Museum. The museum represents Hormel's struggle to keep Spam a relevant American pop cultural icon—like Coca-Cola and Hershey Bars—as opposed to a nostalgic relic.

Hormel is searching for real pop-culture credibility, a way to capitalize on Spam's kitsch value and the public's fond memories of the simple times when canned food was good food.

To clean up Spam's image, some long-standing games, such as the ever-unpopular Spam Gelatin Jump, have been nixed at the annual festival. The Gelatin Jump was basically a game in which the white stuff around Spam was put in a big vat; you stuck your arms in, and if you pulled out a golf ball, you won a prize. But the sticky game is no more.

In less-self-conscious days, massive quantities of Spam were allocated to area sculptors, who carved temporary statues out of the large blocks of processed meat for the festival. One year, Rodin's *The Thinker* was a favorite at the show. Unfortunately for tourists inclined to the visual arts, Spam sculptures are also no longer part of the program. "All that food would be better put to use to feed the hungry," said Hormel representative Mary Harris. "Besides, it just gets kind of gross."

Nowadays, Hormel has pooled its resources for revisionist history in the state-of-the-art museum, which is housed in a building formerly occupied by Kmart. While the museum makes no mention of the pesky labor strikes of the 1980s, much attention is given to former comptroller Cy Thomson, who was put through business college by founder George Hormel and embezzled nearly $1,200,000 by 1916. You can even see the checking deposit slips that nearly ruined the world-famous company.

Apart from a miraculous recovery from that blow, Spam's biggest feat was, of course, saving the planet by helping to win World War II. Tom Brokaw spoke of the greatest generation and, by default, the pork products that made it great. After all, Spammy, Hormel's fighting pig, made the ultimate sacrifice and went to war to feed the troops. Sure, American soldiers turned Spam's company nickname, Miracle Meat, into "the mystery meat that failed the physical," but they probably still welcomed the break from K rations.

Our allies, at least, appreciated Spam. In 1942, Edward R. Murrow announced, "This is London. Although the Christmas table won't be lavish, there will be Spam for everyone." Even Dwight Eisenhower gave Hormel a backhanded compliment in a postwar letter: "During World War II, of course, I ate my share of Spam, along with millions of other soldiers. I'll even confess to a few unkind remarks about it—uttered during the strain of battle, you understand. But as former Commander in Chief, I believe I can still officially forgive you your only sin: sending us so much."

Sadly, the historical photos of the Hog Kill Gang, the

Meat Cooler Gang, the Lard Room, and the Ham Boning Room were not transferred from the old Spam Museum in a suburban shopping mall to the new, cleaned-up, family-friendly digs. Instead, the new museum encourages interaction. Kids, for example, are able to can their very own Spam. If you do it in fourteen seconds—very good time, indeed—there's little satisfaction, since workers at the Austin plant finish a hundred and five cans in the same amount of time.

While kids use a little pink rectangular cushion in the shape of the meat, "Spam is actually in liquid form when it's pumped into the cans," according to a guide at the museum. "The machine fills six cans at a time, kind of like an old-fashioned six-shooter." Behind him, comic drawings of cute pigs show how the happy animals stuff themselves on corn in the pasture. They then joyfully enter the factory and magically come out the other side as big cans of Spam ready for your lunch. The guide explained that 960 hogs are "processed" per hour.

How many cans of Spam does that make? "If all the cans ever eaten were placed end to end, they would circle the globe at least ten times," he offered helpfully. We picture the earth with a glorious belt of blue and yellow cans to rival the rings of Saturn.

The sheer quantity isn't what put the miracle in this meat; it's the versatility, according to one display. Multicultural recipes abound, from Spam sushi to Korean kimchi Spam and Spam pizza. The new prizewinning recipe, however, is Spam cupcakes.

One highlight of the festival is the portly gentleman handing out free Spam magnets. You can't miss him. He wears a vacant smile and a T-shirt silk-screened with the mantra I THINK; THEREFORE, I SPAM.

Holiday on the Range

Persuading kids to vacation on the Iron Range may not be an easy sell, but it's not for lack of trying. A brochure from the Minnesota Museum of Mining in Chisholm sounds like the tagline from a Hollywood slasher flick: "The concentrator. The agglomerator. The pelletizer." These terms may be completely foreign to you now, but after a tour of one of Minnesota's operating taconite plants, you'll be using them as knowledgeably as an Iron Range miner.

The castlelike entrance to the museum lies amid a yard filled with enormous old machinery and railcars from the mines. Inside, the buildings don't offer much of the stomach-turning glee tots love, but they do offer facts about Minnesota iron-ore production. Did you know that nearly seventy-five percent of the United States's iron comes from Minnesota, which is 4.4 percent of world production? Replicas of an underground mine give you an idea of how things were so that you can imagine sleeping in shifts on the floor and breathing in the intoxicating tar fumes.

Also in Chisholm, off Highway 169, is the third largest freestanding memorial in the United States, the Iron Man. This is not a tribute to Ozzy Osbourne's heavy metal ballad but an homage to miners inspired by Veda Ponikvar's poem "Yes, the Iron Man Lives!" Now the kids will be impressed. The eighty-one-foot-tall statue marks the turnoff to the biggest amusement park on the lunar landscape of the range: Iron World Discovery Center.

Iron World guests are greeted by guides dressed in costumes from the turn of the last century. A 1915 tram depot and a 1920s-era electric trolley circle a two-and-a-half-mile manmade canyon on the Mesabi Railway. The big hole in the ground is the enormous Glen Open Pit Mine, advertised as having all the "sights, sounds, tastes and smells of the historic Iron Range." The conductor of the yellow and red train tells stories of the sleeping Ojibwa giant named Mesabi, whose backbone makes up the huge veins of metal from Grand Rapids to Virginia.

One highlight for youngsters here is the bizarrely themed Pellet Pete's 19-Hole Mini-Golf Course. Each hole of the course illustrates a step in the mining process, from exploration through shipping. The Crushing hole comes complete with a mini antique freight car, and the Blasting section has a mini TNT detonator to help kids envision the explosions. You can also take a tour of houses that were built in the area in the past, such as an Ojibwa tepee, a pioneer's homestead, a trapper's cabin, a Finnish Sami camp, and a Norwegian Stabbur house with sod roof and rosemaling on the inside.

Some $8.5 million was allocated for Iron World, whose mission was to recognize the ethnicities of the people who came from forty-three different countries to the Iron Range. Events such as Festival Finlandia, All Slav Day, and Festa Italiana are regular occurrences. The clincher, however, is International Polkafest. For four days at the end of June, thirty famous polka acts come from across the Midwest to participate. The world's first two-step musical and mystery, *Evelyn and the Polka King,* was staged here, enticing audiences with "a five-piece polka band, a missing daughter, and stolen money," according to the show's programs.

To end the Iron World tour on an up note, the Freight Shack Theater has a sing-along, with employees playing the banjo and singing songs in Swedish.

Lark Toy Museum

"*The robots* live together on this wall," Sarah Kreofsky chuckles, pointing to a huge selection of old-fashioned robots that would make George Lucas green with envy.

Also displayed in this playful fantasyland are old metal toys and lunch boxes featuring characters from Betty Boop to Underdog. This is the Lark Toy Museum in Kellogg, started by Kreofsky and her husband, Donn.

Donn Kreofsky had only $700 and a band saw when he decided to create his toy workshop. He was tired of his job as an art professor at Winona State and St. Mary's, so to amuse himself, he got to work carving little hand-painted pull toys for his alternative Toys "R" Us.

"I spend most of the day designing," he says now. "I'll make a sketch, send it down to the wood shop. They'll send it back carved, and I'll decide what colors to paint it." His End of the Tale Wood Workshop now puts out more than a hundred thousand toys a year.

Although the Kreofskys originally set out to mass-produce their handmade toys, they opted out of the wholesale business in 1995. "We used to deal with a hundred and eighty stores nationwide. One day, we'd receive an order for nine thousand pull toys for the Smithsonian, then the next we'd get an order for ten thousand from Neiman Marcus. It got to be too stressful. Now we just do retail through our store and Web site so we can meet the folks passing through," says Donn.

While Father Christmas is busy in his workshop twiddling basswood with his elves, Sarah shows visitors around the best toy shop–museum in the state. She is especially enthusiastic about their pet pig, Gip ("*Pig* spelled backward, because that's how the elves do it"). Kids watch in awe as the miniature potbellied pig spends the day grinding his tusks to sharpen them.

Part nostalgia, part thinking games, the toys range from hula hoops to bicycle bells, from kaleidoscopes to frog habitats. Even "collectible" Jesse Ventura dolls make an appearance. Different stores under the same roof—like the Ticky Tack Tourist Trap—and displays of classic old games lure shoppers all the way from Europe.

The grand finale of the tour climaxes with the hand-carved carousel, which took Donn ten years to complete. A deer, a giraffe, a swan, and even a dragon take a spin every half hour as kids line up to get on their favorite merry-go-round creature.

Nation's Largest Collection of Underwear

"You can smell the underwear," says textile curator Linda McShannock as she opens the door to the nation's largest museum collection of panties, girdles, brassieres, and other unmentionables. We're two stories underground, deep in the bowels of the Minnesota Historical Society (MHS) in Saint Paul, and we can't help but notice that the elastic used to hold up the underwear has been slowly disintegrating over the years.

More than thirty-five hundred precious undergarments are stored in this high-security vault at a constant temperature of sixty-five degrees and with sodium-vapor light, to prevent ultraviolet rays from damaging these priceless pieces. Bust pads and boxers, petticoats and corset covers, and, of course, hoops and tournures for that big-bottom, wide-load look are all stored in these lockers, which are funded, for some reason, by the National Endowment of the Humanities. Of the Historical Society's forty thousand square feet of storage, five thousand house underwear. In other words, one eighth of the museum's collection space is dedicated to undies.

"Munsingwear was as visible in Minneapolis as milling," says McShannock of the underwear giant. You could even say that Minneapolis was founded on underwear, since warm long johns meant the difference between life and death in the frigid winter. George D. Munsing realized this need and marketed his famous scarlet union suit in the 1890s. Finally, farmers could milk their cows and not freeze their tushes off. The farmers were safe, and the city was on its way.

This mother lode of undergarments was bestowed upon the MHS when Munsingwear went out of business, a victim of newfangled underwear trends. But in its day, Munsingwear was a pioneer of the undergarment.

"It's my favorite subject," confesses McShannock, who is something like the underwear curator. After getting a degree from the University of Minnesota in fashion merchandising, she volunteered at the MHS and spent months cataloging nine hundred bras and girdles, a mere fraction of the Munsingwear collection. She dated them, photographed them, described the materials, and put the information in a database. Her meticulous work is now used by underwear researchers across the country.

McShannock slides one drawer open to show corsets stiffened with whalebone, pointing out how women were literally constrained through underwear. Put under too much pressure, the bones could splinter, producing even more

Munsing's famous "itchless underwear" took the country by storm and prevented embarrassing scratching incidents.

Northwestern Knitting Co., which later became Munsingwear, disregarded puritanical objections and was the first company to unabashedly advertise underwear. The drummers (salesmen) hit the road, touting, "Don't say underwear, say Munsingwear!"

More than just freeing women from the confines of corsets, Munsingwear was the largest employer of women in 1920s Minneapolis and the largest underwear producer in the country by 1923. To celebrate its success and show its patriotic fervor, Munsingwear even produced a prototype American flag bra and girdle in 1946, which is carefully guarded by McShannock.

McShannock points out that multicolor underwear was a break with the past, since nineteenth-century underwear was pearly white, scarlet around the turn of the century, and finally peach or flesh color from the 1930s to the 1950s. "There are so many different ways to study underwear," McShannock effuses.

painful results, at least until steel-reinforced corsets were used to keep tiny waists in place.

Enter underwear revolutionary Amelia Jenks Bloomer, who pushed for female physical freedom in the 1850s. Her mutiny against the petticoat and other painful undergarments was unstoppable. The sultry corselet was designed as an all-in-one panty girdle, and the princess style combined a chemise with panties for a convenient one-piece package.

These inventions, often made from cotton, left some skeptics sour. Gustav Jaeger ranted that "only animal fibres prevented the retention of the 'noxious exhalations' of the body, retained the salutary emanations of the body which induce a sense of vigour and sound health and ensured warmth and ventilation."

George Munsing, on the other hand, saw an opening. With silk plated over wool, the silkiness of the garment touched the skin while retaining the wool's warmth.

Milk Carton Boat Races

The big event of Minneapolis's Aquatennial is the Torchlight Parade through downtown, whose oddest attractions are the homemade boats and rafts fashioned out of old milk cartons that are raced on the area lakes. The creative dreams and engineering calculations of ship designers are revealed in the bizarre creations that often barely move once in the water. The fun isn't in who wins the race but in showing off the colorful boats and testing whether they'll actually float. Whoever gets the wettest, wins.

Shellum Bowling Hall of Fame

The walk-out basement looks just like that of any other suburban house in Burnsville. However, inside this door near the Buck Hill ski area lies a collection of bowling memorabilia rivaled only by that of the International Bowling Museum and Hall of Fame in St. Louis.

When Doug Shellum moved into his house, he had bowling on the brain. He needed a large area to display his ever-expanding collection of anything related to bowling. Signed pins, loose balls, and Naugahyde bags clog the entrance. "Here are my Team USA bowling shirts!" Shellum announces enthusiastically. His closet is packed with classic bowling gear from brands such as Hilton, Nadine, Crown Prince, King Louie, Weber, and Hale-Niu. Where else can you learn that the earliest bowling garb consisted of tuxedos, sleek silk shirts, or thick turtleneck sweaters because the lanes often lacked heat?

"Now, that's art!" declares Shellum, pointing to his framed print of a 1950s-era thinly clad lass clutching a black bowling ball. These buxom babes were plastered across early calendars at bowling alleys and the occasional service station. What guy wouldn't want to spend his league nights with women like this? When real female bowlers showed up at the lanes, though, men sometimes teased them—at least until the women outscored them.

Shellum's bowling obsession has compelled him to chronicle every alley that ever existed in the metro area with photos of each site. His historical collection features a wide array of beer-team photos dating from the days when breweries were struggling to get their suds back into the alleys after Prohibition. Every inch of the basement is crammed with bowling paraphernalia, from kids' toys to adults' trophies. The collection ranges from corny postcards and valuable gold medallions to rings from early ABC tournaments. Visitors can even bowl a few rounds on the old miniature barroom bowling alley or tilt the bowling pinball machine.

And it's all going to get bigger and better. Since the advent of eBay, Shellum's Burnsville basement has quickly become too small to contain his dream of a bowler's paradise. Those bowling-museum guys in St. Louis better watch out—Shellum is buying!

Ed's Museum—Wykoff

Donald Eickhoff lifts the cardboard box off the shelf and gives it a sniff: "Yup, Sammy's still in there."

When Sammy the cat's nine lives were up, his owner, Edwin Julius Krueger, couldn't bear to bury his beloved pet. So like everything else Krueger collected, the cat ended up on the shelf. "He loved cats," Eickhoff explains. "The last cat he had, Sammy, he took to the vet. He brought it home in a plastic bag and put it in a box over ten years ago. We found the box in this basement."

Krueger lived with his son above the Jack Sprat Food Store in Wykoff after his wife died, in 1935. He worked odd jobs to pay the bills, running the Amazu movie theater (now the Community Center) and painting steeples. For fifty years, he never got rid of a thing. So when he died, in 1989, he left everything to the town on the condition that his Jack Sprat be turned into a museum—Ed's Museum.

Both a blessing of antiques from decades past and a curse of endless housecleaning, Krueger's collection became the town museum. Luckily, Ester Evers and Cathy Mulhern, the "curators," had a knack for cleaning, and they finally opened the museum after lugging six truckloads of garbage to the dump. As tour guide Eickhoff says, "He never threw anything away. Nothing! Absolutely nothing! We even have all his Social Security envelopes. He had about four television sets. When one didn't work, he'd look at another."

Some people might scoff at the collection in the old store, but to others it's an anthropological gold mine, with every artifact of one man's life. "We don't have anything in here that isn't Ed's," says Eickhoff. Some of the relics are ordinary enough, like the old player piano. Then there's the banana tarantula skeleton secured in a baby food jar. And Ed's twenty-five gallstones.

Much to the chagrin of those who don't see the point

of all this musty old stuff, Eickhoff says, the curators are considering expanding the museum even more because "we have a whole second floor with Ed's stuff that we haven't touched." Now, there's something to look forward to.

Ray Crump's Hall of Fame—Minneapolis

There's Ringo, George, Paul, and John, lounging around with Ray Crump, the center of attention. A few photos show Elvis Presley hanging out with Ray Crump. Leif Garrett relaxes with Ray Crump. Bob Hope jokes with Ray Crump in another photo. Who the heck is Ray Crump?

Ray Crump is the Forrest Gump of the baseball world. He began his career at thirteen years old as a batboy for the Washington Senators. Crump was there when Tony Oliva become the American League Rookie of the Year, in 1964; he attended the All-Star Game at the Met, with Hank Aaron and Willie Mays, in 1965; and he watched Harmon Killebrew smack 573 home runs.

Crump was in Washington the day Mickey Mantle pounded the ball over the fence for the longest home run ever, 562 feet. He was around when Fidel Castro tried out for Calvin Griffith but didn't make the cut. Disappointed with his dead-end pitching career, Castro went home to Cuba and staged a revolution. Crump, on the other hand, started a museum of his personal memorabilia: Ray Crump's Original Baseball Hall of Fame of Minnesota.

Crump moved to Minneapolis with the Twins in the 1960s, as their equipment manager. "I didn't even know where Minneapolis and Saint Paul were. . . . Sports put the Twin Cities on the map!" he says.

While most of Crump's museum focuses on baseball stars, Crump himself is no stranger to fame. His brushes with musicians and entertainers fill his Wall of Celebrities, and he has appeared on television 111 times. Apart from appearances in *Sports Illustrated* and on *Good Morning America*, he's found time to put his life into words in *Beneath the Grandstands*, his autobiography.

In one year, 111,000 visitors toured his collection, thanks in part to his location outside the Metrodome in downtown Minneapolis. Where else can you walk on artificial turf from the Metrodome and admire 10,260 signed baseballs, Kirby Puckett's first uniform, and Harmon Killebrew's last uniform?

If this is too much, rest in a chair made from old baseball bats, and watch a video on how to make a Louisville Slugger. Or slouch in one of the old bleachers from Met Stadium.

Frazee's Metal Moose

Rather than toss metal cogs in the trash or melt them down for recycling,
a sculptor from Frazee collected heavy pieces of scrap and welded them together to
create a mythological moose that guards a pond west of Main Street.

Iggy the Lizard

Describing the two-ton iguana he made from abandoned railroad spikes, creator Nick Swearer says, "It's oiled with human oil." Kids visiting the Science Museum in Saint Paul, who are allowed to climb all over the beast, keep the lizard's exterior rust-free and prevent Iggy from changing color, as most iguanas do.

Swearer began building Iggy when he was fifteen years old. He started out by gathering twelve thousand discarded metal spikes from the railroad tracks near his Northfield home. His pet lizard, Spot, posed as Nick pulled out the acetylene torch and began welding.

Four years later, Swearer's iron iguana went missing during the night. Suspicions fall on industrious Carleton College students with an excess of free time, who allegedly lugged the unfinished lizard a mile away before abandoning the two-thousand-pound beast. Swearer recovered his magnum opus and finished welding the reptile, which measures forty feet from head to toe.

Bird of Goodwill— Saint Paul

This heavier-than-air bird, attempting takeoff, is made of tin scraps, molded brass plates, an empty beer keg, lead pipes, and anything else the sculptor could find. The perfect symbol for the Goodwill store that stands behind it, this phoenix is a reminder that found objects needn't end up in a landfill but can rise up from recycling bins as art.

The Tin Can, aka the Weisman Art Museum

The legend behind the unusual stainless steel Weisman Art Museum in Minneapolis goes something like this: "The architect for the museum took a piece of paper, crumpled it up, and told the construction workers, 'Build it!' "

While architectural students laud the building as a modern masterpiece in which every detail was considered in advance, the building's architect, Frank Gehry, does little to dispel the legend. His original sketch for the Weisman is printed on one of the interior walls of the museum and looks just like a three-year-old's scribble. When the drawing is compared to the actual building, Gehry appears to be either a genius or a trickster.

During a speech in Italy, Gehry showed slides of some models from his rejected ideas, which seemed suspiciously like scrunched-up red construction paper with Popsicle-stick trees around them. Gehry joked, "It's at this point that the client gets nervous, especially after they've invested so much money in the project."

His promise about the Weisman was to not "build another brick lump." Gehry has lived up to his promise, but many unimpressed students simply dub his metal masterpiece "the tin can."

TRAINS & TRANSPORT

B. 4256. Entrance and Waiting Room, Como Park, St. Paul, Minn.

Lake Harriet Trolley and Museum

Terrified pedestrians jumped out of the way of sparks from the tracks and the overhead lines of the early electrical trolleys along the streets of the Twin Cities. In winter, these streetcars were freezing because of the often-windowless carriages. Passengers chewed gum to prevent nausea on the bumpy rides.

Still, this newly introduced form of transport was a step up from the horses that pulled cars down the streets on iron tracks. "Each horse would excrete fifteen to thirty pounds of manure each day, a lot of which was not removed from the city streets," according to North Saint Paul city records. Residents were glad to trade these dirty horses for clanging streetcars.

Five hundred and twenty-three miles of track once crisscrossed the cities. Today, barely two miles of trolley lines still exist. To preserve the memory of these beautiful old streetcars, the Minnesota Transportation Museum has revived one of the most popular lines, from Lake Harriet to Calhoun, and another section in Excelsior, to Lake Minnetonka. Collectors kept three of the old streetcars from being burned and restored the antique cars, which run every evening in the summer.

Enthusiasts at the trolley museum dream of someday extending the line almost into uptown, with another line along the Greenway to connect with the LRT. Along Lake Harriet, a replica of the old depot has been built, housing a mini trolley museum with models of double-decker streetcars and photos of a tram-filled Minneapolis.

The Depot That Time Forgot

Zooming west on old Highway 12 calls for a stop at the Old Depot Museum in Dassel, the "depot that time forgot."

"They came first by horseback and oxcart, letting the moon and stars guide them," says the Old Depot's brochure about the pioneers to western Minnesota. "Then the railroad lines stretched across the state, bringing new settlers by the thousands."

The miniature train in front of the museum shows what carried these settlers to their destinations. Climb up on a caboose from 1922 to get a feel for life on the rails, complete with a stove, desk, and toilet with a hole onto the tracks below. On the side of the museum sits the little railroad station that was moved west from Cokato.

Unfortunately, no passenger trains come through Dassel anymore, and settlers pile into minivans or SUVs instead. At the museum, visitors can reminisce amid a

collection of old railroad paraphernalia and in an unusual railroad scooter that could be pedaled on top of the train tracks—as long as no choo-choos were in sight.

Ten Cabooses in a Row

Just as the horseless carriage made many train routes obsolete, conductors have deemed cabooses no longer useful. Public affection for the rear carriages won't die, though, as seen with this line of colorful cabooses on the east side of Spring Grove.

Minnesota Inventors Hall of Fame

Who'd have thought that Minnesotans would invent the ice cream sandwich, puffed wheat, Liquid Paper, and the Double Chamber Multi Micro Orifice Collector? Every year, eccentric designers converge on Redwood Falls for the Minnesota Inventors Congress to admire new creations and show off their own. The Redwood Valley High School gymnasium is filled with everything from handy-dandy gadgets to Happy to Be Me dolls.

Inventors dream of creating the next Post-it Note or anything else that will make them an overnight millionaire.

And it could happen. For example, Bette Graham used her kitchen hand mixer to stir secret ingredients into a chalky white solution that she used to correct her typing blunders. Her job as a frustrated secretary enabled her to discover her true fate: as the inventor of Liquid Paper. She was helped by her young son, Michael Nesmith, who, upon seeing his mom's success, left town to become the hat-wearing Monkee.

Other recognizable products have also appeared at the convention. Bounce was created by Minnesotan Alice McQueary in 1976. Scotchgard came to light when Patsy Sherman accidentally spilled a chemical on a tennis shoe and couldn't wash it off. No solvents would remove her miracle formula, which caused a splash in the market.

Winners of the annual show are inducted into the Minnesota Inventors Hall of Fame, which is located in the Redwood County Museum. While the museum focuses mostly on local history rather than on these inventing luminaries, the musty building has two rooms dedicated to Minnesota products, with plaques proudly displaying the names of the inventors.

Some of the inventions are downright frightening, like the odd chemical concoction created by Allene R. Jeanes in 1962 for "industrial uses such as film formation as thickeners or bodying agents for edible compositions, cosmetic formulations, pharmaceutical vehicles, and drilling muds." In other words, her "gum polymer derivative" could be used in both your favorite beauty cream and the snacks you pop in your mouth. Display boxes of Duncan Hines desserts and bottles of barbecue sauce show some of the ways her secret recipe is used. Not a comforting thought.

3M—Dwan Sandpaper Museum

When John Dwan saw acres of sand washing up on the shores of Lake Superior, he had a brainstorm: If he smeared paste on some paper, magnetically charged it, and dropped sand on top, he'd make a fortune. Dwan's simple invention turned a little adhesive producer named 3M into a multinational giant.

Constant experimentation led to more inventions, such as wet and dry sandpaper, and kept 3M at the forefront of its field. Scotch tape was introduced in 1928, and magnetic recording tape soon followed. Today, Post-it Notes—invented by a fluke in the lab—are 3M's boom product.

Sandpaper collectors finally have their mecca: Dwan's little house in Two Harbors. At first, a sandpaper museum may seem breathtakingly boring, but don't yawn yet. The house smugly boasts that if the correct kind of sandpaper had been used on the Hubble Telescope, it wouldn't have malfunctioned and cost taxpayers billions of dollars. The museum generously hands out free sandpaper samples for visitors to try at home.

Another calamity could have been avoided as well had NASA given the Sandpaper Museum a ring for advice on the right grade of paper to use when attaching the heat-sensitive tiles that kept falling off the space shuttle. In other words, to avoid future tragedies, pay attention on the field trip, and be careful with your sandpaper!

Pavek's Wonderful Wireless

James Clerk Maxwell's discovery of the relationship between sound and electricity waves in 1865 was initially thought to be nothing more than the dreams of an alchemist. Then, Reginald Aubrey Fessenden of Canada took Maxwell's theory and created the first wireless for boats in 1906. The sirens of the sea began enchanting ships' captains through radio speakers.

The Pavek Museum of Broadcasting in St. Louis Park lines up scores of old radio sets as a huge tesla coil "amplifier" that looks more like a drying rack for clothes. The four different collections at the museum show the evolution of radios, along with weird concoctions such as the strange antenna hats used by the military and shoes that rigged the human body with cable, enabling transmissions to be received.

Not only does the museum have shelves of radios; dozens of televisions, focusing on local TV history, are on display. Huge old camera cranes from WCCO and KSTP give the feeling of being on a real studio game show set, where four thousand young visitors a year can hypothetically win $64,000.

The Pavek gives a glimpse back to the dawn of wireless, before media studies and video spinsters, to the day when Samuel Morse sent those first portentous words: "What hath God wrought?"

Museum of Questionable Medical Devices—Saint Paul

Are your private parts misbehaving or not performing up to par? Bob McCoy, the curator of the Museum of Questionable Medical Devices, can help. Simply insert the frightening, foot-long G-H-R Electric Thermitis Dilator probe in your nether regions and activate your "abdominal brain."

According to the original G-H-R ad, the vitalizing influence of continuous electric warmth directly applied to the prostate helped induce abundant circulation. And with the help of a special ultraviolet comb complete with various accessories, your sex life would make a big leap forward too. But this prostate warmer was soon made obsolete by the Recto-Rotor, "the only device that reaches the Vital Spot effectively."

In the pre-Viagra era, the Vital Power Vacuum Massager showed how to make a "Manly Man" out of Mac by invigorating and enlarging "Shrunken and Undeveloped Organs." Ads for a Vacuum Massager point out: "It is impossible for a woman to love a man who is sexually weak. To enjoy life and be loved by women you must be a man. A man who is sexually weak is unfit to marry. Weak men hate themselves."

If this cure doesn't work, why not try Dr. John Brinkley's radical cure of "implantation of goats' testicles into the human scrotum"? Brinkley's cure was surprisingly popular after articles praised its results. The quack doctor moved (or escaped) from town to town, asking new clients, "Do you wish to continue as a sexual flat tire?"

Now that the Museum of Questionable Medical Devices has left its home at St. Anthony Main and become part of the Science Museum of Minnesota, its more outrageous objects have been shelved momentarily in favor of more family-friendly quackery.

Fortunately, the most memorable piece in the collection is still on display, the bizarre Psychograph Phrenology Machine from 1905, which deduces all thirty-two personality traits and mental faculties—including "sexamity," "suavity," and "sublimity"—simply by reading the bumps on your head. After McCoy received this devilish device, he began collecting other dubious medical marvels. His collection blossomed with dangerous "curative" contraptions culled from the American Medical Association and the Bakken Library in Minneapolis.

Many of McCoy's gadgets, which claim to cure everything from the common cold to unenthusiastic "pelvic organs," date from before the days of the Federal Drug Administration. The FDA began regulating drugs in 1906 and medical devices in 1938. A bona-fide skeptic and jokester, McCoy will tell you to have a seat in William Reich's Orgone Energy Accumulator (probably the inspiration for Woody Allen's Orgasmatron) and feel the "orgone" seep through your pores. He warns, however, that questionable medical devices are still on the market, such as ear candles and magnetic treatments, generating instant profits for snake-oil salesmen from the chronically gullible.

A panel from the Electro Metabograph, dating back to 1940. Its manufacturer claimed that it cured jealousy, impotence, and nymphomania (among other ailments), using AM radio signals.

The Hemodimagnometer, also called the Coetherator, was patented in 1936. The patent calls it an "etheric vibrator," treating "human ailments by the vibration rate of ether." Patients would spit on a piece of paper and put it inside the box though, as with the resonator, a photograph or a handwriting sample was supposed to work equally well. It could also be used for "financial treatments," to make patients richer.

Until the 1920s, female patients thought to be hysteric were treated by having their genitals massaged until they had a "spasm." Early Sears Roebuck catalogs contained a page of vibrators that could be ordered.

Personalized Properties

Dissatisfied with just another boring bungalow in the suburbs? Tired of collecting the same old knickknacks and stuffed animal heads? Or maybe you've had it with those fancy museums and their exhibitions of great artists. So predictable.

Some creative types and home owners feel the same way. They've turned their backs on landscaping with picket fences, collecting stamps, or painting portraits of people and their dogs. Instead, they decorate their houses, their backyards, and even homegrown museums with far-out objects of strange and unusual beauty. Beauty being in the eye of the beholder, of course.

The inspiration for these wacky creations often comes from things other people might regard as, we have to say it—junk: old bowling balls, rusty cars, piles of rocks, plastic Spanish explorers. They merge with the aesthetic spirit of the artist and come out as something unique, a tribute to the individualism we still value here in the Gopher State. Sometimes, whole towns get caught up in the creative frenzy, adopting two-story outhouses or giant balls of twine as their unofficial logo. Only in Minnesota could an outhouse become a proud town symbol.

The neighbors may not always appreciate these unique gardens or homes next door (property values and all that). But we know that you, our discerning reader, will. Many of the sites mentioned here are on private property and may not be long for this world; the developer's wrecking ball is always threatening. So hurry and see them while you still can.

The tiny town of Vining has some pretty big sculptures, including a quirky door and some ever-flowing coffee. Opposite is Molehill in Sauk Rapids.

Itasca Rock Garden

Itasca, in southern Minnesota, was about to become the seat of Freeborn County when the deal was lost to the city of Albert Lea because of a bet on horses—at least that's how the legend goes. From then on, Itasca lived in the shadow of the larger city to its east. But John Christensen believed in the greatness of his town and cemented together fairy-tale buildings to prove its uniqueness to the world. Probably inspired by the Grotto of the Redemption just over the border, in West Bend,

Iowa, and beginning sometime around 1925, Christensen lugged rocks and shells back from his vacations to add to the marvel he was building in the south end of his garden.

Soon, all the neighbors wanted a peek at what was unfolding over the fence. Visitors began coming from across the state to Itasca Rock Garden near Edgewater Park to walk the winding trails alongside mini gnome houses, goldfish-filled ponds, and blossoming flower beds. The paths lead over and under little bridges amid pungent flowers with tiny trolls guarding the lawns and the dwellings tucked into the hillside.

Christensen's work didn't stop in his garden. In search of more living space, he extended his house's basement out from the foundation with fieldstones to make a beautiful greenhouse cellar that fit right in with his rock-garden motif. Christensen's masterpiece is on private property, but the owners keep up the gardens and sometimes allow visitors to take a peek.

AK-SAR-BEN Gardens

The sign TAME FISH ROAD still marks the street leading to the gone-but-not-forgotten AK-SAR-BEN Gardens, located just northwest of Garrison on Bay Lake. This once-famous rock garden compelled celebrities such as Will Rogers, Clark Gable, and Norma Talmadge to pay twenty-five cents to tour its towers, moat, waterfall, and wishing well. And where else but AK-SAR-BEN (*Nebraska* spelled backward) could visitors see two middle-aged brothers dressed in overalls ringing bells as all the bass in Tame Fish Lake swam over for a snack in response, just like Pavlov's dog?

The gardens took eighteen consecutive summers of work for the Vogt brothers, former Nebraskans, to complete. Soon, postcards advertised AK-SAR-BEN, and yellow school buses filled the parking lot with students on field trips to see the spectacular gardens.

We read that nothing remains of AK-SAR-BEN, so we traveled to see what relics might be dug up. The woman at the nursery next door to the famous site told us, "Oh, everything is still there, but AK-SAR-BEN is all divided up now. It's on private property, so no one can visit it anymore. Still, we get at least two or three people a week asking to tour it."

Making a Molehill Out of a Mountain of Rocks

Louis Wippich lived a normal life in Sauk Rapids until 1932, when he became enraptured by the teachings of Madame H. P. Blavatsky. Blavatsky was the founder of theosophy, the "knowledge of the Divine" she had learned from her Tibetan masters. After encountering Madame B., Wippich, a retired railroad worker and Navy veteran, began building a monolithic stone castle on his property, at the corner of Third Avenue North and Sixth Street.

With simple levers, pulleys, and a few hired hands, Wippich built his own temple, featuring two towers, one forty-five feet high. Most of the stones used in the construction were acquired from local quarries or picked up at demolition sites in the area. Some of the larger stones weighed in at well over a ton.

Wippich, the son of immigrant farmers, had quit school after the fifth grade to help his father in the fields. Somehow, without an advanced education, he managed to construct a fantasy cathedral that he christened Molehill. The structure boasts seven Doric columns, a Grecian temple, a Romanesque stairway, and a reflecting pool. A labyrinth of passageways snake through the impressive building.

After Wippich's death, in 1973, at the age of seventy-eight, Molehill fell into a state of neglect, became hopelessly overgrown, and was even used as a dump. Fortunately, though, some of Wippich's descendants have taken it upon themselves to clean up and maintain the property. Though the interior isn't open to the public, Molehill is an awe-inspiring site even when viewed from the street, and it's a fitting monument to its creator, the man who referred to himself as the Clown of Molehill.

Fireplace of States

While most visitors to Bemidji pull over to get their photo taken next to Paul Bunyan and Babe the Blue Ox, those in the know check out the geologist's dream creation inside the tourist center on Highway 197. In the 1930s, Harry E. Roese, a local resort owner, proposed building a Fireplace of States in the town. Roese began collecting rocks to add to the fireplace whenever he went on a trip. He lugged back stones from Yellowstone Park and Old Fort Garry in Winnipeg, which were cemented into the massive chimney alongside dinosaur bones and fossilized sloth tracks. Roese, who had a penchant for tall tales, began spinning yarns of each stone's origin, and curious travelers would stop by to hear his stories.

Warming to his task, Roese sent letters across the country asking for new rocks to complete the collection, aiming to get one stone from each state. As the fireplace gained national fame, politicians sent rocks and stones from all kinds of famous buildings around the country, including the Statue of Liberty, FDR's house in Hyde Park, New York, and part of the north wing of the Capitol building in Washington. What began as a whim became a nationwide effort, with a rock from each of the forty-eight states eventually in place (Hawaii and Alaska weren't states at the time).

The Fireplace of States was completed in 1937. Today, the mantelpiece at the visitors' center proudly displays many of Paul Bunyan's personal effects. The lumberjack's immense razor and toothpaste are there, along with his over-size CB, which kept him in touch with the truckers of the world, and his huge boxers, moccasins, and Zippo lighter.

Outrageous Architecture

Double Johnny—Belle Plaine

Every age has its own bragging points, from the lofty to the mundane. When pioneers first settled this land, social climbers boasted that they had a real outhouse rather than just a hole in the ground. Even Franklin Delano Roosevelt weighed in on the subject by encouraging the building of more hygienic outdoor latrines. He signed a presidential decree in 1933 that a million outhouses were to be built as part of the Works Progress Administration (WPA). It cost those who could afford one just $5 and was free for those in need. While FDR acted bravely to face the nation's latrine problem, he had to live with citizens referring to their biffies as "the Roosevelt."

Two-story outhouses, on the other hand, seemed to be the ultimate joke architecture, as the poor souls below were in danger of getting an unwanted gift from the heavens. In spite of all the guffawing, two bona fide double-decker Minnesota-built johnnies have become symbols of local pride. Rather than builders having to huff and puff to dig multiple holes for multiple outhouses, two-story outhouses did double duty with one hole. The top floor was just set farther back than the floor below to avoid unpleasant surprises for those sitting over the downstairs hole.

A two-story biffy has become the de facto symbol of Belle Plaine. The historic Hooper-Bowler-Hillstrom house contains a beautifully kept working version dating back to 1871, and tour guides explain that the impressive five-holer was essential for the huge family that lived there.

This architectural wonder was tacked on to the rest of the house but far enough away to prevent unwanted aromas from entering. Anyone in town can give directions to the biffy. Belle Plaine even broadcasts its fame as the home of the two-story outhouse on T-shirts.

The National Register of Historic Places was too late to keep another Minnesota two-story outhouse from crossing the border in the back of a collector's pickup. That outhouse has a good home, however, at the prestigious South Dakota Outhouse Museum, in downtown Gregory. A sign explains this architectural oddity:

DOUBLE JOHNNY "Come lately." Dwell on this. . . . 4 feet of snow—an 8 foot drift. How do you open the outhouse door?? Two story Johns were built for stormy weather. Second story holes were located further back than the 1st story holes!! This here 'johnny' was found in Minnesota, dismantled and erected here as you see it today.

The two-story biffy is the centerpiece of the collection of Richard Papousek, the curator of the South Dakota Outhouse Museum. Signs on the top floor of the double johnny caution, WARNING: MEN WORKING BELOW, while a second pleads, NO DUMPING ALLOWED.

Gas Station Pagoda

Passing through the Leech Lake Indian Reservation on Highway 2 in Bena, one might expect log cabins or maybe wigwams to be the unusual architecture of the area. Instead, it's a brilliant red, white, and blue pagoda that catches the eye. The startling structure is the main gas station in the area. Owner Butch Dahl, who helped build the Big Fish Drive Inn west of town, keeps up this Northwoods gas and convenience store, proudly telling all that the building was his grandfather's creation.

Dexter's Windmill

Celebrating its Dutch heritage—and to lure customers to its tables—a restaurant along I-90 in Dexter has raised a nonfunctioning windmill. Munch on some spicy Dutch apple pie as you admire the decorative windmill and remember the boy who saved the lowlands by putting his finger in the dike.

Teddy Bear Picnic

Just past the blue-eyed chicken in Delano sits the teddy bear picnic spot. Grab a shake from the Peppermint Twist Drive-In next door and sit amid the new pink and green mini-putt golf course and kids' playground.

Jungle Safari and UFO Suites

Nick Hook knows how to woo his women. To make lovers out of friends, he dresses in his finest shark-skin suit (no uptight oxford shirt necessary), chills the André champagne, and heads for the exotic theme rooms of the Fantasuites Hotel in Burnsville. Hook confesses, "I prefer the UFO room for the otherworldliness of the lunar lander and the space pod, but I get so absorbed in that huge television set near the moon crater hot tub that I sometimes forget about my date."

With that kind of endorsement, we had to take a look for ourselves. Hook offered to conduct a tour, and the management graciously agreed. We started out with Desert Nights, in which the harem theme is prevalent. "Relax like a sheik in a tented room," beckons the hotel's literature. If tents don't appeal, stay in the Pharaoh's Chamber and "languish inside a pyramid. . . . King Tut watches over all who stay here . . . overlooking murals of the Nile & the Sphinx."

Things aren't quite as serene in the Jungle Safari room, though. Almost buried in the simulated leaves of the tropical forest was a brochure warning, "Look out for the wild animals!" That's a good reason to get out of there and head for the romantic (but prisonlike) Castle Suite. Hook confided that he saves this room for very special occasions. The brochure warns guests: "Beware of the FUN you can have in this dungeon of pleasure. A king size bed guarded by a shining knight in armor . . . surrounded by your favorite night romping creatures! Her golden carriage is your queen bed with TV/VCR drawn by a white stallion."

Another Hook favorite, which calls to mind pliant concubines, is the Eastern Winds room, where "geisha fans and mirrors are just a prelude to the huge tile volcano lava flow like whirlpool. The queen size waterbed will have you never wanting to say Sianara [sic]."

Some of the brochure's descriptions promise maybe a little too much adventure: "If prehistoric is your thing you'll like our authentic cave," called Le Cave. Or "Sleep in a queen-size whaling dingy waterbed before venturing into the mouth of the great white whale" in the Moby Dick suite. For the winter camper, the Northern Lights room prevents hypothermia since "This cozy igloo holds a 7´ round waterbed, outside warm up in a large tiled whirlpool surrounded by mirrors."

But the best room of all, Hook swears, is the Space Odyssey room. "Blast off in our space capsule 7´ round bed," the brochure says. "Complete with TV/VCR &

original Nintendo game. A moonrock tiled whirlpool and murals of outer space complete the out of this world fantasy!"

While true world travelers may turn up their noses at the hokey decorations of the Fantasuites, there's a lot to be said for them. They're only a short ride from the suburbs, so you can save a lot of money on airfare while still putting that hint of the exotic in your love life. There are no terrorists loitering in the lobby of the hotel and no pesky pickpockets in Caesar's Court. And there's an ice machine right down the hall.

"I know some fools don't consider Burnsville particularly romantic," Hook says. "But they don't know what they're missing. Just listen!" He cupped his ear to hear the pleasant white noise of traffic zipping by outside along scenic I-35. "It's just like the ocean lapping on the shores of Venice."

Right.

Nordic Inn Medieval B&B

A chain-saw sculpture of the Viking god of thunder, Thor, stubbornly guards the door. The antler door handles don't budge, and pounding on the huge wooden doors gets no response. Pull the enormous chain to sound a bass bullhorn inside and a man in chain mail and a horned helmet greets you. Remember the password?

Welcome to Steinarr Elmerson's Nordic Inn in Crosby, where B&B translates to "Brew-'n'-Bed" because there are special suds to drink and Viking boats for beds. Inside the former church on First Avenue in a quiet neighborhood, Elmerson helps guests celebrate "the three r's: rowdy, robust, and romantic" in his five guest rooms.

Dinner is Nordic style with "Viking portions!" Lots of potatoes and other root vegetables accompany the meat or fish, but no utensils are allowed, except for an old-style dull knife. Expect to get messy, as napkins are discouraged. Instead, the armor-clad manager offers a slice of birch or cedarwood. Fuzzy Viking outfits complete the experience.

After supper, the fun begins. What was a church sanctuary now has huge stained-glass windows of Odin, the king of the gods, basking in the sun of Valhalla. Under Odin's Scandinavian heaven is a large bar with heavy stools carved from tree trunks. While sipping one of Elmerson's hardy brews, choose from three different interactive dinner theaters as improv actors from the area don Viking garb for a play with you, the guest, as the butt of the jokes. After a brief hop in the whirlpool in the fiberglass cave, it's time for bed in a boat. Tell the front desk if you need a seven a.m. wake-up call, but be prepared for a jolt when a loud Viking horn springs you out of bed.

Pay for a Night in Jail?

The thrill of serving time like an outlaw—if that's your thing—can now be had for less than $100. Best of all, nothing goes down on your permanent record, and you won't be surrounded by scary felons doing the jailhouse rock. Three outdated prisons have been handed over to the tourist trade rather than the wrecking ball and now offer cots to weary travelers.

Just two blocks from Preston's town square sits the Jailhouse Historic Inn, dating back to 1869. The beautiful brick building has been renovated with a plush whirlpool in one room, and the bars have been removed from all twelve suites except for the Cell Block room. Incarceration here requires

some imagination, even if the suite names could cause sleepless nights: the Detention Room, the Drunk Tank, and the Court Room.

Nearby, in tiny Wykoff, the two-room prison from 1913 has been converted into the Historic Wykoff Jail Haus B&B. While some jail-hotels are just a new use of an old building, Wykoff kept its cell complete with iron bars and bunk beds and even added black-and-white-striped sheets and curtains. When it opened, locals staged a trial and a mock hanging to make folks feel at home.

If the Wykoff Jail is full, inmates can be shipped to Taylor's Falls, to the Old Jail Bed & Breakfast. Located along the Mississippi River, the historic building, which was built in 1884, now offers amenities murderers never had but city visitors insist upon.

Thunderbird Hotel

Amid the flak over who has the right to use Native American imagery and who doesn't, the Thunderbird Hotel in Bloomington has stood by its collection of artifacts. The hotel's name stems from the image of the thunderbird emblazoned into stone five thousand years ago on Jeffer's Petroglyphs in southwestern Minnesota. The striking bird, carved by some unknown hand, vigorously flaps its wings as thunder and lightning flash from its eyes. The images are ancient, stretching back to the late archaic–early woodland period. The Thunderbird Hotel, whose fiberglass images date from the mid-1970s, claims its intention is to preserve such Native American artifacts.

Upstairs, past a fountain and a wooden statue of an Indian chief, a passageway leads to the Hall of Tribes, where businessmen and -women head for meetings in the Winnebago Room, the Cherokee Room, the Pawnee Room, and the Menominee Room. Stuffed coyotes, lynx, brown bears, buffalo, moose, elks, wolves, and rattlesnakes line the hallway walls. Small sculptures of Native Americans from various tribes as well as birch-bark canoes and a papoose create a "Distinctive Native American motif," as the hotel describes it.

Three huge fiberglass statues rise over the hotel. The largest is a bare-chested Indian saluting in the direction of traffic passing on the highway below. The second is a member of the Chippewa (Ojibwa) tribe with the description: "They often fought the Souix [sic] and Fox tribes. . . . Members tried to gain long life by using herbs and magic." The third statue, of Chief Thunderbird, is covered with brass paint and stands in front of the entrance to the hotel.

Perhaps one of the main reasons the owners have come under fire for their "Indian" collection is that it is not at all Native American. At least one group of Minnesota social studies teachers thinks the collection is in bad taste and was willing to put their money where their opinions were. The teachers, who had been considering holding their annual conference at the Thunderbird, decided on a different hotel, even though it was more expensive. "The Thunderbird Hotel uses the image of Native Americans to draw in customers and make money," one educator said. "It's incredibly disrespectful of their traditions."

A receptionist at the hotel retorted, "The owners were just really into all the Indian crafts and culture, so they began collecting artifacts. They had a hotel, so why not show it off?" Whether it's offensive or not, aficionados of kitsch can rejoice: The Thunderbird Hotel has kept its collection through a change of ownership and threats from the ever-expanding parking lots of the Mall of America. Experience 1960s tourism at the Bow and Arrow Coffee Shop, the Totem Pole Dining Room, the Peace Pipe Gift Shop, and the incredibly campy Pow-wow Lounge.

Slim's Woodshed and Hobo Jungle

"I was going out now to carve a four-foot gnome," says Slim, who stands more than six feet tall in his cowboy boots and straw hat. He walks with a bit of a limp because of the health problems that made him quit carpentry and take up wood carving full-time. "My medium is stone, bone, wood, clay, and soon-to-be metal." You might say that Slim is the artist-in-chief here in Harmony, the "biggest little town in southern Minnesota." Slim started a kind of woodworkers' cooperative in which twenty-two different artists give workshops and classes. A colorful totem pole and chain-saw-carved Uncle Sam mark the entrance to his woodshed, one block west of the town's Main Street.

Slim grew up in Spillville, Iowa, working for the famous Bily brothers, bachelors who whittled wood into elaborate and sought-after clocks. The brothers refused to part with any of their clocks, even after Henry Ford allegedly offered $1 million for one of their masterpieces. The Bilys obviously inspired Slim to carve, even though he downplays it. "I was allowed to clean up around the saws. You know, they'd let me get the chewing tobacco, get the beer out of the well house."

Slim's museum of wood carving may not have any of the Bily clocks, which the museum in Spillville says are "officially priceless." Slim does lay claim, however, to the largest collection of carvings in

the Midwest. "It's taken me fifty years to collect!" he says as he shows off the novelty clown bottle tops and minuscule wooden chairs made out of toothpicks.

Slim's newest project is the Hobo Jungle, just north of town. Funded by grants from the Jerome Foundation and the Minnesota State Lottery, the Jungle is a series of chain-saw sculptures of famous hoboes. Just as Titian based his paintings on heroes and villains of the Renaissance, Slim uses characters who passed through Harmony for inspiration.

A bike trail now stands where trains once barreled through town. "This used to be where the hoboes camped out because it was near the railroad tracks," Slim tells us. He points out that hoboes have their own language, carving into poles and fence posts to signify whether or not a place is safe. And then a little bit of town history. "The gypsies stayed on the south part of town, and finally someone in town said, 'Can't we all get along? Can't we live in harmony?' And that's how the town got its name," he says. "Or at least that's how the story goes."

Back at the woodshed, Slim has to finish carving the gnome before the end of the day. He pulls out his mini carving chain saw and says something rather unsettling. Because of his health, "I don't have feeling left. I can cut myself anywhere on my body and not feel it. If there's blood flowing, I have to stop my work and look."

Franconia Sculpture Park

As a rebuttal to the success of the Minneapolis Sculpture Garden in front of the Walker Art Center, a group of sculptors decided to exhibit their work away from the prime real estate of downtown. Just outside of Taylors Falls, near the tiny town of Shafer, the Franconia Sculpture Park was formed by sculptor John Hock to support far-out artistic visions.

Two cars getting it on in the field is named *Landing on Eros;* a giant wave made of slabs of wood rises twenty feet in the air and extends seventy-six feet; and three enormous balls made from sticks poke out of the ground. These sculptures are meant to shock and challenge drivers along an otherwise bucolic stretch of Highway 8 near the St. Croix Valley. Supported by grants and foundations, Franconia has attracted artists from as far away as Peru, the U.K., and the Czech Republic, all trying their hand at roadside sculpture.

Big Foot Sighting in Vining!

Ken Nyberg spent ten years as a construction worker. Along the way, he collected metal scraps and other materials that otherwise would have been tossed into a landfill. Nyberg now works part-time and makes colossal sculptures the rest of the time. He welds piles of scrap steel together in his signature patchwork pattern. The enormous sculptures are scattered all around the tiny town of Vining and outside his Quonset hut workshop on the edge of town. Nyberg is unassuming about them, though, saying he makes them just for fun. When asked what the titles of the sculptures are, he replies, "Oh, you can call them whatever you want."

Nyberg's most famous sculpture was also his first big one, but it still goes nameless. "A doctor wrote me a letter

Nyberg's *Clothespin*

calling it a Hawaiian hitchhiker's toe," he says, laughing, because of the painfully distended toe that makes visitors wince in empathetic pain. Most people refer to it as *Big Foot*. The owner of the Citgo Station at the edge of town was so inspired by the sculpture that he renamed his store the Big Foot Gas Station. Now, passersby boast of *Big Foot* sightings after they travel through Vining along Highway 210.

"Different, isn't it?" asks Nyberg. "Can't really go wrong with a foot, since there's billions of them and they're all different."

When he's pressed about the meaning of the *Big Foot* statue, his explanation doesn't reveal much. "I didn't want to do anything with a person in it," is all he'll say. He does say that he thought of doing a statue of a big middle finger once, "But I don't think many people would like that."

Art critics could easily compare his work to that of Claes Oldenburg, whose *Spoonbridge & Cherry* is the prize of the Walker Sculpture Garden and whose *Clothespin* has become the symbol of downtown Philadelphia. In fact, Nyberg welded a huge clothespin as well—a different design, though—which stands in the center of Vining.

Other cryptic sculptures stand in a field outside the Big Foot Gas Station. A huge pair of silver pliers stands ready to crush a large insect. "Some people think it's a beetle, a cricket, or even a wood tick," Nyberg says, preferring to let people construe his work any way they want.

Little by little, his sculptures are becoming well known around the area. Ottertail City commissioned him to construct a giant otter with a fish in its paw as the new town symbol. The local Lion's Club also persuaded Nyberg to weld a (what else?) giant lion that is carried around to local parades on a trailer.

As long as the supply of ten-gauge steel keeps filling up the Quonset hut, Nyberg will fill little Vining with his work until the whole town becomes one big sculpture park.

Artsy Cars

In reaction to Detroit's designs of nearly identical, ho-hum automobiles, some artists have taken this cornerstone of the American dream as their canvas. Springs, cameras, corks, bones, maps, and even grass have been glued to cars in an attack on conformity.

Art cars are the obsessive collector's perfect solution to questions of storage and display. What starts as a small pile of things can quickly snowball into a mountain. Glue the stuff on your car and you've not only freed it from the dusty display case, you've created a flashy work of art.

Obsessive collecting, while a solitary pursuit in theory, seems to beg for an audience. Take the unusual art car that showed up in south Minneapolis in 1998, called the Jerungdu Kale Farm Truck. It was complete with a trailer hauling a musical band of men and women dressed only in kale. When the hot sun started to wilt their green clothes, the Minneapolis police nearly stepped in to make a bold arrest for public nudity.

An easy comparison can be made between these movable art pieces and festival floats, but these altered automobiles usually run year-round. Unlike dragsters, most art cars are often old jalopies on their last legs. However, once artists have spent months altering their autos, a $1,000 engine rebuild isn't so bad (when the alternative is seeing a labor of love smashed by the trash compactor).

Artist Jan Elftmann from Minneapolis was a waitress for thirteen years who collected the used corks from thousands of wine bottles. Many of her earlier art projects involved multiples: paper clips, toys, gum wrapper chains. But Cork Truck has become her signature piece, leading her to use cork in numerous other works of art. Observers wrongly assume that her auto is a tribute to alcohol rather than a means of expressing her artistic vision.

Once in the life of any art-car owner, it's his or her duty to venture to the ultimate art-car attraction: Car Henge, in Alliance, Nebraska—a replica of England's Stonehenge, but with cars. Art professor Ruthann Godollei was so moved by her trip to this masterpiece in the middle of the prairie that she decided to stage a winter version of the Minneapolis art-car parade on the

frozen expanse of Lake Minnetonka. Minnesotan art cars slipped and slid around on the frozen lake, much to the bewilderment of ice fishermen. Not surprisingly, few spectators braved the windchill, but a short film, *Art Cars on Ice,* was created so that the artists would have bragging rights when it was shown at the summer event.

An homage to *Harold and Maude, To Life!* is a mirror-encrusted hearse—a joyful, absurdist take on the final journey we all must make in a culture that tries to hide death behind darkened windows.

Stained-glass master craftsman Ron Dulce covered his VW Beetle in glittering mosaic. The work is so seamless, the viewer forgets that such a curved surface is hard to piece flat glass shards over.

Many collections consist of dated knickknacks; art cars are the perfect medium for last year's castoffs. An aging muscle car covered with Herb Alpert & the Tijuana Brass record covers even uses a fittingly retro art technique, découpage, to hermetically seal the surface of this blast from the past. Tupper Time is Belinda Crimmins's 1964 Ford Fairlane with a picnic always waiting on the hood, complete with fridge magnets, retro plastic dining ware,

and other kitchen kitsch.

Art cars have been covered with Sheetrock screws (a Mad Max mobile), pennies (actually illegal, since money is legal tender), salmon skin (the fish skin is tanned and "perfectly waterproof, more waterproof than a car," claims the artist), nuts (with a plastic illuminated Mr. Peanut on the roof), beans (a Mercedes "Beans"), bones (for Fido to follow), reflectors (to always be seen), Astroturf (for indoor-outdoor protection), cigarette butts (the Stink Bug is a VW Beetle), telephones (PHONE FROM CAR sign included), and much, much more.

At an Art Car Symposium in Houston, art historian Todd Rowan proposed that wearing your identity on your car might be a means of exorcising our common demons, obsessions, fears, and dreams. Many of the items found on these cars are icons of popular culture, loaded with meaning, myth, desire, nostalgia, and the so-bad-it's-good stuff Americans both love and hate. Wearing your issues on your T-shirt has given way to driving them around! To learn how to vent on your own auto, go to artcars.com.

House of Balls

"I just call up bowling alleys for balls, and I leave with a truck full," claims bowling-ball sculptor Allen Christian. "I've got bowlers that come to drop 'em off, but I can't even use them all."

The floor of Christian's studio, in the warehouse district of Minneapolis, is covered with powdery bowling-ball shavings. He's concerned about having inhaled bowling-ball dust over the years, worried about the delayed effects of being a bowling-ball sculptor. He has a ventilation system, but he's not that comfortable with it. "It's my own feeling," he says, "that the balls are probably repositories for nuclear waste."

Christian's brand of found-object art has kept his sculpting going for twenty-four years and the House of Balls alive for eighteen. His balls have toured other states and ten U.S. embassies in Africa, as part of an art show about reusing and recycling materials.

Even Christian's pickup truck is the victim of his bowling obsession: It is adorned with plastic red bowling pins and has HOUSE OF BALLS written along the side in shoe soles. Christian has driven the bowling car across the country, but "only in Minneapolis have I been ticketed. Cops hate the red lights on it, as if only their cars can have red lights." The Bowling Car was the star of the annual Art Cars on Ice festival on the frozen Lake Minnetonka.

Just as Michelangelo insisted on choosing his own marble at the Carrera quarries, Christian is picky about the bowling balls he uses: "You know, they have balls with gyroscopes inside of them. I prefer the old balls, though." The different colorful layers used to construct a bowling ball add to the expressions on the faces of his sculptures, but Christian doesn't know what he'll find inside a ball until he carves it open.

At his studio, eerie music seeps out of the doors. Red and white bowling pins dangle precariously from the ceiling as though ready to bop visitors on the head. Dim lights focus on strained faces carved into the flesh of abandoned bowling balls. This is Christian's House of Balls, named for his penchant for grinding bowling balls into fabulous busts of tormented or placid people.

World's Largest Ball of Twine

Francis Johnson's neighbors knew something wasn't right next door. Johnson flaunted his Swedish background by painting his backyard cupola the colors of his ancestors' bright blue and yellow flag. He collected anything he could get his hands on: pencils, feed caps, ice cream buckets, padlocks, pliers, and especially twine. In fact, he spent four hours a day dutifully wrapping twine. He began wrapping in March 1950, and soon, his vision would shape the identity of the entire town of Darwin.

When Johnson's twine-ball hobby wouldn't fit in his house anymore, he rolled it out into the shed, where he used a railroad jack to continue to wind twine into one continuous string. When he ran out of space in the shed, he brought the ball into his barn, where he hooked up a crane to elevate it for proper wrapping.

At this point, outsiders began to take notice of Johnson's masterpiece. A representative from the *Guinness Book of World Records* snapped a photo, and the ball of twine took its place in the annals of history, outshining the man with the beard of bees and the guy with the longest fingernails in the world. Johnson had made the big time in the record books, but he didn't stop there. He kept winding and winding until the ball reached twelve feet in diameter, weighing eleven tons.

Meanwhile, Frank Stoeber of Cawker, Kansas, was itching with envy as Johnson basked in the limelight. Stoeber had been working on a twine ball of his own for years with no recognition. Thinking Johnson was resting on his laurels, Stoeber wound 1.6 million feet of baler twine night and day. Victory was in sight as his ball reached eleven feet in diameter; then, tragically, in 1974, Stoeber had a heart attack and died.

A shelter for Stoeber's ball was erected in the town square, where residents of Cawker gather at the annual Twine-a-thon festival and add more string to the ball in tribute to their townsman. While Cawker's ball has surpassed forty feet in diameter, Johnson's magnum opus still claims the title of World's Largest Ball of Twine by a Single Person. Francis Johnson could die in peace in 1989 after having wrapped twine for thirty-nine years.

In 1992, *Ripley's Believe It or Not* asked Darwin if it could have the ball for its museum. The tiny town appreciated the offer but flatly refused to let its homespun oddity be shipped away. Undaunted, *Ripley's* turned to Mr. J. P. Payne from Mountain Springs, Texas, to make one that ended up measuring thirteen feet, two and a half inches. But according to the woman at the Twine Ball Souvenir Shack in Darwin, "It's probably bigger but doesn't weigh as much, it's not of twine, and is not done by one person." She laments this copycat ball, since "they took us out of *Guinness!*"

Between selling tickets to the annual chicken dinner, she graciously shows photos of Weird Al Yankovic's visit after he wrote a song about the ball of twine. "It's a good video," she says. "Some of the songs aren't so nice, but his was great. He even projected the twine ball on the screen behind him!" Darwin has embraced Johnson's dream as the town symbol, and Twine Ball Days are celebrated every year. The twine ball now has its own mailbox at its old site, Francis Johnson's front yard, while a Plexiglas silo shelters the actual ball in the main square of downtown (where we hope it will dry out—it was getting a little pungent when we were there).

El Dorado Conquistador Museum—Minneapolis

In 1965, spurred on by the Broadway smash *Man of La Mancha,* industrious entrepreneurs rushed to cash in on the Mediterranean home-décor craze. Cervantes had hit prime time, and all things Spanish were the rage. Black velvet matadors, brass plates imprinted with galleons, and foam conquistadors were swept off store shelves by greedy, if not exactly tasteful, connoisseurs. One could savor the smell of danger and the promise of heaps of gold, all in the safety of your own sitting room.

With floors and walls covered with pressed plastic or black velvet masterpieces, the El Dorado Conquistador Museum boasts the largest collection of conquistador kitsch in the world. Now you can find this ambience at the Kitty Cat Klub in Dinkytown (the same Minneapolis enclave near the University of Minnesota where Bob Dylan first put the moves on long-haired coeds).

The curators' obsession led them to Salvation Armies across the state, scouring for secondhand toss-offs last seen in shag-floored rec rooms in the late 1960s. In the beginning, they absolutely refused to violate their $2 limit per objet d'art in their quest (although they later raised it to $5). The result is one of the strangest anti-art exhibits in the country, comparable only to that found in the Museum of Bad Art in Dedham, Massachusetts.

Inspired by a well-stocked fridge of beer, the curators invented origins for their collection—often involving Nazi art thieves, Sotheby's auction house, and Xanadu, the Foam House of Tomorrow—which they wrote on slick tags for each masterpiece. The newest piece is that of five disembodied conquistador heads on a hardened foam bas-relief. It's named *The Graduating Class: Pizarro, Cortez, Ponce DeLeon, DeSoto, and Columbus in Search of El Dorado, the Legendary City of Simulated Gold.*

This treatment of cheesy paint-by-number knickknacks has landed the museum on the pages of local newspapers and on public radio's airwaves.

"Imperialism has never been so chic. . . . You can almost smell the blood," raved *Minnesota Law & Politics* in 1998. Upon hearing this hype, an outraged ex–elementary school teacher stomped into the museum, questioning this "revisionist history" and commenting, "The conquistadors were explorers, not killers!"

Curator emeritus Scott Wentworth hasn't swayed

Galleon Gallery, simulating battering waves on the bow of a Spanish ship in search of plunder.

But in this more enlightened day of corporate stewardship of public goods, the museum has found a stylish new private-sector home. Curator Dr. Mark Vesley questioned, "Why settle for naming a gallery or a courtyard after a plutocratic benefactor when the entire museum can be subsumed under a for-profit enterprise? *El Dorado* means 'gold,' and the collection can now be inspected during regular business hours amidst the cheery ching-ching-ching of cash registers at the Kitty Cat Klub, a friendly collegiate drinking establishment." This is paradise, found at last.

from his artistic vision of portraying kitschy objects as precious, embellishing with his usual sarcasm, "They're priceless—they have no price."

El Dorado's original home, in the basement of a college bookstore, re-created the unsanitary conditions of a 1970s rec room crossed with the black death–era Middle Ages: The carpet was carefully stained, comfortable plush lounge chairs were seldom vacuumed, and moldy cheese chips were studiously placed under the cushions. In an attempt at a state-of-the-art, interactive, multisensory display, a toilet's flushing could be heard near the

Under the Cherry Spoon

The Minneapolis Sculpture Garden is the largest urban sculpture park in the world, and it has drawn more spectators than ever expected. The centerpiece is a huge spoon with a cherry squirting water, which has become the unofficial symbol of Minneapolis.

Even though this sculpture echoes the fiberglass and cement roadside attractions seen across the state, placing it in front of the Walker Art Center and having two famous artists as its creators (Claes Oldenburg and Coosje van Bruggen) gives *Spoonbridge and Cherry* the label of "fine art."

Perhaps to embrace other roadside archetypes (and to dodge being labeled snooty for snubbing Paul Bunyan in its sculpture park), the Walker also sponsored a hilarious mini-putt course, called Walker in the Rough, with each hole designed by area artists and architects. Since the putt-putt course with enormous moose, cows, and other fiberglass beasts, which once stood near the Minnesota State Fair, disappeared, the sculpture garden's mini-putt is a dead-on stab at the heart of Americana.

Roadside Oddities

Stop *the car!* I just saw a chicken as big as Bigfoot! Wait, that can't be.

Oh yes. Along the roadsides of Minnesota are things that may seem like group hallucinations but are just monuments to the weird bent of some of our inhabitants. There are giant dandelions, huge chickens in full mating display, oversize corncobs, and a particularly beloved forty-foot-long cement otter. And that's just for starters.

These huge beasts are sometimes bait to lure motorists off the road and into the stores lurking behind them. Other times, overflowing ethnic pride urges locals to construct a huge statue to honor their forefathers, like the Swedes in Lindstrom (a tole-teapot water tower) or the Norwegians in Spring Grove (a wild-eyed Viking). Most often, though, these colossi are the visions of individuals who would not go gently into that good night, instead wanting to leave something for all future generations to scratch their heads at and wonder, Why?

Minnesota has the largest number of these roadside attractions per capita in the world, although Wisconsin runs a close second. So hit the road, pull out the camera, and bring back proof that you really did see an orange horse taller than any building in town.

Big Ole

If you dare doubt that Leif Erikson preceded Christopher Columbus in discovering America, you'll have to duel down Big Ole in Alexandria. Town residents go one step further, however, claiming that Norse explorers reached all the way to the middle of Minnesota back in 1362. By that time, the Viking age had long since ended, so these northern explorers were more like curious missionaries than pillaging berserkers. Nevertheless, the statue of Big Ole shows his Norse pride, as he wears the full regalia of his Viking forefathers. History teachers in Alexandria are calmly corrected by students who say, "No, it's not Plymouth Rock, Jamestown, or any of those other historical sites out east. The birthplace of America is in the heart of Minnesota."

Spring Grove's Viking

Not to be outdone by Alexandria, Spring Grove has raised its own statue to secure its claim as the first Norwegian settlement in Minnesota. Never mind that historians have debunked the iconic horns on the helmet, except for perhaps a few Danish Vikings who put gruesome trophies on their hats. Visitors dare not argue with a fifteen-foot-tall Viking with a raised sword and disturbing two-color eyes that, by comparison, make Norwegian bachelor farmers look absolutely cuddly.

Tea for Two Thousand

Showing off its Swedish pride, Lindstrom hired brave painters to dangle from its water tower to adorn the sides with a tole painting. Visible for miles around, the world's largest teapot is just the latest Scandinavian touch in the town. As each new generation slowly loses its ancestors' tongue from Sweden, the road signs in Lindstrom ironically become more Swedish. The town's name has even added umlauts to become Lindström, if only the mapmakers could find out how to type it— or pronounce it.

World's Largest Dala Horse

In Mora, Sweden, during the winter of 1716, hungry soldiers began whittling little horses to swap for soup with the local inhabitants. Sweden's king Charles XII was off seeking his fortune by looting through Europe, so the soldiers back home in Scandinavia took to woodworking to earn their daily gruel. The gift horses carved by the Swedish army became a sort of currency during the harsh winters. In the Dalarna province, these toy horses soon came to be the symbol of Sweden and life-size Dala horses are a common jungle gym for Swedish tots.

In true American fervor—or excess, take your pick—the town of Mora has raised a twenty-two-foot-tall horse to commemorate its Swedish ancestry, along with a smaller painted tole clock. Following Mora's lead, the Scandinavian Heritage Center in Minot, North Dakota, raised an enormous Dala horse, and two Swedish towns in Iowa followed suit. When news reached Scandinavia, a fifty-foot wooden horse was raised in the Dalarna province. No word yet on the latest entry in the giant-horse wars.

God of Peace

Native American Statues

Sculptures of Indians, often deemed offensive because some people think they portray demeaning stereotypes, are under fire. However, a look at a series of them shows that the debate can be strangely subjective.

One argument put forth is that it is insulting if the artist is not actually Native American. However, nearly all of the state's Native American statues were made by European Americans, so if we follow that line of thinking, we'd have to get rid of all the sculptures of Native Americans. Before swinging the wrecking ball, let's look at a few of them around the state.

An important factor in determining if a statue is offensive seems to be the materials used. For example, the enormous and brightly painted Native Americans outside the Thunderbird Hotel in Bloomington were made out of fiberglass by the F.A.S.T. (Fiberglass Animals, Shapes & Trademarks) corporation of Sparta, Wisconsin. Some guests have protested that the big statues are tacky and in bad taste. On the other hand, the *God of Peace* figure in the Saint Paul City Hall and courthouse is regarded as a masterpiece. The sculptor, Carl Milles, a Swede, carved the striking statue, also known as *Onyx John*, in 1932 out of sixty tons of white onyx. The dark blue Belgian marble and mirrored ceiling inside the art deco courthouse adds to the tasteful display of what could easily be called (but isn't) the world's tallest Native American statue.

Sometimes, the materials used to make the statue matter less than the presumed intent of the creator. An Indian chief statue molded in cement by Clarence Prohaska in the 1950s was used to greet tourists as they entered the Mystery Cave in southeastern Minnesota, which was then a private attraction. When the Mystery Cave became part of the state parks system, however, things changed. The book *Monumental Minnesota* reports, "In an article in the *Spring Valley Tribune* the manager of

Chief Kandiyohi

the park said that statues didn't belong in natural settings and what could be considered a stereotype of an Indian might offend Native American visitors." The statue was moved to the tourist information center on Highway 16 in nearby Spring Valley. Now, passing groups of Japanese tourists can be seen getting their pictures taken in front of it.

On the flip side, Two Harbors has a recent chain-saw sculpture of an elongated Indian head with a single feather on top. Sculptor Peter Toth was careful to list his roadside landmark as "a gift to the people of Minnesota" to raise awareness of the plight of the "original Americans." With this disclaimer, he wisely deflects any criticism and can possibly realize his dream to put a similar monument in every state.

Often, the negative reactions come from the commercial use of statues to lure customers, such as the ones at the Thunderbird Hotel or at the Mystery Cave. The *Chief Wenonga* statue in Battle Lake comes from exactly the same fiberglass mold as the Sioux at the Thunderbird but hasn't been criticized, possibly because it stands as a monument to a Native American battle.

And sometimes the statues morph from commercial insult to public tribute. A Native American statue built by Robert Johnson was transformed from a business logo to the symbol of an entire county. *Chief Kandiyohi* (meaning "Abounding in Buffalo Fish") was erected in 1956 in front of the Bank of Willmar but was left homeless when the bank was flattened. The seventeen-foot-tall statue was moved to the lawn of the county courthouse and has become the official logo of Kandiyohi County.

Another roadside salute—this one outside Morell's Chippewa Trading Post, Bemidji

Life in the F.A.S.T. Lane

We Minnesotans admire our enormous roadside sculptures and swell with pride as we imagine that these huge sculptures of fish, voyagers, and other creatures are typical of the Land of Lakes. Look at the labels, however, and you'll find that most of the fiberglass sculptures hail from across the border, in Sparta, Wisconsin.

Do you want a piece of instant roadside Americana so that tourists can't resist taking a snapshot and teenagers can't resist kidnapping your sculpture and dangling it off the overpass for kicks? Stop at F.A.S.T. (short for Fiberglass Animals, Shapes & Trademarks) and browse the brochure for everything from Big Boys to flying saucers. F.A.S.T. has a five-page price list of already made molds ready to form sculptures which cost $700 and up.

A stroll through the "graveyard" of enormous fiberglass figures and molds reveals everything from giant cows to King Kong. "Look! A giant cheeseburger!" exclaimed lead sculptor Jerry Vettrus as he led us around. As we passed a couple of Big Boys, he said, "A guy called me asking for a couple of Big Boys for his yard. He didn't want them painted, he just wanted to look at them."

Vettrus's technique requires "a fiberglass gun and lots of foam to make the mold. It takes $1,000 worth of foam to make a twenty-two-foot-high pirate," he states matter-of-factly. "I've already sent three pirates to Hong Kong, but they wanted one even bigger." Apparently, buying statues in bulk pays off. "The first A&W Bear I made cost $12,000. Since I then had the mold, the second one was only $8,000!"

Vettrus prefers to design original artwork, however. He has books and encyclopedias of drawings he consults for ideas when someone asks for a specific sculpture. "Appleton needed a heart-shaped slide, but it had to be anatomically correct. We consulted with a doctor, and now children can climb right through the aorta!"

Vettrus's two biggest masterpieces date back to the early years, when the company was known as Creative Displays. The forty-five-foot Jolly Green Giant was trucked over to Blue Earth on a flatbed truck just in time to be the de facto golden spike of Eisenhower's interstate highway system, which connected the

coasts in Minnesota. Vettrus's second fiberglass masterpiece—a breathtaking hundred-and-forty-five-foot walk-through muskie—had to be transported in three pieces to Hayward, Wisconsin.

A bit of research reveals that Creative Displays, formerly Sculptured Advertising, began in Minneapolis in 1974; it didn't become the Wisconsinite F.A.S.T. until 1983. Therefore, Minnesotans can boast that the creative spark that launched the business of oversize sculptures did indeed begin in the Land of Lakes.

Norb Anderson, who helped Vettrus form the company, retired from the colossal-statue business when Vettrus bought him out. "As part of the agreement, I have to make him a thirteen-foot dairy cow," Vettrus remarked. Now, F.A.S.T. delivers its statues all over the world, with animal slides destined for Cyprus, a blue aqua splash to Italy, and canine fountains to Brazil. Still, most of Vettrus's work goes to the Wisconsin Dells and small-town Minnesota.

Big Beasts

Paul Bunyan's Cow?

Babe the Blue Ox only had eyes for Lucy the Cow in W. B. Laughead's original tales of Paul Bunyan. Avoiding lowly hay, Lucy filled her four stomachs with trees. Hoping for cream for their coffee, thirsty lumberjacks would reach to the stars to clutch the enormous udders of the colossal bovine. The achy lumberjacks also got liniment from her udders to rub on their sore muscles.

This Holstein in Bongards' Creameries allegedly yields only the finest dairy from her fiberglass udders. (We hope that's not what's for sale in the creamery across the street.) How this lonely cow ended up so far from Paul's sidekick is unknown, but gossip has spread that Babe the Blue Ox had lost an encounter with some sharp snippers, which left him unable to produce progeny with the lovely Lucy.

Big Cement Otter

It was all the otters wiggling around in the rivers that gave Otter Tail County its name. A while ago, schoolteacher and sculptor Robert Burns decided to raise a tribute to the county's namesake. His forty-foot-long cement otter, which stands in Adams Park in Fergus Falls, is lovingly mounted by anyone who can make it up onto his back. In spite of signs warning deviant climbers to keep off, kids and adults alike can't resist clambering up.

In the 1980s, Fergus Falls installed a series of six-foot-long otters along Main Street to inspire town pride. This was years before Chicago erected its series of artist-designed cows and many other towns followed suit. But Fergus Falls wasn't prepared for the onslaught of teenagers with spray paint and baseball bats who sought to personalize each of the otters. The downtown statues lasted only one summer before becoming prized possessions in student dorm rooms or rental houses. Who'd have thought that such playful creatures could inspire such unruliness?

Big Buffalo and Mammoth Mouse

Perhaps to warn travelers along Highway 8 that buffalo have escaped through the fences in the past, this blue-eyed bison stands outside Eichten's Cheese Shop in Center City. The mutant mouse chomps on a big wheel of cheddar under the flags of Scandinavia.

Another famous buffalo statue hasn't survived quite as well as the one at Eichten's. South of Duluth, along I-35, Burko the Buffalo has been splashed with paint and dressed up, and once, it was even kidnapped. Fortunately, the Buffalo House bar, Burko's home, safely recovered the ceramic beast from its delinquent captors.

Smokey Bear

"Only you can prevent forest fires," warns Smokey Bear in the center of International Falls. While Smokey may be a well-meaning bear who wants to save the forests, the drive into Frostbite Falls reveals a different story. Mounds of lumber two stories high cover field upon field, with miles of forest having been clear-cut for the paper mills.

Found-Object Fossils

Geese are welded together out of old watering buckets. A twelve-foot-tall black silhouette of a farm is cut from sheet metal. Metal corn sculptures mimic the surrounding fields. And dinosaurs evolve from dried cow skulls, deer antlers, and lawn-mower blades.

OVERSIZE HUMANOIDS

World's Largest Stucco Snowman

North Saint Paul's Sno-Daze festival was often overshadowed by the much larger Winter Carnival in Saint Paul, with its legendary ice palaces. One winter, when the snow barely dusted the ground and Sno-Daze seemed like a bust, the local Jaycees raised funds to build a permafrost snowman out of stucco so that even in the scorching hot summer, residents would remember winter. Not only does North Saint Paul's snowman sport the requisite black top hat, but the fifty-four-foot Frosty has a secret door in its rear so snowplows can park inside when 'tis not the season.

Belly by Budweiser?

Proof, perhaps, that gnomes should not drink beer and breed with Norwegian bachelor farmers, Spring Grove's statue of a malformed Scandinavian *nissen* stands in front of the town creamery. Maybe by placing this decadent sprite in front of the dairy a statement is being made about drinking more milk to avoid getting a rotund beer gut. Either that, or stick to a strict diet of *rømmegrøt* cream porridge, smoked salmon, Jarlsberg, and aquavit.

Carver's Carving

Unsure what to do with the enormous stump sprouting through the floorboards of this porch, artistic lumberjacks roared up their Stihl chain saws to carve Carver's first settler and attract tourists in their two-tone Volvo Amazons.

One Very Happy Chef

"Never trust a thin cook," goes the old axiom. Not to worry. Mankato's beloved statue has no chance of being mistaken for that rare breed. Instead, the *Happy Chef* joins the ranks of successful chunky chefs Wolfgang Puck, Chef Tell, and Lynne "Never Skimp on Butter" Rossetto Kasper. Alas, *Happy Chef* statues are not so jolly as before, since their numbers have been vastly reduced. Maybe cholesterol has taken its toll and culled the herd of *Happy Chefs* and Big Boys lining the roadsides.

Rocky Taconite

Silver Bay honors its cash cow, taconite, with this metal statue. *Rocky Taconite* stands twelve feet tall (but only about five feet high without its stone base). The statue, built by Village & Reserve Mining Co. out of two steel balls, used to adorn a strip mall in tiny Silver Bay. It was moved closer to Lake Superior to greet visitors entering the town, the Taconite Capital of the World.

Supersize It!

Huge Hockey Stick

After standing in downtown Eveleth for just six years, the world's largest hockey stick was deemed an impending disaster. This regulation 107-foot hockey stick built in Warroad by Christian Brothers was beginning to sag. Perhaps woodpeckers succeeded in punching a hole through the fiberglass exterior to allow rain to soak into the wood. Maybe the hockey gods were angry and lightning had struck the top of the handle. Many theories were put forward, but the only known truth was that the stick had to come down.

Already, Eveleth had succeeded in persuading *Guinness Book of World Records* to disallow a larger hockey stick in Canada because it wasn't regulation. Eveleth's stick wrested the title from its northern brethren and retained the claim of world's largest hockey stick. But it was not to last. While the town was celebrating Independence Day in 2001, the Pro 1000 stick was lowered before it could squash any awed hockey fans.

With the U.S. Hockey Hall of Fame on the hill above the town, Eveleth couldn't let this embarrassment stand. Pieces of the old stick were sold off for $5 a slab to raise money for a replacement. In June 2002, Sentinel Structures of Peshtigo, Wisconsin, finished the new stick and shipped it to Eveleth. Sirens wailed and police lights swirled as the Minnesota Highway Patrol escorted this huge piece to its new home. Once again, the world's largest hockey stick stands above Hockey Plaza, poised for a slap shot of the seven-hundred-pound hockey puck at the mural of the goalie across the street.

World's Second Largest Thermometer

The world's largest thermometer rises above Death Valley because record high temperatures are much more dramatic than record lows. In either case, no one wants to stick around for the extremes. This unusually warm day in Frostbite Falls means it's the peak of the summer tourist season. Swimmers dive into nearby Rainy Lake and quickly come out when they realize that the water temperature stays about the same as that of Lake Superior. In honor of the cold, the world's second largest thermometer was erected in downtown International Falls near the statue of Smokey Bear.

Dandelion Fountain

While gardeners struggle to rid themselves of pesky weeds, in the summer, Minneapolis kids line up to splash in the waters of the world's largest dandelion. Standing above the shuffleboard courts, the Dandelion Fountain has become the symbol of Loring Park and a favorite spot for cooling off during the summer, when the Walker Art Center sponsors movies and music on the nearby grass.

Boots Galore

Pottery and shoes are the products that have earned the river city of Red Wing its nationwide reputation. To honor its famous Irish Setter boot, the town produced a series of four-foot-high footwear to place around its streets. Just as Fergus Falls has its otters and Chicago its cows, Red Wing hired local artists to express themselves with boots as their canvases.

To celebrate its centennial, the Red Wing Shoe Company rolled out huge swatches of tanned leather and stitched together the world's largest boot. "You know, the whole shoe is just like the actual boot, so they used all real leather. The laces are huge! They're like rope," exclaimed an excited security guard at the boot plant, just north of town.

Unfortunately, the authentic Irish Setter would weather quickly if left outside in the elements, so the big boot is brought out only for special occasions such as the Minnesota State Fair. To appease public demand to see the boot, the guard remarked, "I've heard talk that the city of Red Wing will build an atrium to hold the boot, but I wouldn't hold your breath."

apitals of Corn

Festivals across Minnesota celebrate the summer harvest with Corn Feeds, in which bushels of ears are boiled or roasted to feed hungry fairgoers. Certain resourceful farmers selectively harvest their crops to form corn mazes, or "maize mazes," as some advertise. This allows the farmers to collect a few bucks from visitors wandering through the green labyrinths, imagining that they are British hedges. At the end of the mazes, boiled sweet corn awaits wanderers—if they haven't had enough of corn by then.

Anyone can have a Corn Feed, but how many towns are willing to show their love of the cob by erecting a huge yellow statue? The town of Olivia, for one. Amid acre upon acre of cornfields, Olivia installed the world's largest cornstalk. It sits atop the roof of a roadside rest just west of town as an inspiration to the millions of corn seeds sprouting around it.

Olivia has deemed itself simply the Corn Capital and stayed clear of the debate over which town can truly claim the right to be the World Corn Capital. The obvious heir to this throne would be Mitchell, South Dakota, with its Corn Palace decorated with seed art during harvest time every year. Even Lawrence Welk and John Philip Sousa fired up their orchestras in Mitchell to honor the Corn Palace's "ear-chitecture."

The claim of world's largest corncob has not yet been investigated by Guinness but presents a quandary. Rochester has a water tower shaped and painted like an ear of corn—can this cob be entered in the competition? If a farmer paints his grain silo like an ear of corn, would that count? Luckily, no one has taken the debate too seriously.

They're all too busy harvesting and getting ready for the annual Corn Feed.

BIG BIRDS

Virginia's floating loon

Larger and Larger Loons

When Canada released its dollar coin with a loon embossed on one side, Minnesotans were surprised to see another country claim its state bird. Minnesota couldn't retaliate with a loon coin of its own until the quarters for each state were released, a decade later.

Even so, Minnesota takes a backseat to no country — or state — in its number of loon sculptures and events. Nisswa hosts the annual North American Loon-Calling Competition and holds the title of Loon Capital of the World. International Falls and Bemidji have loon statues at their fairgrounds. Vergas has a huge cement statue of the creature overlooking Loon Lake, which appears identical to the sixteen-foot fiberglass loon in Mercer, Wisconsin. Nevertheless, the Mercer folk claim that theirs is the largest and named it *Claire de Loon* in honor of Debussy's lunar composition.

Virginia wanted to build its own loon creation but also wanted to be sure it wouldn't be overshadowed by the other giant loons. A year after Mercer's bird was erected, Bill Martin created a twenty-foot-long, ten-foot-high loon that spends the summer floating on downtown Silver Lake. Tourists zooming down the highway on the way to the Boundary Waters do a double take when looking into Virginia and witnessing the world's largest floating loon towering over tiny canoes.

Loon in Vergas

Chicken Dance in Delano

Tourists speeding along Highway 12 on their way to see the world's largest ball of twine in Darwin are easily distracted by the dancing chicken outside the Tom Thumb Superette in Delano. Erected in 1990, the blue-eyed bird was the dream child of Chicken John, who wanted the world to know that he made the best slow-cooked fried chicken in the state. Giant black chicken tracks inside the store lead to the freezer case, where convoys of truckers from across the country stop to buy some of Chicken John's famous food.

Really Well-done Turkey

Nervous turkeys are hardly news, but Big Tom of Frazee has every reason to be on edge. Just before the Frazee Turkey Festival in July 1998, workers were adjusting the base of the twenty-two-foot-high fiberglass bird with an acetylene torch. A wayward spark flicked up from the flames, landed on poor Tom's fiberglass feathers, and set the bird afire. The workers quickly stepped back and watched as the bird was roasted in a matter of minutes. Motorists pulled over on the highway and took some snapshots of the spectacular pyrotechnics show, but despondent Frazee was left turkeyless for its annual fair.

Creative minds set to work and fashioned an enormous papier-mâché turkey egg for that year's event. "Good thing we already had another turkey on order!" a woman at the Chamber of Commerce pointed out. To help pay for the new bird, T-shirts with a photo of the flaming turkey were sold with the caption WORLD'S LARGEST TURKEY (ROAST).

The new Big Tom, which is slightly larger than the cremated bird, stands at the top of the hill, anxiously watching for men with welding torches.

World's Largest Pelican

Pelican Rapids seems to be into strange pastimes. Just down the hill from where the town holds its annual Ugly Truck Contest stands a fifteen-and-a-half-foot-tall pelican ready to scoop up all the trout jumping at the base of the Mill Pond waterfall. "The pelican is part of all of us no matter how long we've lived here," trumpeted Truman Strand of the Pelican Committee in 1982 to the *Pelican Rapids Press.*

Pelican Rapids's pelican stands as one of the earliest roadside sculptures of an enormous animal. In 1957, Anton and Ted Resset wanted to do something for their town and decided on— what else—a giant pelican. The two employed their metalworking skills to weld the huge bird, which they based on a cardboard cutout. That same year, the white and orange pelican was erected under the Rapids, and since then, it has been chaperone to many bizarre events in the park, including parallel rain gutters filled with water for minnow races and the annual Turkey Festival, with row upon row of roasting birds. Surely, the pelican would not approve.

Remer's Eagle

Although inspired by other towns' enormous statues, Remer couldn't symbolize its name in a sculpture. Instead, Remer erected that most patriotic of symbols, the bald eagle, to grace its Main Street under the stars and stripes.

Prairie Chicken Goes A-Courtin'

Mating season on the prairie finds macho male prairie chickens puffing up their orange wind sacks, flapping their wings, and strutting around making booming sounds that echo across the fields. Female prairie chickens can't resist this mating dance and flock to the largest, loudest roosters for some lovin'.

To honor this bizarre ritual, the town of Rothsay erected a gigantic cement prairie chicken decked out in full mating display along Interstate 94. Art Fosse, a local sculptor, was commissioned to bend steel pipes and mix up thousands of pounds of cement to create the chicken statue. A birder himself, Fosse knew exactly how he wanted the statue to look; he had quietly sneaked out into the fields to witness the mating dance firsthand.

Rothsay declared itself the Prairie Chicken Capital of Minnesota on June 10, 1975, and a year later unveiled the statue with a front-page photo in the *Minneapolis Tribune*.

World's Largest Mallard

"We call them all monstrosities!" jokes the wife of sculptor Bob Burns about the oversize statues scattered around west central Minnesota. Burns is used to the teasing. After all, he's responsible for Fergus Falls's enormous otter as well as the giant mallard in Wheaton.

Burns was commissioned by the Wheaton Lions Club to build the really big bird in 1959. He shirks at taking all the credit for its creation, however, saying, "Two brothers started it in 1959 and finished it in 1961. A couple of other guys did the wire mesh, then someone stuccoed it, and then a group of people painted it three times over the years."

Nevertheless, Burns was the brains behind the duck. After kids climbed all over his otter, he decided to make the mallard less of a jungle gym: "The mallard's wings weren't originally so vertical, but we made it that way so kids wouldn't climb up on it and hurt themselves." Burns's wife interrupts to list some of the other colossal statues in the area: "We have a lot of big things around here, like the pelican in Pelican Rapids and the loon in Vergas. . . . For us, these big statues are normal."

Big Cockerel

Most motorists driving along Highway 61 into Two Harbors are so intent on getting through town to dig their teeth into some blueberry pie at Betty's Pies that they don't even notice the big rooster outside a little antiques store. Well, perhaps the big bird was missing that particular day.

"12 FOOT COCK STOLEN!" blared the newspapers when the icon flew the coop for the second time, or more accurately, was taken home as a trophy. The graduating class from the local high school was blamed for the prank. Eventually, the rooster was recovered.

Weldon Johnson, who erected the bird in 1965, wasn't prepared for its third theft. The police scanners screeched that "a motorist called and reported a brown pickup headed toward Duluth with a giant chicken in the back." Newswires buzzed with the story, and it even ran in the *New York Post*.

Perhaps realizing that hiding a twelve-foot chicken from the law is no easy task, the thief dumped the hot bird into Amity Creek. The chicken had been wrenched from its footings, which tore the fiberglass and resulted in a concussion that broke its red comb. "Workers from the Northwest Airlines A230 maintenance base in Duluth came to the rescue, meticulously restoring the rooster in their fiberglass studio, at no cost to Johnson," according to Joe Pastoor in *The Rake*. Pastoor added that the airline didn't publicize the repair because "flightless poultry, however grand, doesn't generate the marketing image a struggling airline typically wants."

Don't Steal the Teeth!

Fishing capitals in the north woods honor the dangerous creatures who lie beneath the waves by erecting huge statues. Northern pike and muskies look the most menacing, and each town wants to boast the biggest sculpture. Deer River, Minnesota, has a sleek northern pike that parents plop their kids on top of, much like the rideable walleye pike in Kabetogama. In Erskine, Minnesota, a menacing speckled fish next to the public beach warns swimmers that their toes or more could be seen as bait at any time.

Hope, Minnesota, has a twelve-foot-tall chain-saw-sculpted northern pike with a giant Daredevle lure dangling from its mouth. Dale Brooks carved the huge ash stump in 1997 for owners Jim and Millie Stockwell, who, atop their rooftop, placed a silhouette of a fisherman holding a line to the enormous fish in hopes of landing him for supper.

Nevis announced that it has the world's largest tiger muskie, and Governor Luther Youngdahl came to town to inaugurate the cement statue in September 1950. Obviously, picnickers can't resist staging photos of being swallowed by the mammoth muskie.

In 1958, Bena, Minnesota, beat Nevis with a sixty-five-foot fish building that doubled as a drive-in restaurant. The Big Fish Drive Inn began as a shell of bent one-by-four boards covered in tar paper and a coat of paint. The eyes of the fish are round, red Coca-Cola signs. The teeth are made from hand-sharpened pine, painted white, and bear a sign begging visitors not to steal them.

The Fish Are Biting!

Ernest Hemingway's story *The Old Man and the Sea* must have been about a lone Minnesota fisherman. The sparse prose, devoid of adjectives, tries to convey a lack of hyperbole in the fantastic story. Building these extraordinary tales requires deadpan storytelling skills, which sailors and fishermen have used for centuries.

Landlubbers discounted stories of gigantic underwater serpents as hogwash. But who could dismiss an actual photo of the beasts?

Fishermen riding atop colossal

THE FISH ARE HUNGRY HERE!

trout and pike adorned hand-colored postcards prior to the 1920s in Minnesota.

Trick photography— or rather, sleight of hand in the darkroom—made diminutive fishermen into bait for gigantic northern pike. Was this a ploy to keep strangers out of their happy fishing grounds or just another fish story?

HERE'S THE FISH I PROMISED YOU.

GREETINGS FROM AITKIN, MINN.

Somehow, on forgotten paths across the state, the history of Minnesota is laid bare. Travelers who have the courage to leave the superhighways will find the strange, perhaps obscure, but always memorable footprints of those who have gone before. This is where we see the remains of a town swallowed up by an open pit mine, its ghostly lights still shining. Some of these old trails have disappeared and are preserved only through stories. French traders crisscrossed lakes on the Voyageurs Highway in search of pelts. The "roads" they traveled have sunk into frigid waters, but their language survives in the towns and forts along their routes.

Off the Beaten Path

Many of the most mysterious paths lie far beneath our feet, with abandoned staircases leading to underground palaces waiting to be rediscovered. Bat caves and party caves housed brothels or bootleggers' hideouts. These were, and in some cases still are, the routes taken by Minnesota's trailblazers—those who chose to go off the well-trodden path and take the road less traveled to seek their fate.

Houses on Water

Not many places are as remote and deservedly for-saken as a frozen lake in winter, unless, of course, the ice fishermen have found it. Ice fishing has always struck me as the definition of cold tedium. However, with tales of meth labs on the lakes and ice-house hookers, some friends lured me north to Mille Lacs to write about a weekend of this crazy sport. Not that I needed a weekend of illicit debauchery, but I wanted to see if freezing my body parts off in the dead of winter might really be fun after all.

Our destination was a place where the gruff receptionist doubled as the bartender at the year-round resort. At noon, this smoke-filled bar was crammed with snowmobilers, and the tables were already overflowing with beer glasses. The only person who cussed more than these revelers was the bartender himself. We ordered some beer and made small talk, asking how the fishing was. "No one is catching a #@*! thing!" he said. I learned that one of the sick rules of ice fishing is that the walleye bite at the beginning of the season, so die-hard fishermen can't wait to get their houses out and risk everything on the watery ice for a nibble.

If no one was hauling in the lunkers, why were nearly all the ice houses rented out? "Ever heard of fishing widows?" the bartender asked me. Aha! Maybe now I'd see the wild side of ice fishing.

He set a group up with another pitcher of Michelob and turned to us. "Just drive out a mile or so on the lake and turn left," he said. "You're number twenty-six."

Apparently, ice fishing is more about danger than sport. If we didn't fall through the ice, maybe we'd drive into one of those mysterious patches of open water. "Keep your window rolled down a little so you can open the door if we go through," my friend warned me. My friends also told me that a well-built ice house with hefty insulation is hazardous because you can die of asphyxiation from carbon monoxide poisoning. But then, of course, if there are too many leaks, you could freeze to death. Survival lies somewhere between the two.

When we arrived at shack number twenty-six, there was the distinct smell of propane gas in the air. It turned out that the pilot light in the rusty can that doubled as a heater was broken. When we tried to light it, a puff of flame licked out and singed my eyebrows, then the pilot immediately went out again. Back to reception/the bar.

This time, the bartender put us in a "deluxe" shack. Obviously, we weren't tough enough to rough it like real ice fishermen. The only difference between the deluxe and regular shacks was eight holes in the ice and a working heater. We dutifully dropped our minnows in the hole and were instantly bored. A weird existential crisis came over me as we sat in this icebox on a frozen lake with the wind howling and an air temperature of minus fifteen degrees. If we ran out of food, who would I eat first? All the beef jerky we brought was soon digested, no fish would bite our skanky bait, and I started to eye my fellow fishermen nervously.

I remembered Jack London's "To Build a Fire," the story of a man freezing to death in the Yukon. Outside our ice shack, snowmobilers zoomed around like drunken demons.

Luckily, my friends pulled out the bourbon and their Uno cards; the mood instantly changed. Apart from this perfectly mindless game of chance, we engaged in stupid science tricks like freezing soap bubbles, and we bet on whether full beer bottles float (they don't) and how long we could stand outside in our underwear (thirty seconds). The fun had begun.

Knock! Knock! Knock! A drunk guy banged on our door asking if this was where the party was. Luckily, he pushed on to the next shack. No sign of any hookers.

The next morning, the only thing worse than stepping outside to pee was our small shack full of smelly guys. The temperature on the floor was below freezing, and next to the ceiling easily exceeded ninety degrees. The air temp outside hit minus fifteen degrees again, and no one dared measure the windchill when powerful gusts swooshed across the lake. It was frigid, and I was no longer interested in writing on the weekend habits of ice fishermen. We packed up our sleeping bags and the remaining whiskey, and the Jeep barely roared to life. Hmm, broken-down car—yet another way to die out on this lake.

I chalked up the stories of hard-core drugs and hookers to typical fishing tall tales. However, a little research revealed that there was indeed a bust of a methamphetamine laboratory in an ice house in Wright County in 1999. The crackdown couldn't have lasted long, though, since on August 30, 2002, the Minnesota State Supreme Court upheld a decision that cops need permission to enter an ice house.

To get the skinny on crimes on the ice, I called the sheriffs of both Aitkin and Mille Lacs counties, who split jurisdiction on Mille Lacs, but they opted out of speaking on the record, which, of course, furthers speculation by imaginative ice fishermen with too much time on their hands.

In the Lake of the Woods

Minnesota boasts the northernmost point of the continental United States. This geographical oddity sticks up above the forty-ninth parallel and is accessible only by driving through Canada first or by venturing across the enormous and confusing Lake of the Woods.

The tiny community on the Northwest Angle is as remote as any spot in the lower forty-eight. That said, it boasts an extremely old European settlement. In 1737, Frenchman Pierre La Verendrye constructed Fort St. Charles on Magnusson Island as the farthest settlement of Europeans in the northern part of the continent. The fort was used as a base for exploration of the nonexistent Northwest Passage and was financed by its use as a trading post. Today, a reconstruction of the walls of Fort St. Charles stands at the spot with a log chapel.

The Town That Moved

The huge Hull-Rust Mahoning Mine next to Hibbing grew so fast that the entire town had to be moved. In 1918, buildings were uprooted from their basements and dragged two miles away to the town of Alice. Hibbing's houses were the "original mobile homes," with no basements, so they could be moved easily in a day.

Miners became somewhat disgruntled when they would come up from a long day's work and not be able to find their homes. For two years, the town of Hibbing was slowly moved to give better access to the valuable iron ore underground. Some of the houses weren't moved far enough and had to be moved a few more times. No wonder the miners couldn't find their way home! (Sometimes their families could barely recognize the miners, either, as they were covered from head to foot in fine red dust from the pit.)

Today, a few streets of the old town of Hibbing can still be seen next to the edge of the giant open pit mine. Street signs mark the old downtown, and lampposts still light it up. The mine is easy to spot. It is dubbed the Grand Canyon of the North because more earth was taken from this hole than from the entire Panama Canal—1.4 billion tons of earth to be exact, making the Hull-Rust Mahoning Mine easily visible from outer space.

Lost Oxcart Trails

Before James J. Hill laid railroad tracks throughout Minnesota, the best way of reaching the northwest part of the state was aboard a giant oxcart. Steamboats made the journey as far as Saint Paul, but no one dared guide one of the boats up the shallow Red River of the North into Canada. The flat terrain, however, made perfect tracks for wooden carts.

The trail these carts took from Saint Paul to Pembina has all but vanished now. Parts of the historical trail have been turned into roads or highways (I-94), and in more remote sections the giant wheels made ruts so deep that they're still visible. The journey took from thirty to forty days, and the carts, with their wooden axles, could be heard coming for miles. Settlers complained of the awful squeaking sound of the

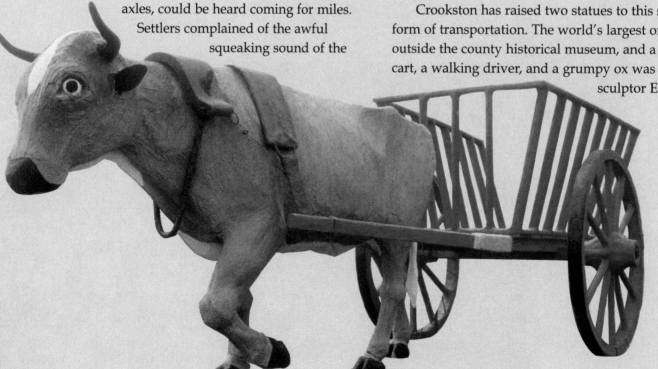

RED RIVER TRAIN.
(In St. Paul.)

From Martin's Gallery of Minnesota Views, St. Paul.

ungreased wheels, which they claimed would make them go either deaf or insane by the end of the trip. A trip to the big city of Saint Paul, then, was the journey of a lifetime.

The Red River oxcarts started rolling in 1844 when the pioneers began plowing the fertile flatlands of northwestern Minnesota and eastern North Dakota. The trips peaked in about 1858 with around six hundred people making the journey that year. The carts may look clumsy, but the six-foot wheels enabled them to travel easily over the thick prairie and wetlands. During the winter, occasional dogsled teams would make the trek but could rarely pull as much as the sturdy oxen.

Crookston has raised two statues to this short-lived form of transportation. The world's largest oxcart stands outside the county historical museum, and a statue of a cart, a walking driver, and a grumpy ox was molded by sculptor E. A. Konickon.

Voyageurs Highway

French-Canadian voyageurs traveled west from Montreal in the 1700s to the pristine waters of Minnesota to trade for pelts with the Indians. Coming across the Great Lakes in enormous canoes, the traders would usually stop in Grand Portage before venturing inland to the border lakes. These were the first Europeans to come in any numbers to explore and trade in Minnesota. Because of them, French names mingle with Ojibwa and Dakota names throughout the state.

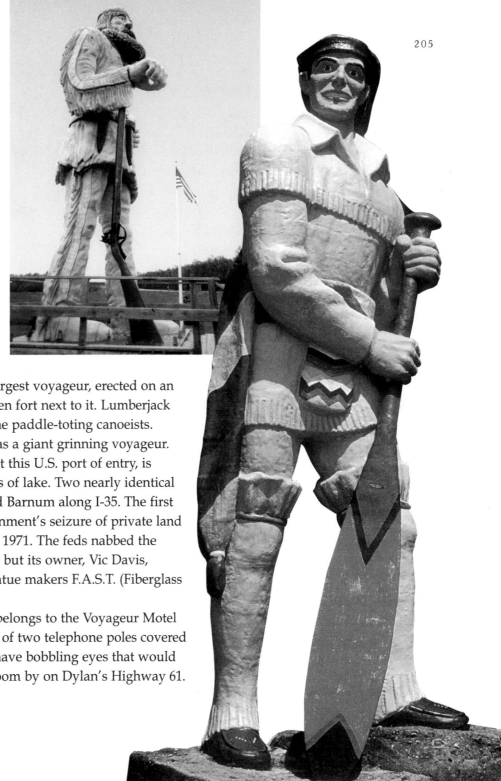

Towns along the waterways erected huge statues to honor the early explorers. Cloquet has what it describes as the world's largest voyageur, erected on an island of the St. Louis River with a little wooden fort next to it. Lumberjack Days are held annually in July, at the foot of the paddle-toting canoeists.

Crane Lake, along the Canadian border, has a giant grinning voyageur. The statue, at right, which guards the border at this U.S. port of entry, is accessible only by water over the vast stretches of lake. Two nearly identical statues stand in Ranier (above) and landlocked Barnum along I-35. The first statue was erected to protest the federal government's seizure of private land when Voyageurs National Park was created in 1971. The feds nabbed the twenty-five-foot-tall statue in a late-night raid, but its owner, Vic Davis, simply bought another one from Wisconsin statue makers F.A.S.T. (Fiberglass Animals, Shapes & Trademarks).

Perhaps the most creative canoeist statue belongs to the Voyageur Motel just west of downtown in Two Harbors. Made of two telephone poles covered in cement, the twenty-foot-tall Pierre used to have bobbling eyes that would jiggle back and forth as he watched the cars zoom by on Dylan's Highway 61.

The Hidden Trails of Gangsters

Minnesota was one of the leaders in the push for Prohibition. It was congressman Andrew Volstead from Granite Falls who sponsored the Volstead Act in October 1919, giving us the Eighteenth Amendment to the

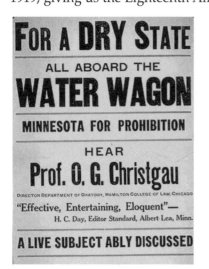

Constitution, which outlawed liquor. (On the other hand, Volstead's vice was chewing tobacco; he went through a pound of plug a day.)

But vice will find its way. Once Prohibition passed, thousands of speakeasies popped up around the state. Winona alone had two hundred banned saloons; when liquor was legal, the town had only forty! Stillwater, another river town, supposedly had Al Capone as a regular visitor, using secret downtown caves to hide his hooch.

Saint Paul became known as Saint Mudd when the cops allegedly struck a deal with gangsters that the outlaws could stay in town as long as no illegal activity took place within city limits. Mobsters would travel up from Chicago for a lengthy stay in Saint Paul while things cooled off. Bootleggers used the town as a stopping point when running moonshine down from Canada. More than a million gallons of booze were smuggled from Canada into the U.S. here each year.

Temperance societies continued the war of words during Prohibition, even though they recognized the presence of illegal speakeasies. An ironic article from *The Boyd Bulletin* in 1932, reprinted in *Coffee Made Her Insane*, had a solution for married drunks:

Own Your Own Saloon

For the married man who thinks he can not get along without a drink, the following suggestion is made as a means of freedom from the bondage of bootleggers: Start a saloon in your own home. Be the only customer. You will have no license to pay. Give your wife ten dollars to buy a gallon of whiskey. Remember there are sixty-nine drinks in a gallon. Buy your drinks from no one but your wife. By the time your first gallon is gone she will have $23.50 to put in the bank and $10 to start business again. (She can throw in two drinks on the house.)

Should you live ten years and continue to buy booze from her and then die with snakes in your boots, she will have money enough to bury you decently, educate your children, buy a house and lot, marry a decent man and quit thinking about you entirely.

The outlawing of alcohol, however, only seemed to encourage dangerous armed criminals to set up distilleries and to transport booze any way possible. Crow Wing County was a hot spot for mobsters. Birchdale Villas on Lake Bertha (part of the Whitefish chain of lakes) was a busy drop-off place for liquor. The booze would be brought down to the Villas either hidden under bags of letters in the mail boat or at night driven down what is called the Old Whiskey Road (County Road 145) through present-day Jenkins.

Another famous drop-off point was the Shawano House just west of downtown Pequot Lakes. The gorgeous stone and whole-log lodge stands on a point on

Lake Sibley at the intersection of West Lake Street and Pequot Boulevard and was used by Chicago bootleggers in the 1920s and '30s.

Just looking at the Pequot Lakes police blotter during Prohibition reveals that this supposedly quiet vacation spot was abuzz with illegal activity. In 1931, burglaries and check forgeries were rampant. The cops reported that six hundred pounds of beef were stolen from the town butcher. In 1933, Mrs. Spangler's Red Poppy Inn was broken into, and her slot machines were stolen. (This in spite the fact that the police and politicians loved to stage photos of themselves smashing piles of slot machines to show the voters how effective they were in ridding towns of gambling.)

In 1932, Franklin Delano Roosevelt was elected president, and he promised to halt Prohibition. By the end of the following year, the Twenty-First Amendment was passed, repealing the antibooze act. Still, the remnants of this lawless period were discovered in 1934 in Crow Wing County when a Chevrolet coupe with bullet marks was found buried northwest of Loon Lake.

CAVING

Underground Wonders

"*I started* when I was fourteen at two a.m. We made boots and waders with garbage bags and duct tape," recalls John (cavers prefer to remain somewhat anonymous because their urban exploration could be considered trespassing) of his first time caving. He remembers being underground on the edge of the storm tunnel for the Minnehaha Creek outfall with a fifty- to seventy-foot vertical drop in front of the "art deco, WPA-style exit." As exhilarating and treacherous as the experience seemed at the time, he later realized how truly dangerous it was. "The guy I did this with then became a serial killer."

With his friend Greg, John has been through tunnels and caves nearly everywhere under the Twin Cities. There are Nina Clifford's Cave and Bordello, the party cave at Shepherd and Otto with the Stairway to Heaven, and a chimney you can climb into that goes up a tunnel with carved candle sconces. There's the Bat Cave under the Washington Avenue Bridge and the three spiral staircases under the Marshall Avenue Bridge that go down a hundred feet amid waterfalls. These are just some of the underground marvels that very few see or even know exist under our feet.

A history buff, John raves about traveling under the Ford Plant in Highland Park in tunnels that are probably a hundred and thirty years old. "These are some of the oldest structures still standing in the Twin Cities."

In the past, with the vicious rivalry between the Twin Cities, Saint Paulites spread a rumor that the enormous F&M Bank tunnel under Minneapolis would eventually give out and swallow all of downtown. Now, the entrance to the tunnel is under a strip club. John remarks that the old F&M tunnel "has extraordinary walking and stooping passages. Large tracts of it are old sewage tunnels filled to the top with swizzle sticks and condoms."

The Mystic Cavern along the Mississippi in Saint Paul, which used to be a speakeasy nightclub in the 1920s, is the "biggest and most accessible cave." But after a couple of inexperienced kids died of asphyxiation from a campfire in Saint Paul caves, the city renewed its efforts to prevent future accidents by blocking off the entrances with iron gates and cement.

There are dangers to underground urban exploration: getting lost, getting trapped, getting caught, breathing asbestos or other hazardous chemicals, drowning, falling, etc. Unless you have someone outside ready to get help, chances are, no one will find you if you get stuck. "Cell phones don't work, or walkie-talkies. Besides, storm tunnels are so loud, even shouting, you can't hear sometimes," John says. As a reminder of how desolate the passages beneath the city are, he lists what he's found underground: "Frogs, crickets, bullheads, animal bones, completely dried-up raccoons, lots of dry skeletons."

Still, he's upbeat about the experience: "A huge part of it is the adventure of finding something completely new."

Spelunking with the Action Squad

More than anyone else in the state, Max Action and his Action Squad have shined a light on what lies beneath our feet. "The term 'urban exploration' was popularized by a zine from Toronto called *Infiltration*," Max tells us. The point is to discover or rediscover lost tunnels, caves, and abandoned buildings.

"We explore mostly in the Cities but have been exploring in Chicago, Duluth, Eveleth," Max says. "I put up on the Web all the maps of the steam plant under the U [university] and pointers about how to do what we do. I didn't think anyone would actually look." In fact, this gave the Action Squad wide exposure and inspired director Melody Gilbert to shoot a documentary about these urban explorers.

Who makes up the mysterious Action Squad? "There's no official membership, it's just whoever is up for it," Max explains. "It's not that secretive, really. The black bars across the eyes [on the Web site photos] don't really do anything because you can still figure out who it is."

Max downplays suggestions that his group is clandestine in any way. In fact, the police almost seem to appreciate that the Action Squad is somewhat visible and has a strict code of conduct not to tamper with or destroy any location. After all, the Squad wants to preserve these finds for future generations. "The history of it makes it more interesting to explore," Max says. He tries to get his hands on any books of maps of the areas the Action Squad will explore.

Thinking about their explorations conjures visions of Jean Valjean of *Les Misérables* trudging through the sewers of Paris, fending off packs of rats. Max is surprised. "Rats? They run away from you. Or if you're in the sewers, they run in the very bottom drain or past you on the ledge. I don't know what they eat. There's just not much down there." Max then shows me a photo of one of the Action Squad with a rabbit skeleton.

Max isn't easily spooked by rumors that some caves or abandoned buildings are haunted. "I don't believe any of that garbage. Although we did find the Bridge to Dimension Zed in Saint Paul. . . . They also say there's a haunted door at the abandoned Martha Ripley Hospital, which was for unwed mothers and later was a nursing home. The door opens up when you walk up to it. The same thing happened to me. I think your weight just triggers the door from the latch."

Before Max leaves, he extends an invitation for a tempting new adventure that night: "I have some friends that are going under downtown tonight who think they have some caves no one has ever seen before!"

The Falls Are Going Out!

The Dakota call the falls at St. Anthony *Owahmenah* ("Falling Water") or *Minirara* ("Curling Water"), and the Ojibwa call them *Kakabikah* ("Severed Rock"). Underneath the falling water lives the god of water and evil, Oanktehi.

When Father Hennepin visited the falls in the 1600s, he recalled that he saw an Indian hang a special beaver robe decorated with porcupine quills for Oanktehi. Hennepin wrote:

I could hear him say as he was addressing himself to the Cascade, with Tears in his Eyes; Thou art a Spirit grant that Those of my Nation may pass here without any Disaster; That we may meet with a great many bulls; and that we may be so happy as to vanquish our Enemy, and take a great many Slaves, whom, when we have made them suffer according to their Merits, we will bring hither, and slay in thy Presence.

How Hennepin knew the Dakota language so well or was able to overhear this personal prayer was rarely questioned. Nor was the idea that the Dakota performed human sacrifice or took slaves, which they rarely, if ever, did. Regardless, Hennepin knew that he needed to sanctify this site, so he named the falls for St. Anthony of Padua.

Even so, dark legends about the falls persisted. The spirit of a Native American woman, Ampato Sapa (Dark Day), is said to haunt the falls. She was heartbroken when her husband, a successful Dakota warrior, decided to take a second wife. In the spring, the tribe was passing by the falls when the water was rushing over it. Ampato Sapa jumped in a canoe with her small son and paddled toward them. Her husband watched helplessly from the shore as Ampato Sapa and their son went over the falls and were crushed by the force of the water. Her ghost still haunts the area, and Spirit Island was named in her honor.

In spite of the macabre stories surrounding St. Anthony Falls, its rushing water gave Minneapolis the power to erect sawmills and gristmills. Lumberjacks used the Mississippi to transport lumber to the mills. These enormous old-growth logs often bashed into the falls with such force that people on shore could feel the earth move. In 1867, errant logs destroyed a wooden apron on part of the falls, resulting in a huge flood along the banks.

Around that time, William Eastman and J. L. Merriam drew up a dubious plan to tunnel right under the falls. By September 1869, workers had excavated two thousand feet of tunnel into the porous limestone under the water. The *Minneapolis Tribune* hailed the construction as "a work of great magnitude and importance, the full extent of which will hardly be realized until it is completed."

Eastman and Merriam began to worry, however, when they noticed water dripping from the ceiling of the huge tunnel from Nicollet Island to downtown Minneapolis. On October 5, 1869, a cry rang out across St. Anthony and the new city of Minneapolis. "The falls are going out! The falls are going out!" Residents rushed to the river. Everyone knew that the Cities' livelihood depended on the falls' waterpower.

According to *The Falls of St. Anthony,* "Proprietors of stores hastened to the falls, taking their clerks with them; bakers deserted their ovens, lumbermen were ordered from the mills, barbers left their customers unshorn. . . . Thru the streets hurrying hundreds were seen on their way to the falls."

The Cities' residents united to haul in hundreds of cartloads of rock to try to shore up what was left of the falls. The erosion subsided, and the workers congratulated themselves on "the triumph of human skill and brain over the dumb force of nature," according to the newspapers of the time. By the next day, though, the falls had collapsed again in a mad torrent.

Eventually, a cement skirt was put in place of the falls; very little of the natural formation remains. Most of the tunnel under the falls was obliterated by the cave-in, but supposedly, part of it still exists under Nicollet Island. Some people call it Satan's Cave. The entrance is accessible by secret hatch doors in houses on the island, which were said to be used by bootleggers during Prohibition.

Gopher State Ghosts

Are ghosts real? Or are they just the product of overactive imaginations fired up by fleeting shadows on dark nights? Certainly, many of the down-to-earth residents of our state have no patience with tales of phantom spirits. But there are many others who believe that souls can, and do, linger behind on earth after their bodily death. These restless spirits may be too tortured by the circumstances of their life—or death—to pass on peacefully to the next realm. Or they may have died before their time and don't even realize that they're actually dead! So they remain in their home, or some other place that's familiar to them, and though they may be harmless, they still scare the daylights out of us.

Following are some of the stories that haunt our state, many of which are appearing in print for the first time. Are they true? We dare not venture a guess. Just light a candle, listen to the thunder shake the windows, and don't bother to lock the doors—ghosts don't need doors to enter your room or your imagination.

The Most Haunted House in Saint Paul

With their turrets and shadows, the old Victorian mansions on Crocus and Summit hills in Saint Paul can't help but suggest tales of murder, treachery, and troubled ghosts. "Oh, they say all these houses down here on Cathedral Hill are haunted and that there has been a murder in every one of them. I don't know how anyone even survived back then if all the stories are true," says writer and Saint Paulite Patricia Hampl.

However, "The house at 476 Summit Avenue may be the most notoriously haunted house in St. Paul," the *Pioneer Press* wrote in 1982. This is the Griggs Mansion, near the top of Ramsey Hill.

The twenty-four-room Romanesque limestone house was built by grocery tycoon Chauncey W. Griggs in 1883. The ceilings on the first floor and in the tower are twelve feet high, and in the third-floor ballroom they're forty feet high. All of the marble fireplaces have cast-iron hearths; the marble mantel in the library even portrays a bloody cockfight. After years of construction, Griggs lived in the house only four years before mysteriously moving out.

Since then, a whole cast of ghosts has been seen wandering about. The parlor is said to be haunted by a ghost named Amy who plays the piano. A thin man in a somber black suit enters and exits the rooms day and night and is unperturbed by anyone who happens to be nearby. Even a disembodied head was reported floating around an apartment in the rear of the house.

The most famous is probably the ghost of a maid who hanged herself on the third-floor landing in 1915. Rumors speculate that she was pregnant by her master, a Union officer in the Civil War, who still haunts the house in his dapper blue uniform, doomed to spend eternity paying for the seduction of his innocent servant.

An unexplained fire struck the house in 1910, killing the gardener, Charles Wade, and destroying the massive library. The gardener's ghost is perhaps the most common visitor to the library, as he returns to browse through tomes on gardening—all of which were destroyed by the fire. Perhaps that's why he continues to come back.

The Griggs Mansion was donated to the Saint Paul Gallery and School of Art, maybe because renting or selling the house had proved sticky. Art students staying in the place, painting late into the night, complained of ghosts and of objects inexplicably moving around the room.

Carl Weschke, the owner of the occult publishing company Llewellyn, bought the house in 1964 and launched an extensive renovation, which some say only increased the number of hauntings. A pamphlet about the house declares that the second floor was covered in metallic wallpaper that later owners dubbed "pornographic" and "psychic." Other rooms were painted red with "gloomy illumination." A large, L-shape room was created for "psychic sessions and séances. . . . It housed some rather unusual social activities."

The house has since been mostly divided up into apartments. When an artist friend of ours moved into one of the top-floor spaces, *Weird Minnesota* asked her if a group of friends could sleep over for a mini séance to try to rouse some of these ghosts. We felt—or imagined we felt—a cold spot on the third-floor landing, so we set up there to meet the dead. The candles were lit, the incense streamed its scented smoke into the air, and the Ouija board was opened up. Nothing. After a bit of wine, however, the cursor began to zigzag across the Ouija board, but it produced only gibberish. Then the knocking in the attic began. No one was up there. Could it just have been the wind, or maybe some bats? Nobody dared venture upstairs to find out, so we lay down in our sleeping bags. No one slept a wink.

Murder, Bigamy, and Arson

Don't ask the guards at the Congdon Mansion in Duluth about the murders. They're not supposed to tell. The gift shop doesn't have any books about the scandalous homicides, either. The dark history of this eerie place is found only splashed across banner headlines in old newspapers.

The fabulously wealthy Elisabeth Congdon was found dead in her bed in the mansion, smothered with her pillow, on June 27, 1977. And on the steps outside her room, another gruesome scene: Her nurse, Velma Pietila, had been brutally clubbed to death.

Congdon had just returned from her summer estate, in northern Wisconsin, to the mansion, which the family called Glensheen, a thirty-nine-room chateau now on the National Register of Historic Places. Elisabeth's father, the iron baron Chester Congdon, built the house just north of downtown Duluth in 1905. When he died, Elisabeth inherited his millions, making her one of the richest women in Minnesota. Although she never married, she adopted two daughters. One was an angel; the other wasn't.

Daughter Marjorie grew up in the luxury of Glensheen and continued her upper-crust habits after she left Duluth. She led her life expecting that her mother would one day will half the Congdon millions to her. In the meantime, she didn't mind spending money she didn't yet have. By the early 1970s, Marjorie and her husband, Roger Caldwell, were deep in debt and overdue on bills. The couple repeatedly asked Elisabeth and her trustees for a loan—but always in vain.

In 1977, Elisabeth was eighty-three years old, and although she was partially paralyzed, she was healthy for the most part. When she was found dead, the mounting evidence pointed to her son-in-law Roger Caldwell.

Elisabeth Congdon

Caldwell, the police said, had sneaked into the house late one night by clumsily breaking a window. (Because of the awkward burglary job, they speculated that he was likely drunk.)

As he sneaked upstairs, a flashlight beam held by the nurse caught him in the eyes. The nurse grabbed at the burglar when he approached, but he clubbed her on the head with a brass candelabrum. The poor woman bled to death on the stairs, still clutching strands of the burglar's hair in her fist.

The man threw open the doors of Elisabeth's room and found her in bed. The frail old woman was no match for the healthy man. The murder weapon was a pink satin pillow; within minutes, Elisabeth was dead. As she lay still warm in her bed, Caldwell pried her shiny rings off her fingers one by one. He then filled a bag with her jewelry and ran out the billiard-room doors.

Caldwell was quickly arrested and sentenced to prison for the murders, but later, when new evidence turned up that allowed him to strike a deal with prosecutors, he was released. Although he confessed to the crimes in court as part of his plea bargain, outside of court he always maintained that he had never killed anyone.

Marjorie was charged with conspiring with her husband to kill her mother to speed up her inheritance. She was acquitted of all charges, however, and the jury even invited her to a party after the trial, out of sympathy. She went on to a new life, fortified by a big chunk of her dead mother's money. Though she wasn't divorced from Caldwell, she married Wallace Hagen in North Dakota. Unfortunately, the two did not live happily ever after.

Marjorie seemed to have a little problem involving fires. She was eventually charged with no fewer than three counts of arson, and in 1992 she was convicted on one of the counts. The night before she was to begin serving her sentence, however, she and her new husband stopped off at home to gather up a few things before she went off to jail. When the police came to pick her up the next day, they found Hagen dead of a drug overdose. Once again, murder charges didn't stick, but Marjorie did serve a lengthy sentence for arson.

The Congdons were perhaps the closest thing Minnesota ever had to royalty, and Glensheen remains open to visitors, now run as a museum by the University

Roger Caldwell

of Minnesota. While you're there, keep a lookout for the ghosts of Elisabeth and her nurse, who are said to haunt the place to this day. Despite the museum curator's efforts to keep rumors of spirits under wraps, tourists have reported seeing apparitions around the mansion and hearing mysterious noises. Perhaps Elisabeth is keeping an eye on her estate to protect it from further plundering by ungrateful relatives.

Bunnell House

The guide in period costume at the Bunnell House in Homer seemed glad to have guests arrive and accompany her through this creepy old home. Rumors of ghosts have plagued the house for generations, and *Weird Minnesota* had to investigate.

Bunnell House was the first permanent dwelling in all of Winona County. Built by Willard Bunnell around 1859, the house, designed in steamboat Gothic style, hasn't changed much since it was constructed. The rough wood exterior has never been painted—which, considering the house's age, gives an unsettling vibe to the already rugged structure. But it's what goes on inside the house that has *Weird Minnesota*, and our tour guide, spooked.

"A lot of people died, and were born, in this house," the guide says nervously. Of the many kids the Bunnells had, the youngest died of a gunshot wound to the leg, and the eldest died in an accident on the Mississippi River, which runs below the house.

The eeriness begins upon entry. The large portrait in the foyer, called *The Discovery*, seems like your everyday innocuous winter scene of two kids trudging along in the snow—until you realize that they've just discovered a dead body, frozen stiff in a snowbank. And thus, the painting gives you your first impression of the house: It seems normal enough, but when you look closer, there's a darker story underneath.

Moving along to the living-dining area, the guide mentions Willard Bunnell's brother, Lafayette, who claimed the house after his brother died. Lafayette was a surgeon during the Civil War, after which he went to California during the gold rush. He ended up penniless and turned to Indian hunting to make money. He slaughtered a group of Native Americans near Yosemite Falls, a bloody act that freed up some of the surrounding land. Lafayette chose to name the future park Yosemite.

The guide admits that she's heard noises in the attic, but she'll never set foot up there; "Sometimes, I see a cat jumping around, but no cat lives here," she says. "In closing up, I go through the house twice to make sure all the lights are out, then two days later, they're all back on. I'm one of only a few people who have a key to this house, and I know no one else comes in here." She adds that she's seen shadows of people in the windows at night, when all the doors and windows are locked.

Some of Willard's and Lafayette's accoutrements are still scattered around the living room, leaving a sense of creepy timelessness. There's a stereoscope with an etching of Abraham Lincoln reading the Emancipation Proclamation, a giant brass spittoon, and a gorgeous old Regina music box. The guide says that the music box is very temperamental and plays only if the people in the room meet the spirit's high standards. She concedes that the evil Lafayette could be the spirit who is still in residence. Perhaps he, too, is haunted by the ghosts of all the Native Americans he so violently killed. She spins the handle and the Regina whirs to life: "Oh, the ghost likes you. The music box is working today."

The Creepy Capital Building

Cass Gilbert, who also designed the U.S. Supreme Court building in Washington, DC, got one of his first big boosts in Saint Paul when he was commissioned to build the new state capital building, in 1895. It was finished ten years later.

Fast forward one hundred years to government staffers claiming to see a hefty man in a bowler hat with a large mustache—who bears a striking resemblance to Gilbert himself—carefully inspecting the workmanship of the structure during late-night legislation.

Another ghostly visitor has been seen wandering the marble hallways of the capital building at night. The regiment from Minnesota was credited with winning the Battle of Gettysburg during the Civil War. A celebration to honor Col. William Covill and his troops was held at the capital building on the day of its groundbreaking in 1905, but the old colonel was too sick to attend. He was so grief-stricken over missing the ceremony that he died shortly afterward.

Covill's corpse was the first to lie in state under the capital rotunda, for all to pay homage to him and his bravery during the war. But even though he was honored in death, Covill's spirit still seems to return to the capital, endlessly seeking the celebration he missed in life.

Last Legal Hanging in the State

The last man to be legally hanged in Minnesota was John Moshik, in March 1898. Moshik murdered a man for the paltry sum of $14. The twenty-five-year-old begged the jury to forgive him because he "inherited insanity." The judge gave Moshik the death penalty. On the appointed day, Moshik was led to the chapel courtroom on the fifth floor of what is now the gothic Minneapolis City Hall. The meticulous Moshik directed the executioners in every

Stairway to Not-Heaven

When Winona burned to the ground in the 1860s, the building at 79 Second St. was the only one to survive. Liquor had been sold out of the building during most its existence, and at one point it had housed a brothel upstairs. The train station was located across the street, so business was brisk. That is, until one of the resident ladies was murdered on the outside stairway. Although those stairs no longer exist, the scent of the unfortunate woman still lingers on, decades after the event. Sometimes, visitors even hear the phantom running on the now-nonexistent steps where the prostitute had been brutally killed.

After a stint as a commune in the 1960s, 79 Second St. became Banger's Pub, but the strange occurrences persisted. Workers constantly complained of odd events. The unplugged jukebox would spring to life and play haunting songs, lightbulbs mysteriously dimmed, and the loud banging of furniture in empty rooms frightened customers. Some employees refused to descend into the basement after seeing objects move through the air in front of their face. Something or someone was heard climbing up and down the stairs—while no one was using them, and no one ever caught sight of anyone on them. Yet the creaks continue.

bit of preparation for his hanging. The noose needed to be tighter, he insisted. The guards hadn't properly tied his hands and feet, he complained. He died in just three minutes.

In the 1950s, stories began to circulate about Moshik's ghost haunting the chapel courtroom. The room was soon "remodeled" out of existence. Still, visitors to the fifth floor, from janitors to judges, report ghost hauntings in the form of cold spots, odd shadows flitting by, and sudden gusts of wind.

Forepaugh's Phantoms

"We'll blow out all the candles, and we'll come back, and they'll all be on," a terrified waitress tells us. These are no trick candles, just regular, long-stem wax ones at Forepaugh's, a high-class restaurant in Saint Paul.

Here, ghosts disturb both the table settings and the waitstaff. "One night, I was putting on my lipstick all alone," the waitress says. "Then I looked in the mirror, and behind me, a single clothes hanger was moving. I don't believe in ghosts, but there was just an overwhelming feeling. This really bothered me."

Forepaugh's, built in 1870, is an Italianate mansion located on the edge of Irvine Park that has since been turned into a fancy French restaurant. The ghostly atmosphere extends even to the area surrounding the building. The Victorian square next to Forepaugh's became the perfect setting for one of Italian film director Dario Argento's horror films because the mood there was so unsettling.

In 1886, before moving his family to Europe, Joseph Lybrandt Forepaugh staged a giant estate sale. The auctioneers wrote that the big move was "allegedly to cure Joseph Forepaugh of 'melancholy.' " They bragged that this was the "finest sale of house-hold goods ever made in the Northwest." Perhaps frontier life in Minnesota had been too rough for Joseph Forepaugh, who sold his giant house to the chief of staff of Civil War general Sherman (who is among those said to have haunted the building).

Forepaugh's melancholy wasn't cured by his grand tour of Europe, so he returned to Saint Paul in 1889. Three years later, the *Pioneer Press* reported that "he found peace" after he turned up dead next to a pond near "the Selby Avenue bridge over the Milwaukee railroad bridge. A bullet wound in the head and the revolver still clasped in the dead man's hand clearly indicated suicide."

But apparently Forepaugh did not find peace, because he came back to his old house—as did the ghost of his mistress/maid, Molly, who committed suicide when Forepaugh left for Europe.

The waitress here reports, "You can still smell her perfume. It's lilac, or one of those Victorian scents."

Gangster Ghost

Bellhop and carnival worker John "Jack" Peifer became a famous gangster in Prohibition-era Saint Paul. Peifer served up moonshine to both mobsters and the well-to-do at the Hollyhock speakeasy along River Road. To earn more cash, he hooked up with the Barker-Karpis gang in 1933; the plan was to kidnap brewery mogul William Hamm. But Peifer was caught and eventually sent before the judge at the federal courthouse, which is now Landmark Center.

Other gangster trials had caused a stir in the building, but Peifer's was the most sensational when it unfolded in 1936. He was found guilty and sentenced to thirty years in Leavenworth Penitentiary in Kansas, but he never had to serve time there. Instead, he took a lethal dose of cyanide in his cell at the Ramsey County jail.

Peifer's spirit is said to roam the halls of Landmark Center, breathing down beautiful women's necks, tipping over numerous trays of champagne glasses, and playing with the elevators by bringing people to the sixth floor, which can be accessed only with a special key.

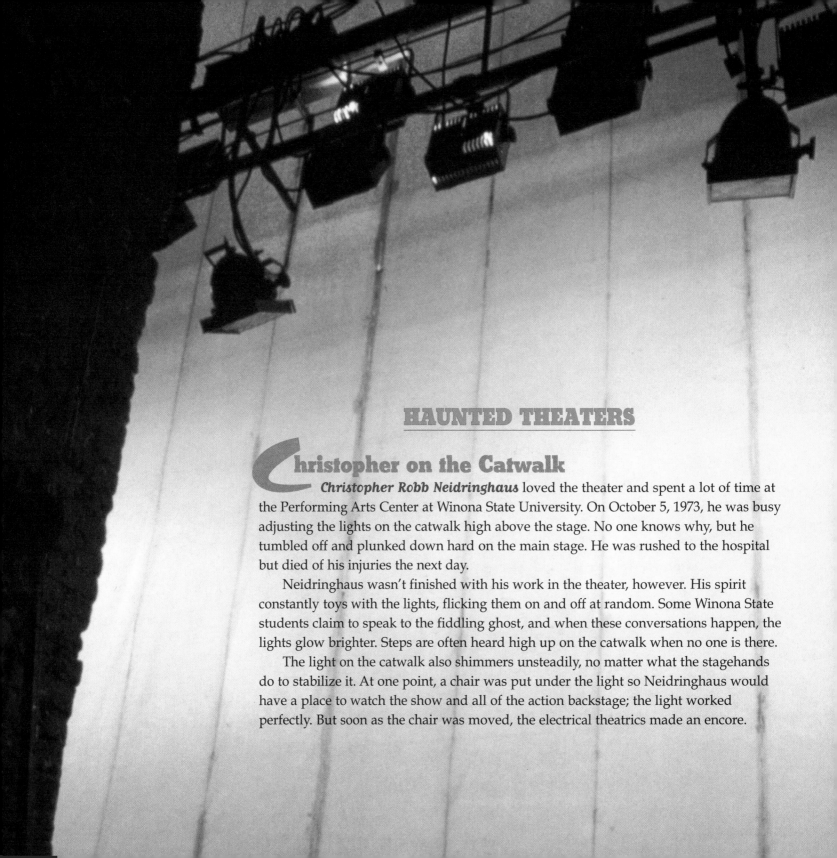

HAUNTED THEATERS

Christopher on the Catwalk

Christopher Robb Neidringhaus loved the theater and spent a lot of time at the Performing Arts Center at Winona State University. On October 5, 1973, he was busy adjusting the lights on the catwalk high above the stage. No one knows why, but he tumbled off and plunked down hard on the main stage. He was rushed to the hospital but died of his injuries the next day.

Neidringhaus wasn't finished with his work in the theater, however. His spirit constantly toys with the lights, flicking them on and off at random. Some Winona State students claim to speak to the fiddling ghost, and when these conversations happen, the lights glow brighter. Steps are often heard high up on the catwalk when no one is there.

The light on the catwalk also shimmers unsteadily, no matter what the stagehands do to stabilize it. At one point, a chair was put under the light so Neidringhaus would have a place to watch the show and all of the action backstage; the light worked perfectly. But soon as the chair was moved, the electrical theatrics made an encore.

Quiet, Ghostbuster at Work

Carol Margaret is a professional ghostbuster: "Ghosts come to me and ask, 'Can you help me? Are you of the light?' When I was little, I thought it was just my imagination." Margaret has been teaching classes on ghosts for fourteen years and earns her living ghostbusting and doing hands-on healing in the Twin Cities area.

A protégé of famous local ghostbuster Echo Bodine, Margaret has perfected her clairvoyance so that she can commune with the dead. "When I started doing ghostbusting," she says, "I wasn't very good at protecting myself. Now, if I feel them starting to take my energy, I do a cord cut." She swoops her arm in front of her body as though cutting an invisible umbilical cord.

Ghostbusting conjures images of Dan Aykroyd and Bill Murray blasting poltergeists with giant stun guns, but Margaret's approach is nothing like Hollywood's vision. "First of all, I don't banish anyone," she explains. "Living and dead people all have free will." Margaret prefers to persuade her ghosts to clear out voluntarily. She tells of a house she was called to, in Northfield, that had a ghost hiding in the attic. The spirit "told me that she couldn't go over to the other side because she was helping the owner of the house tidy things up," she says. "Then, her husband came from the other side and helped her leave this side."

Margaret agreed to give a demonstration of her ability to commune with ghosts at the notoriously haunted Mounds Theater on the east side of Saint Paul. She'd already taught a couple of classes there because of the generally friendly spirits in the theater. The bathroom, she said, was the haunt of a large woman who loves the theater. "She was telling me that she likes to wear the boas," she added.

The owners concurred, "Yeah! We keep finding feathers on the floor. We clean up the feathers all the time."

Margaret explained that there were three ghosts, two women and a man, watching us. "Last time I was here, they showed me that they lived down the block. I know she was going down to the corner to get her friends. They come and party. It's like their social event. They'll sit in the chairs, watch the play, mingle with the guests, and have a blast."

The Spirits Just Aren't That into You

Many of the stone buildings in downtown Mantorville are teeming with ghosts. The Hubbell House restaurant, which dates from 1856, has a little old lady ghost milling about. The Opera House has a woman dressed in a long black dress who is said to wisp up to the rafters and hide props or turn on all the lights late at night.

"I've lived here my whole life, and I've never heard such nonsense," says the woman running the antiques store in the center of Mantorville.

A man shopping in the store rebuts, "Come to think of it, I do remember some stories when a Rochester troupe came through. All sorts of strange things happened."

The man points to an old white house on the hill and says that the Old Manor is the real haunted house of Mantorville: "There were all sorts of strange stories. A woman was buried in the basement. Then an old car was buried under the basement. They wanted to shoot a movie there, but that never worked out."

The woman scoffs at his credulity: "I've been top to bottom, from the attic to the basement in that house, and I've never felt any ghosts."

The man smiles and says, "Maybe you're just not sensitive enough."

Hauntings at the Fitz

The World Theater in downtown Saint Paul was badly in need of repair. Garrison Keillor's radio show *A Prairie Home Companion* was growing in popularity, but its home theater (now called the Fitzgerald) needed a complete renovation.

The revamping began in 1985. When a false ceiling was removed, construction workers discovered another balcony that had been covered up. A note, written to a stagehand named Ben, who was surely long dead, was found. That's when the hauntings began.

A theatrical ghost, who has been called Veronica, sings eerie old tunes late at night that echo through the empty theater. Cold spots and dark shadows move restlessly about. Tools and props are moved or simply disappear. Ancient bottles of muscatel wine appear but are always empty. Maybe Ben the stagehand was a drinker?

And was it the awakened stagehand who dropped a large piece of plaster from the catwalk high above the stage, almost hitting a couple of modern-day stagehands? When the near victims looked up, they saw a shadowy figure disappearing from the catwalk. Then they realized that the ceiling in the Fitzgerald isn't made of plaster. Where had this old material, which nearly crashed down onto their heads, come from?

Some theatergoers think the theater is visited by the ghost of author F. Scott Fitzgerald because he was so honored to have the theater renamed for him. In the meantime, stagehands watch their heads.

Usher in the Ghost

Richard Miller was a bit of an outcast at Morningside High School in Edina. When his passion for downhill skiing ended with a bad accident on the slopes, he turned to the theater. He landed a job as an usher at the premier venue in the state, the Guthrie Theater, where he wore the standard blue coat with red patch on the pocket.

Miller still had the job when he enrolled at the University of Minnesota and moved to a dorm room in Territorial Hall. He remained an outsider and fell into a deep depression. On February 5, 1967, the distraught student-usher bought a Mauser rifle at the Sears on Lake Street. While wearing his Guthrie usher's uniform, he shot himself in his car in the Sears parking lot. His body is buried at Fort Snelling National Cemetery.

A short time later, theatergoers at the Guthrie complained about an annoying usher in row 18 who kept walking around during the middle of a performance. The management was baffled, since no ushers were assigned to row 18, which happened to be Miller's old area. After everyone left the theater one night, another usher looked back before turning out the lights. There was Richard Miller, standing next to row 18 in full usher uniform—a telltale large mole on his cheek.

Another sighting occurred when a visiting opera troupe was heading to their cars after a performance. One of the singers noticed a distressed usher weeping in his car. When she approached him to see if everything was all right, the vision disappeared. She described the driver to people in the Guthrie, who recognized the figure as Miller.

One late night in the theater, the living ushers wanted to conjure the dead usher's ghost. Row 18 was chosen as the perfect spot to ask the Ouija board if there were any spirits present. The board spelled out G-H-O-S-T and got as far as M-I-L when the frightened ushers ended their séance.

Other times, misty formations have appeared mysteriously onstage. Once, napping ushers were woken up by a ghostly presence that descended down the stage to energetically play the piano. Spooked workers in the theater finally held a makeshift exorcism in the early 1990s in an effort to banish the ghost.

Though the Guthrie Theater was a favorite venue for many musicians and actors, the management decided to give it up for a new location downtown. Perhaps in an ironic finale, the last show performed there was Hamlet.

THE OTHERWORLDLY OUTDOORS

Ghostly Ships Defy the Waves

Maybe the many ghost-ship sightings on the north shore of Lake Superior have something to do with the weather. Maybe it's a trick of driving rain, or fog, that creates these apparitions. Then again, maybe not.

A schooner crew once saw a phantom ship, cut apart in three different sections, sailing across the lake. Magically, the ship then united into one large sailing vessel. When the crew tried to hail it, the ghostly craft disappeared.

Sailors know that mirages, common as they may be, impart terrible luck, and there are many stories of ships sliding beneath the waves of the lake after one of these ghostly sightings. The most dreaded phenomenon of Lake Superior is the Three Sisters. Two giant waves rock a boat so that it tips violently from port to starboard. Just when the crew thinks they're safe, the third Sister capsizes the whole ship.

One sign of good luck on the lake is when the top of a ship's mast or a spar glows with an eerie light called Saint Elmo's fire. Also known as corposants, the Corpse Light, and Jacob's Lantern, the greenish-yellow light is believed to be the soul of an old crewmate offering protection.

Ghost Photographed Near White Bear Lake

The dawn of photography sometimes presented unexplained images on photo plates. At the time, these could be explained only as actual images of the dead among us. In this photo, from 1890, Truman Ingersoll is visited by a ghost at his home near White Bear Lake. Images like these were printed in newspapers across the country and used by psychic mediums to prove to skeptics that our deceased ancestors still existed and were all around us.

Many were unwilling to believe and regarded these images as hocus-pocus. An article in a 1903 issue of *Scientific American* revealed how to shoot a black-and-white photo plate of a ghost: "The object representing the specter is mounted on black cloth, preferably black velvet, so that no other object than the specter will be represented by reflection" in a small mercury-covered mirror in front of the lens. To trick the person sitting in the photo into thinking that a ghost was indeed next to him or her, "a screen may be placed between the sitter and the specter, so that the delusion may be made complete . . . the trick will not be discovered by the sitter."

Guess they settled that, but tell that to Truman Ingersoll.

Sunken Flying Dutchman?

In 1902, talk spread that the steamship *Bannockburn,* nicknamed the Flying Dutchman of Lake Superior, was lost somewhere in the enormous lake. The families of the crew members received telegrams informing them not to worry about their relatives because the ship was perfectly safe in spite of rumors to the contrary. Yet the *Bannockburn* disappeared, and no trace of the wreckage has ever been found. When mist rises above the surface of Lake Superior, other ships' captains have reported seeing the speedy 245-foot-long *Bannockburn* zoom past and disappear out on the lake within minutes.

Ghost Train

The train connecting Marine-on-St. Croix to Osceola, Wisconsin, runs only for special occasions, like three-course dinner trips, weekend excursions in the summer, and the annual Wheels and Wings festival. Even so, people who live near the train hear the chugging engine and the toot of the horn regularly, all year round. To spook youngsters, the classic old train leaves the station every Halloween for a ride over the St. Croix River and through the fall colors in search of the phantom train.

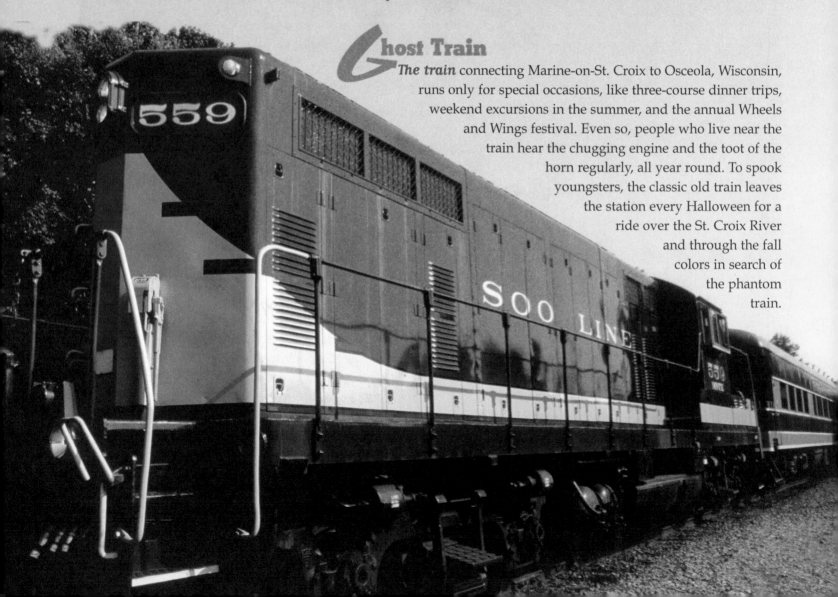

HAUNTED CAVES AND MINES

Castle Royal Rubout

A variety of confused ghosts are said to wander around the Wabasha Street Caves in Saint Paul, unable to find the exit. A phantom couple often appears late in the evening. A man in a panama hat likes to

make the rounds as well. And then there are the victims of a Mob shoot-out: mobsters killed in a notorious triple murder in the middle of a crowded nightclub.

During Prohibition, the caves were taken over by bootleggers and used as a giant speakeasy nightclub. The Castle Royal, "the world's first underground nightclub," opened in 1933 with a huge 1,600-square-foot dance floor where revelers could do the two-step to tunes played by the big bands of the day. Gangsters flocked to the hottest nightspot in town, especially since the Saint Paul police had struck a deal with the mobsters that they wouldn't be touched within city limits as long as they behaved themselves.

That all changed in 1934, when three men were shot down with machine guns while standing in front of the fireplace of the Castle Royal. The crowd screamed and ran out the doors in a panic. By the time the police showed up, no trace of any incident remained—the bodies had been whisked away and the blood mopped up. Look closely at the fireplace, though: The bullet holes, which couldn't be removed, still bear silent witness to the crime. The three men were probably buried in cement deep in one of the unfinished caves.

Lost Forever in Boomsite

Just north of Stillwater along the St. Croix, long caves weave underground for hundreds of yards. Not all of the nooks and crannies in the Boomsite caves have been charted, because many are too small and treacherous, especially if rainwater from aboveground seeps into the soft rock.

Ignoring that danger, three spelunkers from the University of Minnesota set out in the 1960s to explore the mysterious caves. The soft rock suddenly collapsed around them and trapped the cavers. Two of them managed to dig themselves out. The third screamed and screamed for help that never came. He died in Boomsite, but his cries echoed for days afterward. Some claim they can still hear the anguished sounds echoing around inside the dark caves.

HAUNTED SCHOOLS

Rubbing William Mitchell's Nose

It's tradition for students entering William Mitchell College of Law in Saint Paul to rub the nose of the bust of the school's namesake, William Mitchell, in the entryway. The students hope that this will not only bring good luck on tort exams but also protect them from the spirit that lives in the basement of the L. E. C. building.

William Mitchell was elected to the Minnesota Supreme Court in 1881, after which he became the first dean of Saint Paul College of Law (one of the schools that would later make up William Mitchell College of Law). His body was buried in Winona in 1900, but his spirit still seems to watch over the school on Summit Avenue.

It's a good thing, too, because this building, once a Catholic girls school, has many ghosts milling about in the basement where the bowling alley used to be. I speak from experience, having worked in the bookstore that sold used law books. I would hear constant complaints from law school employees about spirits in the storage rooms.

One of the spirits might be of fairly recent vintage. One day, when I came in to work, a policeman came into the store and asked to use the telephone. As he dialed the precinct station, I asked if there was anything wrong. "The guy in the new bookstore down the hall dropped dead," he said. Apparently, the bookstore manager had had a heart attack and died while the bookstore was being held up. Whoever did it had gotten clean away.

Over the next few months, the plot thickened, though the law school managed to keep the sordid story out of the newspapers. The killer was an alleged prostitute who knew the manager because he supposedly dealt drugs. She locked the door of the bookstore behind her and threatened him with a razor blade. The man had been complaining about numbness in his arms in the previous weeks, and the stress may have triggered the heart attack. As he lay dying on the carpet, his attacker took money out of the cash register and stole his wallet.

The woman was eventually caught and allegedly confessed to everything. However, the story goes, the police forgot to read her her Miranda rights, so she walked away from what would have been second-degree murder charges. Whether or not her victim is one of the spirits who now wander and wail in the dank storage rooms, we don't know. But it's no wonder the students keep rubbing William Mitchell's nose before venturing into the basement.

The Burning Priests

On August 27, 1915, Bishop Patrick Heffron was kneeling in front of the altar in the empty chapel of St. Mary's College in Winona. It was dawn, and the bishop liked to come here early to pray, before the day began. His head bowed in the quiet chapel, Heffron heard the door creak open behind him but assumed it was just another early riser making the most of the morning. When he heard the slow steps coming toward him, the bishop turned to find the fifty-five-year-old Father Laurence Michael Lesches aiming a revolver at him. Lesches pulled the trigger three times. One shot blasted the altar, another hit Heffron in his left thigh, and a third punctured his lung.

Lesches ran out of the chapel, the wounded Heffron stumbling after him. The bishop collapsed in the doorway of the chapel. When Lesches was picked up by the police and asked why he would commit such an outrageous act, he complained that the bishop had told him he was cut out to be a farmhand more than a priest. Heffron had refused to give Lesches his own parish because the bishop viewed him as emotionally unstable, an insight that proved to be all too correct. Heffron recovered from his bullet wounds, and Lesches was sent to the State Hospital for the Dangerously Insane in Saint Peter.

Then, on May 15, 1931, another of Lesches's enemies was found dead in Winona. Father Edward Lynch, a good friend of Bishop Heffron, had roomed with Father Lesches. When the two were roommates, Lynch professed his love of sports to Lesches. The unpredictable Lesches swore that Lynch would burn in hell for his deviant love of athletics.

While Lesches was still locked away in Saint Peter, a nun discovered Lynch's body in his bedroom in Winona — completely charred. The bed wasn't burned in the least, but the priest's body lay as though in the shape of a crucifix. The coroner was stumped and could surmise only that Lynch had been electrocuted by the little ten-volt lamp on his bedside table. The theory was generally regarded as hogwash, but no one had a better explanation.

That same year, another priest at St. Mary's College was burned to death, and three more were killed in a fire. While everyone suspected Father Lesches of the crimes, his alibi was airtight, as he was confined to Saint Peter and had never been allowed to leave. He lived the rest of his life in the asylum, dying in 1943, eighty-four years old.

The stories of these poor priests haven't been forgotten. A new dormitory was built on campus in 1921 and named for Bishop Heffron, who had been integral in the founding of the college. Today, stories still circulate about ghostly presences haunting the building. A student punched the face of what looked like a darkly cloaked ghost in Heffron Hall but broke every bone in his hand. Unexplained cold spots have been charted in the dormitory halls before two a.m. every morning. Students swear that the third floor is haunted by the ghost of Lesches, still searching for revenge against Bishop Heffron.

Cemetery Safari

t's hard not to get spooked in a cemetery. All those people lying only six feet under as you walk nearby. Once, they were just like you and me. Now, only their dried bones are left behind, seeming to reach out to us from beyond the grave. But these dearly departed probably mean us no harm. They ask only to be remembered.

Dotted around Minnesota are many strange burial sites, some devoted to those celebrated—or reviled—in life, some the final resting places of the humble or unknown. Whether lying beneath a simple tombstone, in an elaborate mausoleum, or buried deep within an ancient mound built by some civilization long past, these dead speak to us of lives lived and a fate that awaits us all. What are they trying to tell us? Walk softly in these places, and perhaps you will hear.

Here Lies Paul

In the tiny town of Kelliher, in a forty-foot-long rise in the park on the south side of town, lies what's left of Minnesota's most famous lumberjack. While other towns have Paul Bunyan's earthly artifacts—ax, ox, anchor, duck—Kelliher has the otherworldly: a tomb and stone inscribed with the simple epitaph HERE LIES PAUL, AND THAT'S ALL. The mythical woodsman died in 1899. His best buddy, Babe the Blue Ox, was buried in western South Dakota, leaving behind a massive mound that is now called the Black Hills.

Tortured Poet

Students at the University of Minnesota fondly recall how Regent's professor John Berryman shook when he gave lectures. He chain-smoked in front of students and dismissed one of his classes early when he found out that only a small fraction had ever read Cervantes. He said lessons would be resumed once they'd all read *Don Quixote,* which wasn't even on the syllabus.

Berryman's tormented, searching poems in *77 Dream Songs* won him the Pulitzer Prize for poetry in 1965, and he won the National Book Award in 1969 for *His Toy, His Dream, His Rest.* In spite of his success, Berryman struggled with the demon drink and once spent five months in a hospital for alcoholism.

Berryman's father committed suicide before his son was even a teenager, and the boy was subsequently sent off to boarding school in Connecticut. His poems envisioned death as a welcome repose from life's pain and rare joy. Berryman taught at the university for seventeen years. Then during the frosty Minnesota winter of 1972, he jumped off the Washington Avenue Bridge into the frigid Mississippi River. He is buried in Resurrection Cemetery in Mendota Heights.

Sea Wing Disaster

The Mississippi meets the St. Croix River at Lake City and there forms the placid expanse of water called Lake Pepin. Ralph Samuelson invented waterskiing here amid sailboats taking advantage of the breezes. The lake hides a tragedy, however—the worst water accident in the history of the state.

Around the turn of the century, wooden tourist boats carried visitors up and down the rivers to see the sites. One of the most popular ships was the *Sea Wing*, which the captain thought could easily handle a hundred people. When the wind picked up and the waves bounced the little boat, the passengers panicked. They desperately ran from side to side in the cabin of the boat, trying to stay on the high end, away from the roiling water. Their weight proved to be bad ballast and caused the ship to capsize, taking ninety-eight passengers to a watery grave at the bottom of Lake Pepin.

VERY CLIMAX OF HORROR.

The Tornado on Pepin's Treacherous Bosom the Crowning Calamity of All Minnesota's Annals.

At Least One Hundred and Twenty Lives Swallowed Up by the Angry Waters of the Fatal Lake.

An Appalling Sacrifice to One Man's Determination to Brave the Fury of a Storm Irresistible.

y Miles of River Line Plunged Into the Gloom of Mourning for the Fearful Death of Loved Ones Lost.

Red Wing Bowed Down With Grief and All Business Forgotten in the Presence of the Sublime Horror.

Above, a contemporary lithograph depicting the 1862 Dakota Uprising. Left, President Lincoln's letter to General Silbey ordering the execution of the 38 Native Americans found guilty by the military tribunal.

Mankato's Missing Monument

After the 1862 Dakota Uprising, relations between Native Americans and the white settlers were bad indeed (see "Local Legends"). During the brief war, about three hundred settlers died, and estimates put the number of Indian deaths at twice that number. Thirty-eight Dakota were hanged in the town of Mankato for their part in the uprising; four thousand citizens watched the proceedings. After the hangings, the dead were kept in the Quarry Hill Park caves in Rochester, a spot also used for keeping food fresh.

During the winter of 1862 to 1863, Fort Snelling became an internment camp for the Dakota. Over a hundred Indians died in captivity there. The 1,300 who managed to survive the brutal winter were loaded up on two steamboats in the spring. The boats traveled down the Mississippi to St. Louis and then up the Missouri River to a dry, dismal land called Crow Creek, in South Dakota. Three years later, the Indians who had remained in this desolate place were transported farther west to the Santee Reservation in Nebraska.

To mark the fifty-year anniversary of the largest mass execution in the United States, a monument was erected to the Dakota in 1912 at Front and Main streets in Mankato. Many outraged citizens demanded that the five-foot-long, two-foot-wide plaque be moved because they didn't want a reminder of the horrible events in such a prominent location. The stone marker became a common target for symbolic red paint during the events at Wounded Knee in South Dakota. Finally, the city stepped in and put the plaque "in protective custody," according to government officials. No one knows where the missing monument now stands; it was probably lost in a warehouse somewhere and is gathering dust. In 1997, a large granite buffalo was erected near Main Street in Reconciliation Park as a goodwill gesture to Native Americans.

The small town of Morton near Redwood Falls chose a different approach. They decided to honor only the Native Americans who helped the settlers during the conflict. The "Friendly Indians" to whom the controversial monument was dedicated include John Other Day and others who had converted to Christianity and accepted the ways of the white man.

Good Indian
ANPETU-TOKECA, (Other day.)
Who rescued Sixty-two persons from the *Indian Massacre* of 1862, in Minnesota.

WHITNEY'S GALLERY.   SAINT PAUL.

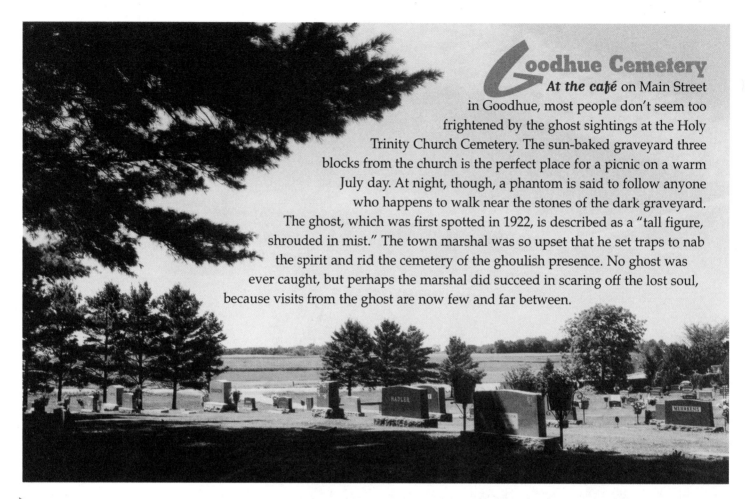

Goodhue Cemetery

At the café on Main Street in Goodhue, most people don't seem too frightened by the ghost sightings at the Holy Trinity Church Cemetery. The sun-baked graveyard three blocks from the church is the perfect place for a picnic on a warm July day. At night, though, a phantom is said to follow anyone who happens to walk near the stones of the dark graveyard. The ghost, which was first spotted in 1922, is described as a "tall figure, shrouded in mist." The town marshal was so upset that he set traps to nab the spirit and rid the cemetery of the ghoulish presence. No ghost was ever caught, but perhaps the marshal did succeed in scaring off the lost soul, because visits from the ghost are now few and far between.

Norsk Cemetery

Spring Grove, Minnesota's first Norwegian settlement, didn't want its earliest residents to be forgotten. So old tombstones were brought into the downtown park and lined up very close to each other. Peruse the names and discover plenty of old Oles and Lenas, along with a couple Torvalds, Dagfinns, and Oddbjørgs.

Lies in Lakewood with His Stuffed Rabbit

Herbert Khaury was born in New York City, but he changed his stage name often, according to the crowd for which he was performing. Rollie Dell, Larry Love, the Singing Canary, and Emmett Swink are all onetime monikers. The one that stuck, though, as he strummed his little ukulele and sang in a wavy falsetto, was Tiny Tim. His famous version of "Tiptoe Through the Tulips" made him a regular on television. When he married Victoria "Miss Vicki" Budinger, in 1969, live on *The Tonight Show* starring Johnny Carson, more people watched it than watched the moon landing.

Tinyheads, or Tiny Tim groupies, followed his career religiously in spite of, or perhaps because of, his belief that aliens lived on the moon and that Richard Nixon was perhaps the nation's best president ever.

Tiny Tim married Minnesotan Susan Gardner (not live on television this time) in 1995 and moved to the Twin Cities area. He made local headlines when he borrowed an electric cart at the airport—perhaps after having had a couple of drinks—and had a slow-motion accident. Toward the end of his life, the Twin Cities showed a renewed interest in his music, and he made a comeback. At the Woman's Club of Minneapolis, he sang a hearty version of "Tiptoe Through the Tulips" and then collapsed. Tiny Tim died on November 30, 1996, just sixty-four years old. He was buried in Lakewood Cemetery with his stuffed rabbit, his ukulele, and six tulips.

Winona's Revolutionary War Hero?

The only Revolutionary War veteran buried in Minnesota fought under George Washington as part of the First Massachusetts Regiment of the Continental Army. Stephen Taylor was one of the heroes of Ticonderoga, serving alongside Ethan Allen as a member of the Green Mountain Boys.

Or at least that's how the story goes. The true extent of Taylor's military prowess is unknown, but historians doubt that he was actually there to take Fort Ticonderoga from the British in 1775. After the war, Taylor moved to the Minnesota Territory with his large family and received 160 acres of land around Winona as part of the government's gift to veterans. For his military service, Taylor has been honored with a unique tombstone in Winona: a miniature replica of Fort Ticonderoga.

Annie's Grave

When I was in high school, back around 1980, a couple of my girlfriends and I drove out to Sleepy Eye (at night, of course) to check out Annie's Grave. The story was that Annie died back in the 1800s, and a few days or weeks after she was buried, it was reported that she had been buried alive. So she was dug back up, and sure enough, there were clawing marks on the casket.

Well, my girlfriends and I didn't really believe it, but we brought a couple of bent coat hangers along to see if her spirit was still around. Well, I was the one holding the coat hangers (kind of like divining rods), and they whipped around so hard that it was like a force beyond anything I had ever experienced! One of the rods actually hit me hard in the face. My girlfriends witnessed this. We all felt it and got out of there. We were absolutely shaking. I never picked up divining rods again except to find the occasional lost pair of keys. The grave is still there—you won't have to ask too many people around Sleepy Eye before you find someone who knows about it and could probably take you there. It's kind of creepy even in the daylight because the grave isn't even in a cemetery. It's just sitting out along a gravel road next to a cornfield. I'm guessing that her family didn't belong to a local church, so she was just buried on what was their property at the time.—*Kay Kalthoff*

Satirist's Ashes in Sauk Centre

When Sinclair Lewis revealed the small-mindedness possible in the little towns of Minnesota, he was no longer welcome in his hometown of Sauk Centre. His "fictional" novels, especially *Main Street,* had casts of characters that bore a bit too much resemblance to living persons. Besides, why did he take on the stuffy-sounding Sinclair when his real first name was Harry?

When Lewis died in Rome, on January 10, 1951, however, his fellow townspeople seemed ready to let bygones be bygones. After all, he'd been awarded the Pulitzer Prize for *Arrowsmith*—which he turned down—and was the first American writer to win the Nobel Prize for Literature, in 1930. His ashes came home to rest at Greenwood Cemetery in Sauk Centre.

Fire! Fire! Water! Water!

When loggers began clear-cutting the forests of Minnesota, they left behind fields of scrap lumber that dried in the hot summer sun. These scraps needed only the slightest spark or bolt of lightning to ignite a massive blaze. The fires spread as fast as the wind could take them, and any towns in their path were doomed. The settlement of Virginia on the Iron Range burned to the ground twice, in 1893 and 1900. The horrific Moose Lake Fire of 1918 killed 453 people. A twenty-eight-foot granite memorial marks the spot in the Moose Lake Cemetery.

The Hinckley Fire Museum depicts the "greatest tragedy in Minnesota history," which ravaged this former "Town Made of Wood" on September 1, 1894. The town has gone a long way to set the scene: Pick up an old-fashioned phone in the museum and you'll hear a crackling fire and desperate screams. Then a low voice booms: "This is a true story of gruesome loss of life, miraculous salvation, and ultimately, a new beginning for both survivors and the earth itself."

The day of the fire was oppressively hot. Only two inches of rain had fallen since spring, and temperatures had climbed to over a hundred degrees in some towns. While all the good wood from the area was floating downstream to lumber mills, the ground was covered with small, dried-out branches, a tinderbox ready to explode. Sparks from passing trains probably ignited the kindling, and the inferno swept from town to town. Engineer James Root and his "rescue train" managed to carry some people to safety, but his hands were seared to the burning throttle of the train. Residents of Hinckley jumped in the local gravel pit or swam in the lake until the fire subsided.

Tommy Dunn of the Depot Agent's Office in Hinckley sent his final message of warning to the next depot in Barnum: "I think I've stayed too long!" His bravery allowed people in neighboring towns to escape the flames while his own depot was engulfed in flames, with him inside.

The smoke was visible deep into Wisconsin and all the way south into Iowa. The fire scorched 320,000 acres and destroyed six towns: Mission Creek, Sandstone,

BURYING THE DEAD—90 IN ONE TRENCH UNIDENTIFIED.

Miller, Partridge, Pokegama, and, of course, Hinckley. The official "Coroner's Tally" put the number of dead at 418.

Following the fire, legends arose telling of the bravery of some and the fates of those left behind. Locals reported seeing a mysterious figure whom they dubbed Wolf Boy foraging through the woods and making frequent stops to drink from the lake. The story goes that Wolf Boy was so horribly burned in the fire that he couldn't—or wouldn't—rejoin society. And in the scorching days that followed the inferno, the residents of Hinckley shivered as they heard the howls of Wolf Boy, mourning his lost life.

ERECTED
TO THE MEMORY OF THE
MEN, WOMEN
AND
CHILDREN
WHO PERISHED IN THE
FOREST FIRE OF
OCTOBER 12, 1918

Lola and the Landscapers

As teenagers in the late 1980s, my sister and I were hired by a family friend to help with a landscaping job in the town of Bellingham. We were to mow a cemetery lot for the princely sum of $50. We started on a beautiful August morning with two lawn mowers at our disposal: one push and one riding. About an hour into the job, the riding lawn mower suddenly stopped and would not start again. We thought it was simply a mechanical problem, pushed it back onto our pickup truck and called it a day. When we brought the mower in for service the next day, it started right up. The mechanic checked it over just to make sure, but he could find nothing wrong.

Rider mower fixed, we started the job again early the following day. It was as sunny and clear in the cemetery as the first time we were there. I was using the push mower, and as I walked by one of the headstones, I noticed it had the name Lola on it. I called my sister over, and we joked about it as we sang the popular Kinks tune.

We started to mow again and were about one quarter done when the riding mower stopped dead. It was followed just five seconds later by the push mower—dead too. At the same time, a strong, cool breeze started blowing in the cemetery, making the entire atmosphere ominous, and we freaked out. We didn't even use the ramp to get the riding mower in the pickup truck; we lifted it on pure adrenaline! We took off as fast as we could and did not return. I called the landscaper and told him that the mowers weren't working and that we couldn't finish the job. We never stepped foot in that cemetery, or in Bellingham, for that matter, ever again. It taught us both a great lesson: Never make jokes about the dead, as they may be listening!—*Mark J. Schneider*

Giants in the Earth

In his book *The M-Files,* Jay Rath writes about the supposed giants unearthed from Indian mounds across Minnesota. Moose Island Lakes uncovered a seven-foot-tall skeleton in 1861. Eight-foot skeletons were found in Dresbach, and Rainy River unearthed a whopping nine-footer in 1896. Pine City also had its own gigantic skeleton.

Rath reports that in 1884, fifty-two men of "exceptionally large stature" were uncovered in Le Crescent, having been buried eighteen feet underground. Even more impressive are the six hundred huge skeletons that were found in Lanesboro. Rath explains that "George E. Powell, writing in 1907, said that 27 years earlier he had heard oral histories representing a battle said to have occurred 200 years before then. The dead were supposedly strangers slain by Ojibwe; the story comes from a 100-year-old Ojibwe."

During an era when archaeological hoaxes filled the newspapers, the discovery of these giants seems likely to be either poor science or clever storymaking. Rath suggests a different possibility: Neanderthals or *Gigantopithecus* (another humanoid that evolved in Asia nine million years ago and survived until one million years ago). These giants, says Rath, "could have crossed the land bridge between Siberia and North America. That would have been a trip of merely 52 miles."

Mounds Park

More than ten thousand Indian mounds have been uncovered around the state, and many more have probably gone unnoticed. Most of these graves were plowed over by new settlers eager to reap as much from the land as possible. Only a handful of the mounds remain, and excavation of them is now illegal. Archaeologists maintain that many of the mounds stretch back three thousand years, but dating the finds is often difficult because many different generations were buried in the same spot.

Saint Paul's Mounds Park has six giant mounds overlooking downtown and the Mississippi River. Originally, eighteen mounds filled the area, with an additional nineteen along Dayton's Bluff. That any were saved in Saint Paul is thanks to the editor of the *Pioneer Press*, Joseph Wheelock, who set up the parks system in 1893.

The earliest reference to the mounds comes from explorer Jonathan Carver, who gave his name to the famous cave beneath the Indian graves in Mounds Park.

Unimpressed, Carver described what would be named Carver's Cave as a "dreary cavern" in his journal from 1766. He went on to say, "At a little distance from this dreary cavern is the burying place of several bands of the Naudowessie [Dakota] Indians; though these people have no fixed residence, living in tents, and abiding but a few months on one spot, yet they always bring the bones of their dead to this place."

INDEX

Page numbers in **bold** refer to photos and illustrations.

WEIRD MINNESOTA

by

ERIC DREGNI

Executive Editors
Mark Moran and Mark Sceurman

ACKNOWLEDGMENTS

Thanks to:

Max Action and his Squad of Spelunkers, Sigrid Arnott, Sasha Aslanian, Tracey Baker and Brian Szott at the Minnesota History Center, Carol Berg, Fred Case and his sign house, Hillary Churchill, Dr. Demento, Michael Dregni, Capo Dregni (traveling companion extraordinaire), Nicolino Dregni for clues on prosthetic photos, John Dregni for spelunker clues, Hans Eisenbeis for keeping me motivated with articles, Scott Fares for clues on the mummy, Prof. Godollei and her car of many colors, Trish Hampl, Geoffrey Johnson, Piccola Katy—the best traveling companion ever, Garrison Keillor, Leif Larsen, Mark "Shaky Ray" Lindquist, Paul Lundgren and the Geeks, John McClellan, Bob McCoy and his collection of quackery, Nan Nelson for the LSD tips, Ken Nyberg, Lib Peck, and John Pierson for leads on punk rockers stealing prosthetics, John Perkins and Nick Hook for theme music about foam houses, Dennis Pernu for the latest on the hockey stick, Karl "Son of the Baron" Raschke, Brian Sanderson, Kathryn Slusher, Ma Sommers, Dr. Sphincter for hating everything, Kaia Sveien, Margaret Tehven and her alleged incorruptible, Mark Vesley for linking the Conquistadors to the Vikings in Egypt, Jerry Vettrus at F.A.S.T. and his splendid "graveyard."

Publisher:	Barbara J. Morgan
Managing Editor:	Emily Seese
Editor:	Marjorie Palmer
Production:	Della R. Mancuso
	Mancuso Associates, Inc.
	North Salem, NY

BIBLIOGRAPHY

Bergheim, Laura. 1997. *An American Festival of World's Capitals: Over 300 World Capitals of Arts, Crafts, Food, Culture, and Sport.* New York: John Wiley & Sons, Inc.

Blashfield, Jean F. 1993. *Awesome Almanac Minnesota.* Fontana, Wisconsin: B&B Publishing.

Breining, Greg. 1997. *Minnesota.* Oakland, California: Compass American Guides, Fodor's Travel Publications, Inc.

DeGroot, Barbara, and El-Hai, Jack. 1995. *The Insiders' Guide to the Twin Cities.* Manteo, North Carolina: Insiders' Guides.

Dickson, Paul, and Skole, Robert. 1995. *The Volvo Guide to Halls of Fame: The Traveler's Handbook of North America's Most Inspiring and Entertaining Attractions.* Washington, DC: Living Planet Press.

Dierckins, Tony, and Elliot, Kerry. 2001. *True North.* Duluth, Minnesota: X-Communication.

Donnelly, Ignatius. 1882, reprinted 1976. *Atlantis: The Antediluvian World.* New York: Dover Publications.

Donnelly, Ignatius. 1888. *The Great Cryptogram: Francis Bacon's Cipher in the So-called Shakespeare Plays.* Chicago: R. S. Peale & Co.

Dregni, Michael, ed. 1999. *Minnesota Days: Our Heritage in Stories, Art, and Photos.* Stillwater, Minnesota: Voyageur Press.

Fedo, Michael. 2002. *The Pocket Guide to Minnesota Place Names.* Saint Paul: Minnesota Historical Society Press.

Gauper, Beth. 1996. *Midwest Weekends: Memorable Getaways in the Upper Midwest.* Kansas City, Missouri: Andrews McMeel.

Gurvis, Sandra. 1998. *America's Strangest Museums: A Traveler's Guide.* Toronto: Citadel Press.

Hansen, Nicole O. 2003. *Out and About in Rochester & Southeastern Minnesota.* Cambridge, Minnesota: Adventure Publications, Inc.

Harris, Moira. 1992. *Monumental Minnesota.* Saint Paul, Minnesota: Pogo Press.

Hauck, Dennis William. 1996. *National Directory of Haunted Places.* New York: Penguin.

Holbert, Sue E., and Holmquist, June D. 1966. *A History of 50 Twin City Landmarks.* Saint Paul: Minnesota Historical Society Press.

Hollatz, Tom. 2000. *The Haunted Northwoods.* St. Cloud, Minnesota: North Star Press of St. Cloud, Inc.

Holub, Joan. 2001. *The Haunted States of America.* New York: Aladdin Publishers.

Holzer, Hans. 2002. *More Where the Ghosts Are.* New York: Citadel Press.

Kane, Lucile M. 1987. *The Falls of St. Anthony.* Saint Paul: Minnesota Historical Society Press.

Kimball, Joe. 1985. *Secrets of the Congdon Mansion.* Minneapolis: JayKay Pub. Inc.

Lavenda, Robert H. 1997. *Corn Fests and Water Carnivals: Celebrating Community in Minnesota.* Washington, DC: Smithsonian Institution Press.

Lee, Carvel. 1990. *36 One-Day Discovery Tours.* Minneapolis: Nodin Press.

Maccabee, Paul. 1995. *John Dillinger Slept Here: A Crook's Tour of Crime and Corruption in St. Paul, 1920–1936.* Saint Paul: Minnesota Historical Society Press.

MacDougall, Curtis D. 1958. *Hoaxes.* New York: Dover Publications.

Marks, Susan. 2005. *Finding Betty Crocker.* New York: Simon & Schuster.

Marling, Karal Ann. 1990. *Blue Ribbon: A Social and Pictorial History of the Minnesota State Fair.* Minneapolis: University of Minnesota Press.

Marling, Karal Ann. 1984. *Colossus of Roads: Myth and Symbol Along the American Highway.* Minneapolis: University of Minnesota Press.

Meier, Peg. 1988. *Coffee Made Her Insane.* Minneapolis: Neighbors Publishing.

Millett, Larry. 1992. *Lost Twin Cities.* Saint Paul: Minnesota Historical Society Press.

Norman, Michael, and Scott, Beth. 1994. *Haunted America.* New York: Tom Doherty Associates.

Norman, Michael, and Scott, Beth. 1985. *Haunted Heartland.* New York: Warner Books.

O'Reilly, Jane H. 1998. *Quick Escapes: Minneapolis/St. Paul.* Old Saybrook, Connecticut: Globe Pequot Press.

Rath, Jay. 1998. *The M-Files: True Reports of Minnesota's Unexplained Phenomena.* Madison, Wisconsin: Wisconsin Trails.

Ringsak, Russ, and Remick, Denise. 2003. *Minnesota Curiosities.* Guilford, Connecticut: Globe Pequot Press.

Rubin, Saul. 1997. *Offbeat Museums: The Collections and Curators of America's Most Unusual Museums.* Santa Monica, California: Santa Monica Press.

Rubinstein, Sarah P. 2003. *Minnesota History Along the Highways.* Saint Paul: Minnesota Historical Society Press.

Rule, Leslie. 2001. *Coast to Coast Ghosts: True Stories of Hauntings Across America.* Kansas City, Missouri: Andrews McMeel.

Shepard, John. 1989. *Minnesota: Off the Beaten Path.* Guilford, Connecticut: Globe Pequot Press.

Simonowicz, Nina. 1996. *Nina's North Shore Guide.* Grand Marais, Minnesota: Many Blankets.

Stein, Gordon, and MacNee, Marie. 1995. *Hoaxes: Dupes, Dodges & Other Dastardly Deceptions.* Detroit: Visible Ink.

Stelling, Lucille Johnsen. 1988. *Frommer's Guide to Minneapolis and St. Paul.* New York: Simon & Schuster.

Stonehouse, Frederick. 2000. *Haunted Lakes II.* Duluth, Minnesota: Lake Superior Port Cities, Inc.

Teel, Gina. 2001. *Ghost Stories of Minnesota.* Edmonton, Canada: Ghost House Books.

Thornley, Stew. 2004. *Six Feet Under: A Graveyard Guide to Minnesota.* Saint Paul: Minnesota Historical Society Press.

Warren, William W. 1984. *History of the Ojibway People.* Saint Paul: Minnesota Historical Society Press.

White, Helen M. 1984. *The Tale of a Comet and Other Stories.* Saint Paul: Minnesota Historical Society Press.

Wilkins, Mike; Smith, Ken; and Kirby, Doug. 1992. *The New Roadside America.* New York: Simon & Schuster.

Williams, J. Fletcher. 1876. *A History of St. Paul to 1875.* Saint Paul: Minnesota Historical Society Press.

Wilson, Blanche Nichols. 1950. *Minnetonka Story.* Minneapolis: Ross & Haines.

Winter, Laurel. 1990. *Minnesota Trivia.* Nashville: Rutledge Hill Press.

Works Progress Administration. 1941. *The W.P.A. Guide to the Minnesota Arrowhead Country.* Saint Paul: Minnesota Historical Society Press.

PICTURE CREDITS

All photos by the author except for public domain art and as indicated below.

SHOW US YOUR WEIRD!

Do you know of a weird site found somewhere in the United States, or can you tell us about a strange experience you've had? If so, we'd like to hear about it! We believe that every town has at least one great tale to tell, and we're listening. It could be a cursed road, haunted abandoned site, odd local character, or bizarre historic event. In most cases these tales are told only in the towns in which they originated. But why keep them to yourself when you could share them with all of America? So come on and fill us in on all the weirdness that's lurking in your backyard!

You can e-mail us at: Editor@WeirdUS.com,
or write to us at:
Weird U.S., P.O. Box 1346, Bloomfield, NJ 07003.

www.weirdus.com